HENRY SIEBEN

AND THE MONTANA STORY

Ciara Ryan

The Foundation for Montana History

ISBN: 978-1-59152-360-4

Researched and written by Ciara Ryan
Design by Steph Lehmann

Cover photos courtesy Hibbard family private collection.

Subjects: LCSH: Sieben, Henry, 1848-1937 I Montana – History – Biography I United States – History (1864-1937) I Montana - Agriculture – Ranching I Montana - Pioneer

Library of Congress Control Number: 2025908016

For more information or to order extra copies of this book
call Farcountry Press toll free at (800) 821-3874.

Produced by Sweetgrass Books
PO Box 5630, Helena, MT 59604; (800) 821-3874;
www.sweetgrassbooks.com

Produced and printed in the United States of America.

29 28 27 26 25 2 3 4 5 6

In memory of
Emily Stonington Hibbard

CONTENTS

—ACKNOWLEDGMENTS—

This project began as a conversation between the staff at the Foundation for Montana History and Henry Sieben's great-grandson Chase Hibbard. Chase asked if anyone would have an interest in the steamer trunks bursting with Sieben family history stored in his airplane hangar. The team thought the whole state of Montana might have an interest! The Foundation is grateful to Chase and the many Hibbard, Baucus, and Sieben family members who generously shared their collections, time, and memories about Henry and his adventures. The Foundation is especially thankful for the family's trust and patience in the process of researching, writing, and publishing Henry's story.

I was assisted in the research by clerks and recorders, librarians, and archivists across the state who opened their facilities and shared their expertise. My research benefited from the deep historical knowledge of Ken Robison, Ron Lee, Ellen Baumler, Owen Robinson, Ike Kaufman, and Garvey Wood who answered many questions and generously searched their own research notes for mention of the elusive Henry Sieben. Sadly, Ellen, Ike, and Garvey died before the manuscript went to press. Whitney Hibbard offered access to his oral history interviews with Montanans who remembered his great-grandfather. Whit also generously supported the digitization and transcription of these wonderful interviews. Montana historians David M. Emmons, Amy McKinney, and Mark T. Johnson all read and commented on early versions of the story. Thank you to Judge Robert Holter for his feedback on early drafts.

Foundation president and CEO Charlene Porsild shepherded the project from beginning to end, providing direction, support, and vision to keep the project moving. She also called on friends and colleagues for help along the way. Karen Fred typed the oral history transcripts. Tom Ferris digitized the Hibbard and Baucus family photographs. J.M. Cooper shared images from a modern-day Adel Ranch shearing. Lynn Thompson Baca provided invaluable developmental edits.

Finally, I thank my husband, Tony Zammit, our children Aisling and Philip, and our extended family for their support and encouragement. I am forever grateful for their good humor and patience as I jabbered on about Henry's adventures.

Of course, none of the above would have been possible without the many donors, friends, and board members who provided financial support to the project. Thank you all! ❖

INTRODUCTION

Henry Sieben arrived in Montana in 1864 as a seventeen-year-old with a goal of making his fortune. At that time, the Montana Territory was just beginning to experience the influx of westward settlement that would change it forever. And so, Henry's story and the story of Montana are inextricably linked. From gold mining to freighting, from open range to homesteading, and from soldier/bachelor society to permanent family farms and businesses, Henry Sieben participated in all the major economic and social developments of Montana itself. While thousands of settlers buckled under the uncertainty and danger of the tumultuous new territory, Henry capitalized on every opportunity, growing out of his dusty traveling clothes and cowboy boots into a business suit and a bowler hat to become one of Montana's most successful and respected businessmen.

Henry Sieben's relative absence from the historical record is understandable, given that he avoided the limelight for most of his life. We encounter him in a few of his contemporaries' autobiographies, including Granville Stuart's well-known *Forty Years on the Frontier* and the autobiography of Conrad Kohrs, but almost nowhere else. Even in two more-recent works, the biography of Nelson Story and a history of two of Sieben's neighboring families, Henry is mentioned in passing or not at all.[1] Historian Dick Pace's "Henry Sieben: Pioneer Montana Stockman" (1979) was the sole published article seeking to explore Sieben's life and contributions to Montana's history. Since then, however, interest in Henry's tale has lain fallow. The reason for Sieben's obscurity is largely by his own design. He did not pay to have his biography published in the subscription histories of the era, so he is not featured in *Progressive Men of Montana* and similar volumes. Henry was not motivated by adulation or notoriety. He was quiet, reserved, and most at ease when he was working, mostly behind the scenes.

Delving into his business records, personal papers, and the personal reminiscences of those who knew him reveals Henry Sieben to be a fascinating character who turned critical moments in Montana's history into golden opportunities for himself and his family. Seemingly from nothing, Henry Sieben built a lasting and thriving enterprise that survives today in two of Montana's largest family ranches. This work focuses on bringing that story to life. The first half of this book explores Henry's modest march to affluence from his difficult immigrant childhood through the opening years of Montana's territorial history. A rich collection of primary sources never before seen by researchers was generously made available to this project by Henry Sieben's descendants. These sources reveal the remarkable story of an orphan from Germany who journeyed to Montana and stayed to create a remarkable ranching legacy.

Henry began a career that spanned most of the components of the fledgling economy. Henry and his older brother, Leonard, spent the 1860s freighting, farming, and mining in the new territory, learning to bet on themselves. By the start of the next decade, the brothers were ready to establish their own cattle enterprise. Freighting and ranching taught them to endure the bitter cold and wicked heat, pushing through blizzards, dust storms, and driving wind. Montana was a rugged place. Rugged folks were required to thrive in this environment. The Siebens learned quickly that fortunes could be made (and lost!) on the open range. Eventually, Leonard would return to the East, but Henry understood that he and Montana crossed paths at the right time. Henry put his money on Montana, and he made good on that bet. Once he caught the ranching bug, Henry had it for life. When he became concerned about overgrazing in one area, he never hesitated to move his cattle hundreds of miles in search of quality grass. Henry ranched near and with some of the greatest pioneer Montana stockmen. Together, they fought back against the invasion of the large Texas cattle barons, took the issue of cattle rustling into their own hands, and helped organize the Montana Stockgrowers Association.

According to his contemporaries, Henry Sieben was ambitious, canny, honest, and intelligent in work ethic and business.[2] He had the ability to take full advantage when opportunities presented themselves.

Henry was also almost universally liked and admired by his peers. He never forgot the favor of a friend and tried to help hardworking ranchers who found themselves in dire straits. The aid was usually financial, sometimes earning him the nickname of "hip-pocket banker." Henry also realized that diversification was key to business success and having a family was key to personal happiness. Over the years he invested in cattle, sheep, real estate, mining, banking—he invested wherever he saw an opportunity to increase his holdings. He also searched for and found a wife in Miss Alberta Gordon. Henry and Alberta welcomed two daughters—Berneice and Margaret—and built an impressive home in Helena that showcased their wealth as well as their confidence in the capital city. Henry and his family made Helena their permanent home, though his ranching and business dealings spanned the entire territory.

The second half of the book examines Henry's and Montana's growing stature and importance. As Montana grew into statehood in 1889, Henry Sieben's business also came of age. His Culbertson-area Diamond Ranch grew to become one of Montana's largest cattle operations, though he eventually returned to the Chestnut Valley area to establish a sheep business. It was a calculated and brilliant move. As Montana became the nation's number one wool-growing state, Sieben became one of its top wool producers. At the end of the narrative, readers will find three appendices. The first is the Sieben family tree. The second is an illustration of most of the Sieben livestock brands recorded in Montana. The third is a cast of characters Henry met and interacted with throughout his long life in Montana.

The ultimate legacy of Henry Sieben was created when he purchased the Mitchell (later Sieben) Ranch near Helena, followed by the purchase of the Adel Ranch near Cascade. He stocked both ranches with sheep. By 1910, he had helped to establish the Montana Woolgrowers Association and had successfully navigated a number of legal cases surrounding water ownership and conflicts over fences. Henry was aided in this legacy-building by his wife, Alberta, who established the family within Helena society. From this firm social and business base in Helena, Henry was able to withstand the booms and busts of the Montana economy that came with World War I, drought, Prohibition, and the Great Depression.

By design, Henry Sieben built and expanded two prosperous ranches, one for each of his daughters. In 1922, he transferred operations of the Sieben Ranch to his daughter, Berneice, and her husband, Fred Sheriff, and the Adel Ranch to his daughter, Margaret, and her husband, Alfred T. Hibbard. Henry died in 1937 and the two ranches have been continuously operated by Berneice and Margaret's descendants ever since. Henry Sieben's intrepid story thus reaches even beyond today.

While the family papers are extensive, Henry himself left no personal journals or correspondence, only pocket notebooks. Relative Peggy Gordon Lestz later recalled Henry as a private person who ". . . didn't think that it was anybody's business what he thought about something."[3] Lestz claimed Henry destroyed his correspondence and made sure what survived was inaccessible. Whether Henry really did destroy his own records is hard to confirm, but by using a wide variety of other surviving records related to him and his businesses, we have been able to recover much of the story of this significant pioneer businessman. ◈

1852–1864

STARTING OUT

In August 1852, Apollonia Gabel and Joseph Sieben wrangled their seven children aboard a steamer and waved goodbye to their family in Mainz, Germany, headed for their new life in America. They kept waving, long after their loved ones were too tiny to discern among the crowd of well-wishers on the dock.

The steamer chugged slowly along the Rhine River on that hot summer's day, away from the Sieben family home in Abenheim, a small village in the present-day state of Rheinland-Palatinate. For years Joseph and Apollonia had eked out a meager living as farmers in the area's fertile valley. But the Revolution of 1848 and the subsequent riots had torn their quiet region apart, and crop failures and food shortages were a constant worry for the young family. The couple must have been both frightened and excited as they left their land, family, language,

Postcard views of Abenheim, Germany (undated), where Henry and his six siblings spent their earliest years. Courtesy of the Hibbard family private collection.

and culture behind. Like the nearly one million Germans who followed in their footsteps that decade, the Siebens hoped this risky and bold move would ultimately offer them a better life.

From Mainz, the Siebens traveled to the coast to board an ocean liner. Once aboard, they had little time for regrets. Their seven young children—John (aged 16), Theresa (14), Valentine (12), Margaret (11), Leonard (8), Henry (5), and Jacob (2)—were unsettled and anxious. Joseph and Apollonia comforted the children as best they could, but the couple was exhausted. They had spent months saving for passage money, packing, and planning for their journey and new life. Unfortunately, the conditions on board were miserable. The ship was filthy, the food was stale, and there was a lack of potable water. Apollonia, like many on the overcrowded vessel, was ill for most of the forty-eight-day voyage.

When the vessel docked at New York harbor in September 1852, the Sieben family eagerly disembarked and scrambled to find their bags amidst the chaos on shore. As planned, Theresa Sieben stayed in New York to visit friends, while the rest of the family continued by train to Chicago. When the Siebens arrived in Chicago a few weeks later, Apollonia was still ill and unable to continue. The family was forced to stay in Chicago where she died and was buried in January 1853.

Joseph ached for his lost wife and the familiarity of home, but felt he had no other choice than to forge ahead. In February 1853, he and his six children left Chicago driving a team of horses from Chicago to Dutch Bottom on the Rock River near Crandell's Ferry in Whiteside County, Illinois. The region earned its nickname for its large number of immigrants from Germany and the Netherlands. It wasn't home but it would have to do for Joseph and his children.

Illinois had a large German immigrant population in the 1850s, drawn by the Illinois Railroad's promises of free public education and abundant and affordable land. The German-speaking agents for the railway extolled the virtues of the "Garden State of the West," and Joseph Sieben believed he could easily purchase land and then use his large family and German farming skills to establish their new life in northwestern Illinois.[1] Alas much of this rhetoric was false, and when he arrived in Dutch Bottom, Joseph was frightened and broke. He had gone into debt covering the family's room, board, and medical bills in Chicago.

Like so many other immigrants, Joseph was tenacious and resourceful. With the help of his German friends and neighbors, he soon rented a farm and took possession of a vacant, dilapidated cabin. He put the children to work updating the structure and chinking it with mud to make it as weather-proof and comfortable as possible. He also secured a job on a neighboring farm, earning 50 cents per day. The two eldest boys—John and Valentine—went to work, as well, earning 30 cents and 24 cents per day tending to more affluent farmers' crops. The younger children—Margaret, Leonard, Henry, and Jacob—were thus often left to their own devices.

Finding it difficult to manage his large family, Joseph sought a wife. He remarried in 1855, and the Sieben children soon had a stepmother and a new half-sibling. Apollonia's children did not warm to their new stepmother, and instead of the union providing security for the children, life became fractious and unhappy. Tragedy struck in 1856 when their cabin burned, destroying the entire contents. Unable to provide for them, Joseph was forced to send his children out to live with and work for various friends around Dutch Bottom. Joseph never recovered from the loss and disappointment of the fire, and he died three years later. Family lore suggests his new wife was purposefully responsible.[2]

The Sieben children were orphaned but young, resilient, and now familiar with this new land. The eldest siblings John, Theresa (who had rejoined the family), Valentine, and Margaret took their younger brothers Leonard, Henry, and Jacob under their wings. They all knew how to work hard, thus they continued working for neighboring farms, though this often meant that they were unable to attend school. Two of the younger Sieben boys, Leonard (aged 19) and Henry (aged 16), were coming up on registration age in 1863 when the civil war began, so enlisting in the Army was an option. They could continue to work as farm hands. Leonard had worked for a family friend, Lyman Warren, and Henry had worked for William Bessie and John Hoover, as well as for his older brother, John Sieben, who had managed to secure his own land. But, like their parents, Henry and Leonard Sieben began to imagine a better life elsewhere. When their friends, Louis Heller and Louis Arnett, secured a prairie schooner and four horses in order to travel west, the Sieben brothers pooled their money and joined them. Also like their parents had been, Henry and Leonard were nervous about the journey, but they had nothing to lose. The West held a promise of a better future. Little did they know that Henry was about to begin his modest march to affluence.[3] ❖

Chapter 1

1864–1870

THE LAND OF GOLD

Faced with the options of military service, continued work as a farm laborer, or travel to the West, Henry chose adventure. With that decision, his personal story became intertwined with the story of Montana.

A month before Congress formally established the new territory of Montana on May 26, 1864, Henry Sieben was headed for its gold fields. His companions included his brother, Leonard, and two friends, Louis Arnett and Louis Heller. The four men had heard many tales of the fabled land of gold nuggets for the taking, and they were optimistic they would be successful in making their fortunes. On April 18, 1864, the four young men embarked with a group headed west over the Mormon Trail, paying $90 (approximately $1,700 today) apiece for their passage, including meals. They took turns driving and walking to ease the strain on their horses. The journey offered Henry plenty of time to imagine a future of wealth and promise.[1]

Details are scarce about Henry's overland trail experience. He and his friends likely began their journey by following the Mormon Trail from Nauvoo, Illinois, through modern-day Nebraska to the Platte River, approximately 500 miles. They had plenty of company on this section, as nearly 40,000 migrants poured over it that summer. Half of them split off at the fork of the North and South Platte rivers to take the South Platte Road to Denver. The other half, headed for the Montana and Idaho territories, turned north toward Fort Kearny. When Henry and his party reached the Platte, they followed the north bank of the river to Fort Kearny. Established in 1848, Fort Kearny was the first fort built to protect Overland Trail travelers. Henry recalled that they met a band of Pawnees shortly after the ferry crossing at Council Bluffs, the first Native Americans they encountered on the journey. Henry was relieved the meeting yielded an evening of rapport and merriment, and the two groups spent a cheerful time together racing and engaging in other athletic contests.[2]

Once they and their horses were rested, Henry's group continued the journey on the Platte Road, reaching Fort Laramie in May. This fort was the second military post established on the Overland Trail and was an important stop on the Platte Road. It was also the site where the Fort Laramie Treaty was signed on September 17, 1851, between United States treaty commissioners and representatives of Native nations of the North American Plains. The treaty set forth traditional territorial claims of the nations. The United States acknowledged that the land covered by the treaty was Native American territory and did not claim any part of it. Native Americans guaranteed safe passage for settlers on the Mormon Trail and allowed roads and forts to be built in their territories in exchange for annuity payments of $50,000 (approximately $2 million today) for fifty years. The treaty made the journey west possible for Henry and thousands of others.

Having rested and re-provisioned, Henry's group prepared to continue west to the gold fields. Before they could get underway, however, the officers in charge at Fort Laramie announced that single outfits would not be allowed to travel due to signs of unrest brewing with Native Americans. Since the army could not escort the many settlers flooding in, and thinking there would be greater safety in numbers, they instituted a requirement that travelers form large wagon trains as they headed west. Now the question became which wagon train to join. There were groups already committed to the 800-mile Mormon Trail to Corinne, Utah, while others were considering one of the two newly established and more dangerous northern cutoff routes to the Montana Territory. These became known as the Bozeman Trail and the Bridger Trail.

The Bozeman Trail left the Mormon Trail and headed north-west, following the valleys of the Powder, Bighorn, Yellowstone, and Madison rivers to the gold fields near Virginia City. The route crossed

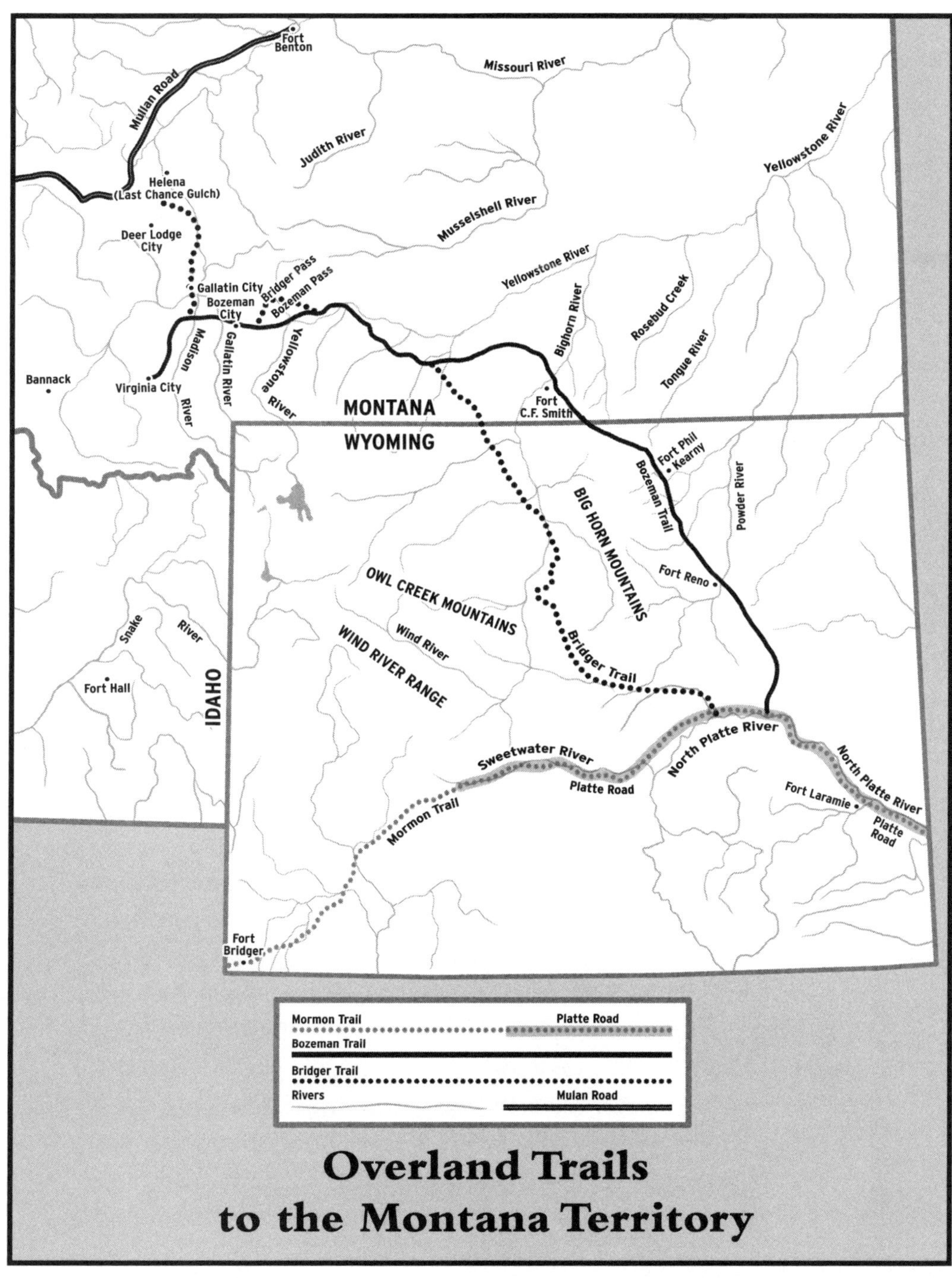

Fort Benton
Missouri River
Mullan Road
Judith River
Yellowstone River
Helena (Last Chance Gulch)
Musselshell River
Deer Lodge City
Yellowstone River
Bridger Pass
Bozeman Pass
Gallatin City
Bozeman City
Bighorn River
Rosebud Creek
Tongue River
Madison River
Gallatin River
Yellowstone River
Bannack
Virginia City
Fort C.F. Smith
MONTANA
WYOMING
Fort Phil Kearny
Bozeman Trail
Powder River
BIG HORN MOUNTAINS
Fort Reno
OWL CREEK MOUNTAINS
Wind River
WIND RIVER RANGE
Bridger Trail
Snake River
Fort Hall
IDAHO
North Platte River
Sweetwater River
Platte Road
North Platte River
Fort Laramie
Platte Road
Mormon Trail
Fort Bridger
Mormon Trail
Platte Road
Bozeman Trail
Bridger Trail
Rivers
Mulan Road
Overland Trails to the Montana Territory

one major pass (now known as Bozeman Pass) dividing the Yellowstone and Missouri River basins. This region was controlled by the Sioux, Cheyenne, and Arapaho tribes. The Bozeman Trail was named for John Bozeman, who made a living guiding wagon trains west to the gold fields. Bozeman (1835–1867) was born in Georgia and abandoned by his father at the age of 14. He left the tumultuous South in 1860 to search for gold in Colorado, abandoning his wife and children. He earned a reputation as a gambler, ladies' man, and self-promoter. He also established and promoted the town that bears his name, which later served as a service and supply center for the growing mining operations in Idaho and Montana territories. While he was adept at "mining the miners," and seemingly always had a new scheme, Bozeman never amassed significant wealth and his colorful life came to a mysterious end in 1867 when he was murdered while traveling to Fort C.F. Smith.[3]

The Bridger Trail, by contrast, ran north through the Big Horn Basin along the western edge of the Big Horn Mountains. The trail ran approximately 425 miles parallel to the Bozeman Trail and also crossed the traditional lands of the Sioux, as well as the traditional lands of the Crow, to the gold fields of the central Montana Territory.

Jim Bridger (1804–1881) was a mountain man remembered for his talents as a guide and a storyteller. He was born in Virginia and orphaned at an early age. He spent twenty years working in the fur trade traversing between the British and American territories to the north and the Spanish and American territories to the south. He established Fort Bridger (a waystation he named for himself) on the Oregon Trail in southwestern Wyoming and established a reputation for providing reliable information and hospitality to those stopping at his fort. He also established the Bridger Trail, using a new cutoff in 1864. In his later years, Bridger worked as a scout for the U.S. Army, though he eventually returned east to Missouri and died on his farm there.[4]

There were many rumors and concerns about "Indian troubles" on both the older and longer Mormon Trail and the two cutoff routes, but the more established route at least offered travelers some confidence in knowing many had gone before them. Clarissa Elvira Shipley and her family, for example, decided that the "farthest way round [was] the safest way home," on their journey from Iowa to Idaho Territory, reflecting the belief that the new shortcut routes were simply too dangerous to attempt.[5]

While Henry and his party grappled with the decision over which route to choose, parties formed for both trails. Bridger gathered 300 men and 100 wagons to take on his new route west of the Big Horn Mountains. The party left Fort Laramie on May 20. The Heller-Sieben party decided to hedge their bets on John Bozeman. Bozeman had been circulating among the wagons, assuring emigrants that there was plenty of grass, water, and wild game on his new cutoff. Bozeman convinced Henry and the hundreds of others gathered at the bridge that with a strong party they could stand off any potential conflicts with Native Americans. Bozeman was tall, good looking, and wore a suit of fringed buckskin. He made enough of an impression on Henry and his party that they chose to follow Bozeman along his shorter but more perilous route.[6]

Bozeman gathered his wagon train at Richard's Bridge, a point northwest of Fort Laramie. Allen Hurlbut, a gold prospector, was also organizing his wagon at the bridge. When Hurlbut's party left on June 16, it was the first to take the Bozeman Trail in 1864. Two days later, Bozeman's train of approximately eighty wagons departed and followed Hurlbut's tracks. Each wagon paid Bozeman $5 ($100 today's value) to lead them across terrain known only to them by rumor and guidebooks. Henry, Leonard, and their two friends were now headed for Virginia City. Little did they know they were partaking in history. This journey turned out to be John Bozeman's first and only guided trip over the entire Bozeman Trail with a wagon train. By the end of 1864, more than 4,000 emigrants took the Bozeman and Bridger Trails into Montana Territory.[7]

Henry Sieben himself shared only brief reminiscences of the remarkable journey. Fortunately, a fellow passenger, John T. Smith, recorded his memories of the trip for the *Bozeman Chronicle* in 1891. Additionally, Abram H. Voorhees, a member of Captain Allen Hurlbut's wagon train, kept a diary of the journey. After departing from Richard's Bridge, Bozeman followed Hurlbut's tracks to Salt Creek, then continued to the Powder River crossing where he stopped to wait for the train that John T. Smith was on to catch up. The second train consisted of about twenty-five wagons and while it did not actually join Bozeman's train, it stayed close behind for mutual support. The Bozeman-Smith trains trailed Hurlbut's party to a few miles south of the Tongue River crossing, halfway between present-day Ranchester and Dayton, Wyoming. On July 2, Bozeman passed the Hurlbut train, which had stopped at Wolf Creek so that passengers could prospect in the Bighorn Mountains. As a result, Bozeman became the trailblazer.[8]

The journey offered an endless sequence of wonders for Henry, Leonard, and their friends. Henry could not help but be struck by the richness of nature they saw the farther they journeyed north from the Mormon Trail. What a sight to see the abundant bison and elk, sometimes a grizzly bear or moose, and wolves circling in packs. Some of Hurlbut's train had joined Bozeman's group and the train now included approximately 108 wagons, or about 360 people. The group reached the Bighorn River on July 4 and reportedly celebrated by killing over 100 bison. This was not an uncommon activity. Many male emigrants enjoyed hunting game along the Bozeman Trail, often just for sport. This behavior was one of the reasons for the depletion of the animals Native Americans subsisted on. By 1868, the Crow Tribe reported they were starving because of the lack of game.[9]

The next morning, Henry and his party experienced their first difficult river crossing at a place now called Spotted Rabbit Crossing on the Bighorn River. The Bighorn was a fast and turbulent river, and the crossing was extremely hazardous. They spent considerable time and effort navigating the crossing. Once across the Bighorn, Bozeman was unsure of the route. He decided to follow Native American trails, leading his wagon train across extremely rough terrain. Henry, Leonard, and their friends were relieved when they finally reached the Yellowstone River opposite present-day Billings.

The wagon train continued its journey up the north side of the Clarks Fork River where they intersected Jim Bridger's route at Rock Creek. Henry recalled that Bridger and his train were just a few days ahead of them at that point. From Rock Creek, Bozeman followed Bridger's trail. The wagon train passed many signs of Native American presence along the trail, including just-abandoned campsites. As the train advanced, they reportedly had three encounters with Native American tribes and at one point were driven off their route east of Rock Creek. Henry recalled they met a band of Crows on Rosebud Creek. At the first sign of conflict, John Bozeman advised the group to be calm and avoid trouble. Henry stated: "Those Crows were a sassy outfit, but we managed to get along with them by giving them a little food from our stores. Candy seemed to please them especially."[10]

Once they were out of danger, Bozeman led his train to the Yellowstone crossing and down the steep, winding descent of Bridger Canyon. Henry and his companions were thrilled when the trail brought them to a warm creek and hot springs (later known as Hunter's Hot Springs) where they rested a little. The group split at the mouth of Shield's River with some travelers going up the Yellowstone River to Emigrant Gulch.[11]

Henry, Leonard, and their two friends continued with John Bozeman over Bozeman Pass and into Virginia City, Montana Territory. They arrived on July 25, 1864, three months and seven days after leaving Illinois.[12] As they completed the last leg of the journey through the Madison River valley and on to Alder Gulch, Henry reveled in the extraordinary profusion of flowers and delighted in the melodious bird song. He would remain in this territory for the rest of his life, witnessing and participating in all the changes that were to come. Until after the Civil War, the place now known as Montana seemed remote and dangerous for newcomers. Native Americans—especially the Piegan, Gros Ventres, Sioux, and Northern Cheyenne—defended their territory well. In the aftermath of the fur trade that had essentially ended in the 1850s, fewer than 1,000 non-Natives lived in the region. Fur trappers and traders such as Malcolm Clarke established livings by marrying Native women and learning how to peacefully negotiate places to trap.

Everything changed with gold. Once gold was discovered in large quantities in 1862, attention to the region quickly increased. The Union seized on an opportunity to use the gold to finance the Civil War. Entrepreneurial farmers flooded in to help feed the miners. Montana became a booming place where the adventurous and desperate alike could start over and perhaps escape the ravages of the Civil War. The non-Native population surged from fewer than 1,000 to more than 20,000 within just a few years. By 1870, that population broke down into 18,306 whites of varying European ethnicities, 1,949 Chinese, and 183 African Americans.[13]

The trail-weary Sieben-Heller party arrived at the chaotic and multicultural town of Virginia City in the summer of 1864. It had been just a few months since a desperate group, known later as the Vigilantes, had banded together and wiped out a gang of road agents. These road agents had murdered at least 100 people in robberies the previous fall. The group had been run under the secret leadership of Sheriff Henry Plummer and had terrorized the surrounding areas for some time. The Vigilantes took the law into their own hands, capturing and hanging twenty road agents of the Plummer gang in the first six weeks of 1864. They were still doling out justice when Henry reached Virginia City. He would later declare that finding himself in a country where bad men had been hanged so recently only added to the thrill. The cutthroat operation was still the topic of discussion at every gathering.[14]

The remote mountain town was established just the summer before, after a gold strike at nearby Alder Gulch. In total, miners would recover an estimated total value of $4 billion worth of gold from the area. People flocked to the new camp from every direction.[15] The Sieben brothers looked wide-eyed at the boisterous world of Virginia City. They noticed the greed, the hard work, the exhaustion, and the hurdy-gurdy houses, as well as the casual fist-blows and gun shots. As they absorbed their new surroundings, the Illinois group tried to get their bearings. During the mild winter and spring since Virginia City's founding, the newly arrived miners had worked tirelessly constructing residential and commercial buildings. Every kind of business from banks to saloons to dry goods were now present. The town held a bookstore, a stationery shop, a bakery, lumberyards, a druggist, hotels, and a reading room.

Henry and Leonard Sieben arrived in Virginia City, Montana Territory, in July 1864 with a wagon train much like this one. Courtesy of the Montana Historical Society Library and Archives, 956-113.

Freight teams from Salt Lake were making noisy, regular arrivals with supplies. Luxury goods were few and far between, but there was no food shortage.[16]

By the following year, the town would begin to take shape. The territorial capital would move from Bannack to Virginia City in 1865, and the territorial legislature would meet on the second floor of the Stonewall Hall on Wallace Street. Local citizens also founded the Montana Historical Society with leading pioneers such as lawyer Wilbur F. Sanders assuming role of president (Sanders was the lawyer for the Vigilantes when Henry first arrived in Virginia City), Judge H. L. Hosmer as historian, and Granville Stuart as secretary. Mr. A. M. Smith would arrive in Virginia City with a camera and photographic supplies to open a gallery over "Con" Orem's saloon. The gallery was crowded with people every day, all anxious to have likenesses taken to send home. Granville Stuart remarked that "most of us had a tintype taken and then this enterprising man, Smith, would place it in a little black case lined with red velvet, call it a 'daguerreotype' and charge us $5 for the same."[17] The photograph gallery was as profitable as a mining claim. Unfortunately, no daguerreotypes of Henry or Leonard have survived. Henry had little money and his childhood had taught him the value of frugality. He viewed photographs and keepsakes as flamboyant unnecessary purchases.

As vibrant as the town was, Henry and his party quickly discerned they would not make their fortunes in Virginia City. They observed how newly arrived miners worked six days a week gathering together some gold dust. Gold dust was the sole medium of exchange at the time, and it was valued at $18 (approximately $350 today) an ounce. Every business house had gold scales for weighing the dust. When miners had cleaned up their gold dust, they placed it in a buckskin sack and went to a gambling den or dance hall where they remained until they had spent the contents of the sack. Miners indulged in every sort of gambling game, and it was not uncommon to see $1,000 bet on the turn of a monte card. These gold seekers would then return to their diggings to repeat the same thing over and over as long as their claim lasted. When it ran out, they started out again, belongings on their backs, in search of new claims.

However, Henry's group had not traveled this far to jump into a tumultuous and unstable world. Gambling for a quick thrill held little interest to them. Instead, these plucky young men chose to gamble on themselves. The group split up and Louis Heller and Louis Arnett continued south to Utah. Leonard Sieben's keen eye quickly observed that just as important as extracting the precious metal from the streams and hillsides was the need for supplies in the mining camps. Shortly after their friends left, Leonard got a job with the Diamond R Company freighting goods and supplies to Montana's mining towns. Henry fell back on his skillset, working as a field hand.[18]

Henry and Leonard were nervous yet excited as they parted ways in the summer of 1864. There would be no government mail route to Virginia City until November of 1864, but they knew it would be established before long. Once that happened, they would keep abreast of their comings and goings by depositing mail for one another at the

An early view of Virginia City, Montana Territory, as Henry Sieben would have known it. Courtesy of the Montana Historical Society Library and Archives, 956-063.

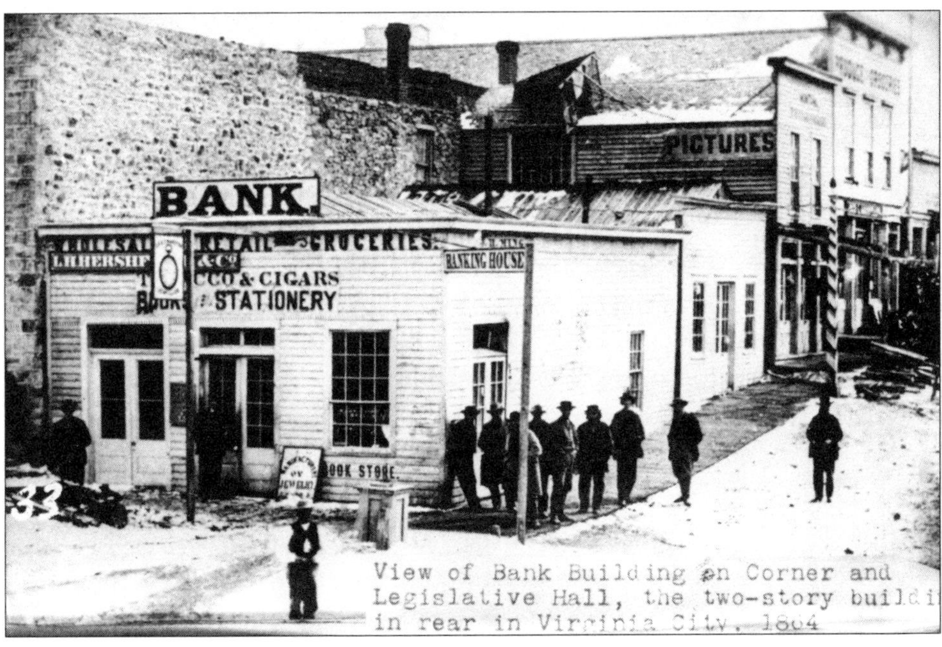

L.H. and Aaron Hershfield were two of Virginia City's earliest entrepreneurs and were close associates of Henry Sieben. Pictured here, the Hershfield dry goods store and bank in Virginia City, 1864. Courtesy of the Montana Historical Society Library and Archives, 956-102.

post office. All they would have to do was consult the "Letters List" in the territory's first newspaper, *The Montana Post* (there are two notices of mail waiting for them at the Virginia City Post Office in 1865 and 1866).[19] Until then, it was time to roll up their sleeves and get to work in this new land.

Henry secured his first job with two ranchers named Joe Goey and Jeff Gowan. They paid him $50 per month ($1,000 today's value) and put him to work cutting hay with a scythe and raking it with a hand rake on their ranch at Meadow Creek, just north of Virginia City. Henry easily settled in, assisting his employers in baling and hauling hay to Virginia City where there was a ready feed market for stage and saddle horses.

The balmy fall of 1864 stretched well into November. There was no severe weather until about early December, when a sudden storm arrived. The thermometer dropped to thirty-seven degrees below zero, and a foot of snow fell in the valleys surrounding Meadow Creek. That first snow lay on the ground and daily storms added to it until there were two feet of snow in the valleys and from five to six feet on the divides. As the work on the ranch receded, Henry's bosses cut his pay to $25 ($500 today's value) for the duration of the winter. This didn't sit well with the ambitious immigrant.[20]

Just like Henry, Montana's future was also in flux. The growing territorial population of 20,000 resulted in new and important gold discoveries. As claims around Bannack and Virginia City filled up, miners moved on to make gold strikes on Prickly Pear, Last Chance, Silver Bow, and Ophir creeks. As mining operations moved to new locations, boomtowns sprang up nearby to support them. To make sense of the chaos, law and order had to follow.

The first Montana territorial legislature met in Bannack in December 1864. Governor Sidney Edgerton from New York convened the proceedings, having been named territorial governor by President Lincoln earlier the same year. The lawmakers who assembled in Bannack from December 12, 1864, through February 9, 1865, set about defining the more practical aspects of governance: the number of counties (nine), the number of judicial districts (three), a prohibition on gambling scams, policies for managing livestock, taxing mining properties, and assuring the administration of justice in the rough and tumble mining towns.[21]

Henry was unsure of his next move and so he stayed on the Meadow Creek Ranch for the winter. This choice provided him with time to establish friendships and business associates. He also visited Virginia City for supplies and news of Leonard.

While he waited, Henry witnessed a disaster unfold that would set him on his first business venture. Several wagon trains traveling from Salt Lake loaded with flour and other provisions were snowed in at Beaver Canyon, Idaho, and all their oxen had perished. Provisions of every kind became scarce in Virginia City and the surrounding area. The price of flour—one of the most essential supplies for any community—skyrocketed. In fall 1864, a ninety-eight-pound sack of St. Louis flour was $26.50 ($500 today's value). By early April, the price had risen to more than $40 ($800 today's value) a sack, and by the end of the month, the price rose to $100—even $150 ($2,000 to $3,000 today's value). That was more than twenty times the price in the rest of the country. Most people were unable to purchase provisions and were reduced to a diet of only beef. Thanks to newly arriving cattlemen, beef was plentiful, selling for $0.15 ($3 today's value) per pound. Henry listened, observed, and started thinking about the essential and lucrative business of transporting goods.

The scarcity of provisions led to great distress and tension in Virginia City that winter, and that stress resulted in a riot. Sheriff Neil Howie, aided by the Vigilance Committee, supervised the first "flour riot." More than 400 people marched into Virginia City residences and public buildings and confiscated all the flour they could find. Ultimately, the rioters rounded up more than eighty sacks of flour, stockpiled them, and then redistributed the flour to the town's residents.[22]

Henry's takeaway from this incident was that there would be a lucrative future in freighting, and he devised a plan to start his own freighting business. In typical resolute style, Henry walked approximately seventy miles to the Gallatin Valley in the spring of 1865 and used the money he had saved working on the ranch to secure himself a wagon and a team of oxen. This marked his first business venture in Montana, and it set the pattern for many subsequent ventures: intentional, considered steps toward a calculated risk.

Soon Henry was following in Leonard's tracks running freight over the Mullan Road from Fort Benton to Helena and Virginia City. He also traveled the Montana Road bringing supplies from Salt Lake City and Corinne, Utah, to Montana's mining camps.[23] Connecting roads branched from the Mullan and Montana roads to the mining camps, the Gallatin and Missoula valleys, and Fort Benton. Montana's road system originated as aboriginal trails used by generations of Native Americans as they followed the bison herds. The fur trappers later used those trails, and in 1860, Montana's first road engineer, John Mullan, developed some of them for wagon use. Today's highways follow these same routes.

Henry freighted goods between Virginia City, Helena, and Fort Benton with an outfit similar to this team of oxen shown on Front Street in Fort Benton, Montana Territory, 1865–1877. Courtesy of the Montana Historical Society Library and Archives, 947-075.

Henry Sieben was not the only one with this bold idea to freight supplies through Blackfeet and Bannack country. The Mullan and Montana roads were clogged with wagons and stagecoaches endeavoring to reach the mines. Henry's ears vibrated with the sounds of snapping bullwhips, squeaking wagon wheels, and the gruff encouragements of bullwhackers, muleskinners, and stagecoach drivers to oxen, mules, and horses. He heard the bullwhackers long before sighting the wagons.[24]

Like the others, Sieben's outfit consisted of three wagons coupled together with the largest wagon at the rear. Trains usually consisted of twenty-five sets of wagons. Each wagon was overseen by a driver who walked alongside it. Six or sometimes seven yokes of oxen towed each wagon set. Each team of oxen could haul up to 20,000 pounds of supplies. If hauling perishable goods, freighters used smaller wagon sets and faster mule teams.

Part of doing business from 1865 to 1870 for freighters like the Sieben brothers and migrant travelers was navigating a maze of unsurveyed toll roads and bridges. These were literally a pay-as-you-go system—toll collectors built the roads and bridges around geographic obstacles and then charged travelers for their use, and price gouging was a common occurrence. For example, when Henry loaded a wagon, he could expect to pay $40 in tolls on Montana Road between Helena and Corinne, Utah. That would roughly translate to $800 today. Of course, the freighters passed on these costs to their customers, making goods and supplies even more expensive.[25]

Once Henry had purchased his first freighting outfit, he and Jeff Gowan, the rancher who had hired Henry at Meadow Creek, made their first stop at Virginia City. In a poignant passage, evocative of a young boy's longing for company and celebration, the eighteen-year-old Henry recorded with special clarity this welcome spectacle in Virginia City:

> I drove back to the same ranch and Mr. Gowan and I pulled out for Virginia City, March 17th, 1865. The reason I remember the date is that it was St. Patrick's Day and the Irish miners had a

> parade and displayed their beautiful green flag, which I thought was the most beautiful thing I had ever seen. The next day we loaded up some freight for Last Chance Gulch (Helena).[26]

It took Henry and Jeff seven days to reach the camp at Last Chance Gulch. Henry later recalled that this was a pretty good time for the 130-mile journey. The camp was just about a year old and there was a high demand for lumber. Henry and Jeff secured a contract to haul and cut logs for a sawmill located a few miles away at the mouth of Lump Gulch. They would then haul the finished lumber into the camp at Last Chance Gulch, which Henry later noted was "the starting point of Helena."[27]

The town of Helena began with the lucky strike by a group of four gold seekers on July 14, 1864, in the Prickly Pear Valley. They named the location Last Chance Gulch and soon thousands of prospectors descended on the area. The Prickly Pear Valley and surrounding mountains had been a prime location for Shoshone, Pend d'Oreille, Salish, and Blackfeet hunting parties for generations. It was a crucial place, the site of converging trails to bison, elk, deer, antelope, and wolves. Once gold was struck, it also became a vital service and supply center for miners, freighters, merchants, bankers, and ranchers. And it was here that Henry Sieben eventually made his home.[28]

Although Henry Sieben had a partner and a freighting operation, he spent the rest of 1865 trying his hand at various other enterprises, as well. His first job was as a laborer at the new sawmill in Last Chance Gulch where he and Jeff Gowan worked from April to June 1865, producing lumber to build the new community. When June rains flooded out the dam at the mill, putting everyone out of work, Henry decided to try his hand at mining. He started at Ophir Gulch on the west side of the divide and mined there briefly before hearing of another strike on nearby Madison Gulch at the head of Nevada Creek. Like many others, Henry threw in with two partners named Day and John Brown, and they worked the placer mine claim at Madison Gulch until October of 1865, but with little to show and winter coming on, the trio dissolved their partnership. Henry then made his way southeast to Crow Creek to hunt. He later recalled that he spent the winter hunting in the area with an Irishman named Collins and another man named George Powell. Together, they provided game to Virginia City and Helena, earning between "1 to 20 cents per pound."[29]

Henry realized that supplying the miners was more lucrative than mining his own claim, and he was content to let his mining interests lapse. He was not alone in this realization. During Henry's 1866 freighting season, an estimated 2,500 wagons pulled by 20,000 oxen and driven by 3,000 bullwhackers traversed the Benton Road to the camps in central Montana.[30] Of course, many of Henry's contemporaries did find success in the mines or combined mining with other enterprises. William Andrews Clark began freighting goods in Montana Territory then quickly diversified his operations. Clark's rise was spectacular; he pocketed $42,000 (approximately $800,000 today) from his placer mining near Bannack, ran a successful freighting business to the camps, built his fortune in banking, then capped his rise by purchasing four promising copper mines. Clark became one of the famed Copper Kings of Butte.[31]

During the winter of 1866, Henry and his freighting companions who were hunting in the Missouri River area between Fort Benton and Last Chance Gulch occasionally encountered Native American hunting parties. These encounters were usually friendly, and Henry recalled one interaction where a group traveling by foot asked for some meat. Henry gave them a deer, which they cut into chunks so they could carry it more easily. Henry described each of them as having a good lariat, which made a number of the members of Henry's outfit extremely suspicious. Two days later this same group returned and stole fourteen of Henry's fifteen horses. Henry and his companions pooled their resources and hired a "Frenchman" by the name of Vel (probably a Métis, a person of mixed European and Indigenous heritage) to "act as interpreter and they went out on the Marias River and succeeded in trading for the horses. They cost us about $13 per head to get them back."[32] The experience opened Henry's eyes to the reality of the conflicts

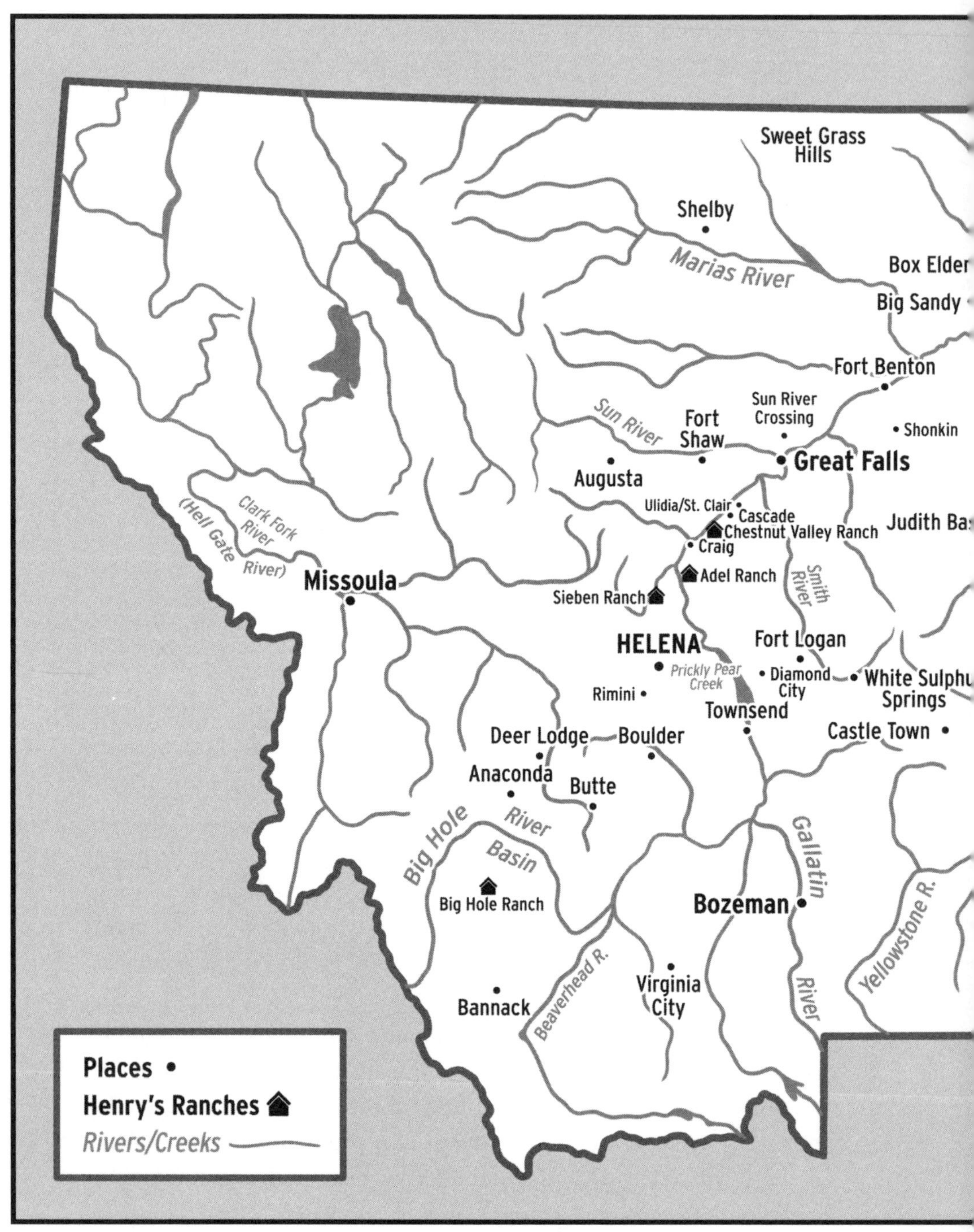

Sweet Grass Hills
Shelby
Marias River
Box Elder
Big Sandy
Fort Benton
Sun River Crossing
Shonkin
Sun River
Fort Shaw
Great Falls
Augusta
Ulidia/St. Clair
Cascade
Chestnut Valley Ranch
Judith Ba
Craig
Adel Ranch
Smith River
Sieben Ranch
Clark Fork River
(Hell Gate River)
Missoula
HELENA
Prickly Pear Creek
Fort Logan
Diamond City
White Sulphu
Springs
Rimini
Townsend
Castle Town
Deer Lodge
Boulder
Anaconda
Butte
Big Hole River
Basin
Big Hole Ranch
Gallatin River
Bozeman
Yellowstone R.
Beaverhead R.
Virginia City
Bannack
Places
Henry's Ranches
Rivers/Creeks

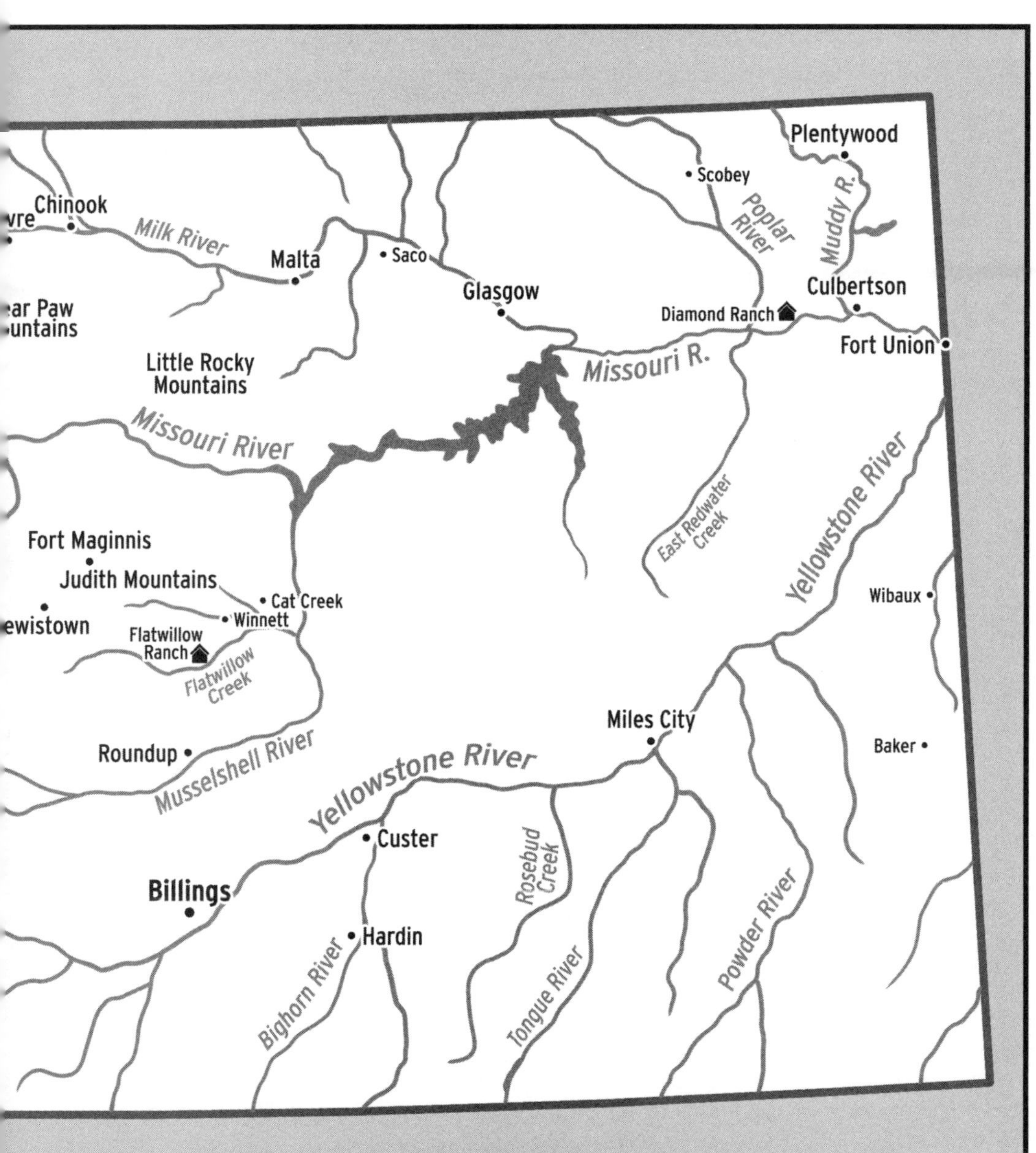

Henry Sieben in Montana
1864–1937

between Natives and non-Natives. Although a number of his partners favored violence over bartering when it came to horse theft, Henry preferred a non-violent approach. He later recalled that in all his years on the range, he never had a violent confrontation with Native Americans.

While Henry had been mining, hunting, and freighting to survive, Leonard had been crisscrossing the territory hauling goods for business magnate Charles A. Broadwater (1840–1892) at the Diamond R Freighting Company. When Leonard joined Henry at Crow Creek in spring of 1866, the brothers decided to enter a partnership together and start their own freighting business. However, before they could start, the brothers split up to gather the necessary capital for the venture. Henry later remembered:

> In the spring [Leonard] went to Utah with the team, and I hired out by the month to Swett and Metzger, driving team. That trip took us until July before we got back. Then we got together at Helena. He came up with a load of barley and sold it to Nick Kessler and then we bought another team from Billy Lemon. He sold it to us on time and agreed to furnish us freight from Salt Lake City up here and we made that trip in the fall of the year and earned money enough to pay for the team, six yoke of cattle and the wagon.[33]

Henry and Leonard spent the rest of 1866 developing their freighting business, making trips from Salt Lake City and Ogden, Utah, to Deer Lodge, Virginia City, and Helena and from Fort Benton to Helena and Virginia City, as well. Fort Benton was a special place. The town began in 1846 as an outpost of the American Fur Company. As the head of navigation on the Missouri River, Fort Benton quickly shifted from a fur trade center to a service and supply center for the miners. The Sieben brothers rushed in to help move those supplies. As the supplies flowed in, gold flowed out. In fact, at least 200 tons of gold flowed out by this route between 1862 and 1869. In August of 1866, Granville Stuart witnessed the arrival of a freight wagon in Fort Benton. Drawn by four mules and escorted by a company of miners, the wagon was loaded with two and a half tons of gold dust, valued at $1.5 million ($30 million today's value). The gold came from Confederate Gulch in the Big Belt Mountains and was to be shipped downriver by steamboat.[34]

Not surprisingly, such cargo shipments made Fort Benton a lively scene for thieves. The town had a similar rough-and-tumble feel to Virginia City. People and materials flew through town at a remarkable pace. Henry did not stay long in either place, freighting frequently from one to the other. He left Fort Benton in May 1867 and made two trips to Helena and one to Deer Lodge, all in just a few weeks. He then traveled to Fort Peck, a landing point south of present-day Glasgow, Montana, where the steamboat *Fort Peck* had just arrived but was unable to continue upriver because of low water. Along the journey, Henry met a team of Garrison & Wyatt freighters who were returning from a freight trip to Fort Union. Henry was warned to turn back due to the presence of hostile Natives. Henry recalled, "They tried to prevail upon us to turn back and not go down, but we concluded to take chances and make the trip all right. The freight we got belonged to the firm of Kenny & Jack, a hard-ware firm in Helena."[35] Luckily, Henry transported the freight to Helena without incident.

As the 1860s drew to a close, Leonard and Henry realized they needed to focus their business interests elsewhere. The transcontinental railroad was nearing completion in 1868, and the Sieben brothers knew that when the train arrived in Montana Territory, overland freighting would be largely unnecessary. So, they turned their attention to the cattle industry. Cattlemen had entered the Montana Territory area before the gold rushes of the 1860s. In 1850, recognizing an opportunity, enterprising former fur-trader Richard Grant and his sons began acquiring cattle through trade, driving them north to the Beaverhead Basin area of southwestern Montana for grazing. The Grants then herded the fattened cattle back to the Oregon Trail the following spring, trading one fresh animal for two that were trail weary. By the mid-1860s, the Grants had several thousand head of cattle in the Deer Lodge Valley. In 1864, William C. Orr, of California-based Poindexter and Orr partnership, drove a herd into the Beaverhead Valley for wintering. Soon they were running one of the territory's largest cattle and sheep operations. Other savvy businessmen including Conrad Kohrs and Philip Lovell had also turned to raising and selling livestock. Kohrs bought Johnny Grant's ranch in 1866 and soon after ranked among Montana's leading stockmen. Texas cattle rancher Dan Floweree bought a cattle herd from Missouri in 1865, and cattle rancher and vigilante Nelson Story (1838–1926) drove the first Texas longhorns into Montana, locating in the Gallatin Valley.[36]

Henry and Leonard closed out a successful freighting season in 1867 and then returned to their wintering headquarters on the Missouri River to prepare for their new enterprise. They made two trips from Fort Benton to Helena and one to Virginia City in the spring of 1868 before buying approximately 100 head of cattle. Then they hauled 200 cords of wood from below Sun River Crossing to Fort Shaw in order to spend the winter hunting and looking after their herd. Henry remembered that "in the spring, Brother Leonard went to Fort Benton and made a contract with the butcher, Mr. Stockings to deliver these old work oxen for beef at 10 cents per pound. We bought the cattle the year before. They cost us $10 to $12 per head, and when they butchered them at the rate of 10 cents per pound they netted us $90 to $100."[37] That settled it: their next venture was cattle raising.

As a new decade stretched out in front of them, the Sieben brothers, now in their mid-twenties, were becoming seasoned pioneers, with farming, freighting, mining, and cattle experience under their belts. ◈

Chapter 2

1870–1879

"I PADDLED MY OWN CANOE"

With the dawn of the new decade, Henry and Leonard Sieben were ready to diversify their family business operations. The railways were offering cheaper and faster freight and supplies, and the brothers saw demand for their wagon transport diminishing. Meanwhile, Montana's growing population was creating a strong market for beef, something Henry and Leonard were anxious to supply. In what would become a familiar pattern, the brothers pivoted to a new business gradually, continuing to take on freighting contracts while simultaneously building a cattle operation.

In the spring of 1870, the brothers readied their teams and freight wagons and headed south to Corinne, Utah, in search of goods and supplies. Corinne was a Union Pacific freight and supply station where freighters offloaded goods and supplies from the trains to wagons headed for the gold camps. Here the brothers learned they had only half the freight they had expected. So, they pivoted. While Henry took that load, Leonard rode to Bear Lake Valley some seventy miles northeast to purchase cattle.

Bear Lake figured prominently in the great migration on the Oregon and California trails. By the early 1860s, European settlers had fanned across the valley and created towns along the edge of the lake, growing hay and grain, and running cattle and sheep across grassy meadows. Leonard was encouraged by the quality and price of the stock he saw at Bear Lake and purchased 160 animals. Then he returned to Corinne where he hired Henry Schrammeck to help him trail animals, mowing machines, rakes, wagons, and other equipment back to Montana. Schrammeck stayed on to assist the Sieben brothers in the Chestnut Valley and served as their first ranch manager.[1]

Long cattle drives characterized Montana and the West during the prosperous years of the industry from 1860 to 1890. The movement of large herds of cattle, ranging in numbers from 100 to 2,500, required teams of men, wagons, horses, equipment, and provisions. Leonard and Schrammeck traveled about ten miles a day from Corinne to the area near present-day Cascade, Montana, a distance of about 500 miles. The nearly two-month-long journey was difficult. On a typical day, the team broke camp at daybreak, grazed their herd on the move throughout the day, took a brief break at noon, and then stopped early for the evening. At night, a pair of mounted cowboys took turns circling the herd to keep the cattle together. The "night hawk" was usually the youngest or most inexperienced cowhand, and he was tasked to stay up all night to guard the herd and the horses.[2]

The Sieben brothers needed capital to launch the new cattle operation. While Leonard was driving cattle, Henry continued to haul freight to help pay for them. That summer, one of his contracts was with Charles Broadwater, who contracted Henry to take a load of government freight from Corinne to Fort Ellis in the Gallatin Valley, the base of operations for the settlement and for exploration of the Yellowstone region. At Fort Ellis, Henry found a strong demand for his wagon and team. Local farmers were anxious to transport barley to Nickolas Kessler's brewery in Helena, now a thirsty town of 3,000 some eighty miles to the west. Kessler had immigrated to the United States from Luxembourg in 1854, followed the gold rush west to Bannack in 1863, and later moved to Helena where he purchased an interest in a fledgling brewery located on Ten Mile Creek.

Gallatin Valley barley was not Henry's last freight load. That same summer of 1870 he acquired a contract from Lewis & Reese, a mining outfit from St. Louis, Missouri, to move a ten-stamp quartz mill from Georgetown in southwest Montana to St. Louis, Montana (now Hassel), a mining camp on Indian Creek just west of present-day Townsend, Montana. This was a trip of nearly 140 miles. The ten-stamp quartz mill consisted of ten heavy steel columns called stamps along with two large frames in which the stamps would slide up and down to crush ore. It took

Henry two trips to transport the heavy mill over rough and primitive roads. As soon as the stamp mill parts were unloaded, Lewis & Reese hired Henry to freight 3,000 feet of timber to construct the mill. By the time he finally pulled into winter quarters in the Chestnut Valley in the fall of 1870, Henry had not seen Leonard in months, but his pockets were full.[3]

As the Sieben brothers started their cattle business, conflicts between the U.S. government and Native Americans shifted from control of the roads and trails to control over the land itself. By 1870, there were over 20,000 non-Native residents in Montana Territory and railroad, mining, and ranching interests were insisting the government open more land for settlement. In 1873, President Ulysses S. Grant signed an executive order establishing most of Montana north of the Missouri River as a reservation for the Blackfeet, Gros Ventres, Assiniboine, and Sioux. A year later, he issued another executive order shifting the boundary of that reservation north to the Marias River—cutting out some of the best traditional Blackfeet hunting lands and opening it up to stockmen such as the Sieben brothers.

Native Americans stood their ground, many times refusing to be relegated to the ever-shrinking reservations. The resulting tensions caused much bloodshed. Among the most notorious episodes was the Marias Massacre. In 1869, a handful of Blackfeet men killed Henry's business associate, Malcolm Clarke, at his ranch north of Helena, a site that would eventually be part of the present-day Sieben Ranch. Clarke and his family are buried in a small plot that remains on the ranch. When the Blackfeet refused to turn over the men involved in Clarke's killing to the government, federal troops were sent from Fort Ellis to retaliate. In January 1870, under the command of Major Eugene Baker, the U.S. 2nd Cavalry launched an attack on a peaceful Blackfeet winter camp. Baker's men killed 173 people that day including elders, women, and children, none of whom had been responsible for the death of Malcolm Clarke. The 2nd Cavalry had attacked the wrong camp.

Other tragic battles followed. In order for the Sieben brothers and thousands of other ranchers, miners, and homesteaders to settle the territory, the federal government had to settle significant issues with western tribes. Events such as the Battle of the Little Bighorn in 1876 and the Battle of the Bear Paw in 1877 were among the many conflicts that ultimately cost countless lives, relegated Native Americans to reservations, and made more land available to settlers in Montana Territory. The expanding livestock industry demanded that land. Once there was beef, hay, and grain available, more settlers arrived and they, too, sought new land.[4]

The cattle industry developed rapidly. The fertile Sun River Valley served as the main portal for the northeastward movement of the cattle industry. Conrad Kohrs, for example, brought 1,000 head of cattle to the south bank of the Sun River near Fort Shaw in 1869. From the beginning, water was a top priority for ranchers in Montana. As the Sun River Valley filled up, others pushed beyond the Missouri into the sheltered confines of the Smith and Musselshell rivers, settling on creeks with various springs and water resources. In the 1870s most of the breeding stock were Shorthorn, Hereford, and Angus cattle, and they grazed on open, unfenced range. The animals largely fended for themselves, with natural barriers such as forests and rivers limiting their movements. This allowed ranchers to cut small amounts of hay, establishing a pattern of driving herds to the high country in the summer and back to the lush valley floors for winter pasture.[5]

The Sieben brothers studied these patterns, watching and planning. By the spring of 1871, they were ready to focus exclusively on raising and selling livestock. They sold their freighting outfit to Thomas Clary, a wagon master with the Diamond R Freight Company, for $3,750 ($95,000 today's value), which included twenty-one pairs of oxen and nine wagons, using the proceeds to send Leonard and the ranch manager back to Utah to buy more animals. The pair bought and trailed 400 head of cattle back to the Chestnut Valley, while Henry oversaw ranch operations and put up hay for the winter. By the fall of 1871, the brothers' herd had grown to more than 600 animals.

The daily work of the open range suited Leonard and Henry. The brothers were strong, excellent horsemen, and accustomed to Montana's extreme weather. In the spring of 1872, the Sieben brothers sold seventy-five beef cattle to a butcher in Helena, and Leonard used

On Montana's open range, cattle were annually rounded up, roped, and branded to identify the owner. Photo by L.A. Huffman, ca. 1880, courtesy of the Montana Historical Society Library and Archives, 981-439.

the proceeds to make a third trip to Utah, securing and trailing another 300 animals from Bear Lake to the Chestnut Valley.

The cattle industry in Montana was growing up, and it was a competitive business. At the same time, the placer mining boom waned and many of the miners left, reducing some of the demand for beef. The Sieben brothers persevered. They sold beef each spring to butchers in the still-busy mining towns of Diamond City, Marysville, Helena, and Butte. They also sold cattle to purchasers who shipped the animals down the Missouri River from Fort Benton to Bismarck and from there to Chicago by rail.[6]

In 1872, Montana established a brand office and made brand registration a territory-wide requirement. Now that they were becoming significant players in the cattle business, the Siebens needed to create and register their brand and, in 1874, Leonard and Henry recorded their first brand: a diamond. (See Appendix II on page 218.)

When word of Leonard and Henry's success in Montana reached their family in Illinois in 1872, their younger brother, Jacob "Jake," decided he would also take a chance on seeking his fortune in Montana. After eight years in the territory, Leonard and Henry finally received their first family visitor from Illinois. Unfortunately for Jake, his first winter was bitterly cold. Conrad Kohrs remembered the winter as one of the coldest he ever experienced:

> My brother and I were out one day. We were well clad, wore mocassins [*sic*] and buffalo overshoes, had a blanket from our saddle that we wrapped around our legs and thighs. We experienced no trouble except with our mouth and eyes. The breath froze on our lips and we had trouble keeping our eyes open. All the quicksilver thermometers in Deer Lodge were frozen and the way we found out how cold it was by Chris Wibeau's thermometer at Silver Bow which registered sixty below.[7]

Now three in number, the Sieben brothers built a substantial operation in the Chestnut Valley, Henry's first real home in Montana. The Chestnut Valley was one of the earliest European settlements in the state of Montana. It lies along the east side of the Missouri River, approximately 30 miles south of present-day Great Falls, and was described by Lewis and Clark in their *Journal of 1805* as a "handsome level plain." It is located on what was a main overland route that connected Fort Shaw on the Sun River to the mining camp of Helena. The first settler was the valley's namesake Robert Chesnut, who built a cabin in the area in the fall of 1868 (the spelling without the first "t" is the correct one, but long usage has made Chestnut universal). Lush grass in the lowlands along the river, and trees and brush for shelter made it an ideal place to winter oxen.

More and more immigrants and families, from Europe and the East Coast, settled here in the 1870s, thus transforming the area into a stable community where the Sieben brothers could operate their cattle business. An original settler of the valley, Eva Nolan, recalled that there were numerous German settlers here, including the Siebens, Henry Burmeister, and Robert Abel. The newcomers multiplied rapidly. Over the course of the 1870s, sheep ranchers increased in numbers and holdings throughout the territory, following the same path of geographic expansion into central Montana as the cattlemen. Well-established investors began to take notice of the potential of the sheep industry, especially when John Healy, a representative of a major wool-purchasing concern, opened a depot at Helena in 1878. Montana investors stocked the ranges by sending buyers to California and Oregon mostly. Drovers trailed sheep to the territory in bands of 2,000 to 6,000, sometimes stretching out fifty miles. By early 1879, 15,000 sheep were grazing on the Smith River and 60,000 were on the Musselshell River.[8]

Already learning to be at the fore of emerging industries, the Sieben brothers floated the idea of adding sheep to their operation in 1875. It was Jake who first proposed the bold business venture at a time when the brothers were navigating a national economic downturn that had begun with the Panic of 1873. Large banks on the East Coast that were financing the railroads began to fold, and the collapse sparked high bank withdrawals, failed brokerage firms, and halted railway construction. The downturn lasted until 1878 or 1879. While other outfits tightened their purse strings, Leonard, Henry, and Jake bet on themselves and expanded into the sheep business.

In the mid-1870s, there were no sheep for sale in Montana. In fact, Henry would later recall that there were only one or two bands in the entire territory. But Jake was resolute that the future was strong for sheep. In 1875, Leonard and Henry agreed to finance him, and Jake traveled to Red Bluff, California, to purchase 2,225 Merino ewes at an expense of $6,000 (approximately $170,000 today). Since construction on the Northern Pacific Railroad had halted in 1873, he had no choice but to trail the sheep back to Montana—a trip of 1,000 miles.

Jake struggled in the first few years. The weather was so bitterly cold in December 1875 that he was forced to stop with his sheep in the Prickly Pear Valley near Helena. Leonard rode down to meet him and found the sheep in such poor shape that he postponed a trip east in order to help care for them. He hired a rancher to haul hay to the sheep, but they became so badly infected with mange that half the flock died before spring. In desperation, they called on help from I.G. Baker & Company in Fort Benton to bring them up two hogsheads (large barrels) of scrap tobacco from St. Louis to dip the sheep and cure the mange. When the tobacco arrived, Henry traveled north with four horse teams to pick it up and haul it back to the valley. The three brothers built vats of two-inch lumber and dipped the sheep twice in the summer of 1876. The dip cured the animals, and Jake was able to save the remainder of the flock. It was a hard lesson. Interestingly, the location of the dipping vats eventually became part of the modern-day Sieben Ranch, and the vats remain near the Towhead buildings east of Interstate 15 on the Sieben Flats.[9]

Jake's poor luck with the sheep continued and he suffered another heavy loss in 1876. One particular winter morning, his herder turned a band of 1,200 sheep out of the corral and then returned to his cabin for breakfast. While he ate, a storm drove the sheep across a half-frozen slough. The ice gave way and the sheep plunged into the freezing water, drowning 400. A Helena news article that reported on the incident offered the following advice to new ranchers: "Never let the flock out of the corral until the herder is ready to go with them; and then see that the herder never leaves the sheep until they are back in the corral."[10]

Despite these setbacks, the Sieben brothers' operations grew. Their reputations as businessmen also grew and their activities were often reported in the local papers. At the end of 1875, the Republican newspaper, the *Helena Weekly Herald,* made sure to let its readership know that Henry Sieben had dropped into their offices to renew his subscription to the paper. When Leonard visited Fort Benton in the winter of 1876, the *Benton Record* reported his arrival and quoted him as stating that "everything is lovely and the sheep run high on the hills for there is no snow worth mentioning."[11]

In March 1876, Leonard and Henry along with their neighbor and friend Charles W. Swett arrived in Helena with sixty head of beef cattle and sold them to Guthrie & Norris, a local market. *The Herald* covered the business deal made by the "famous stockmen" who drove the cattle "directly from the bunch grass ranges of Sun River and the Missouri, where they have run during the entire winter, receiving no other feed besides that supplied from the fields."[12] In the same edition, an overly excited journalist wrote that one of the Siebens' seven-year-old cows weighed 800 pounds; these shrewd businessmen couldn't have asked for better—or more hopelessly exaggerated—publicity.

Ranchers on the open range had to cooperate in segregating animals and determining ownership, resulting in the tradition of the roundup. The roundup was a twice-annual cooperative effort to gather all the cattle in a region, sort them out, brand new calves, and trail each herd to its winter or summer range. The roundup was a regular feature of the Sieben brothers' year in the Chestnut Valley. It usually lasted weeks and meant hard work for everyone. Large roundups were colorful affairs, employing as many as seventy men and hundreds of horses. A roundup captain oversaw the entire operation and held the authority to hire, fire, and command the help. Cowhands were up at 4:00 a.m. to look for stray cattle and herd them back to the roundup area. After the spring roundup, the cattle were turned out or trailed to summer pasture. The second roundup in the fall allowed ranchers to select cattle for market and then trail them to the nearby towns or a railhead.[13]

Henry participated in the hard work of making and breaking camp on numerous cattle roundups over the years. Roundups required a large number of hired hands and horses as shown here ca. 1890. Courtesy of the Montana Historical Society Library and Archives, 981-451.

The roundups required the Sieben brothers to be away from their ranches for significant periods of time throughout the year. While the Sieben brothers were away on roundups, Jake's wife, Sylvia, and their two sons, Robert and Charles, oversaw the running of the Chestnut Valley operation. Sylvia and the boys had arrived in Fort *Benton* in May 1876. Like so many others, Sylvia had boarded the steamer Benton with her children at St. Louis, Missouri, for a two-and-a-half-month journey. When they arrived in Montana, it had been four years since the family had been together. Jake temporarily moved them into the one-room cottonwood log cabin he shared with Leonard and Henry in the Chestnut Valley.

The newcomers had little time to adjust to their surroundings as four feet of snow fell the first of June. Workers arrived in droves to the valley, having come down from the mountains to get out of the snowstorms. They slept in wagons and tents near the small Chestnut community, and Sylvia used both fireplace and cooking stove to help them all. When the snow melted suddenly, they used boats to travel around the ranch. Jake soon moved his family and their sheep to a nearby cabin known as the Cobell Place, located at the mouth of Hound Creek, approximately fifteen miles east. They stayed there for a few weeks and then returned to the Chestnut Valley where they lived in tents until the haying was done. In late October, the brothers moved the Cobell Place cabin to the tent site and built another room for Leonard, Henry, and others to occupy as needed.

Women worked hard on the ranches. Sylvia washed clothing and household linens by hand and hung them out to dry in all weather. She served as doctor and pharmacist for the cowboys and sick neighbors. She cooked for family members and the hired help. She grew and preserved fruit and vegetables and raised chickens, milk cows, pigs, turkeys, and geese for the family to eat and to sell. Luckily for all, life on the ranch suited Sylvia, and despite the long hours of hard work, she found time to enjoy the natural beauty and expansive horizons their new home offered. Sylvia also helped improve the Chestnut Valley community by providing much-needed social outlets for the young

Robert Thoroughman and his family, pictured here on their ranch in the Chestnut Valley in 1888, were early neighbors of the Sieben brothers. Standing at center are Robert and Anna Thoroughman with their children Joseph and Anna (at left with the horses). Courtesy of the Montana Historical Society Library and Archives, PAc 74-41 07.

and old. Shortly after the snows and flood of her first few weeks, Sylvia turned her home into the local community hub. She began hosting regular socials for local families and the many bachelors in the Chestnut Valley. Sylvia was also a musician and acquired an organ, which provided entertainment for dancing.[14]

Never idle, Sylvia also organized the first school in the Chestnut Valley. The local families gathered in 1876 to elect "Messrs William Allin, Jake Sieben and Thomas L. Gorham as trustees and Mr. J.A. Harris as clerk."[15] Jake successfully petitioned Meagher County commissioners for a school district, and the first days of school were held in the Siebens' cabin. Sylvia taught school and Sunday school until 1879. Anna E (Bickett) Thoroughman described Sylvia as "at all times public spirited and by nature an industrious capable woman, she has been the greatest possible blessing to her less energetic neighbors in organizing and carrying out schemes of entertainment for the public good."[16] In 1879, Sunday school moved to the nearby John House Ranch, and in 1884 the community built a new, designated school building.

Education was important to Montana ranch families, but children also played important economic roles on the ranch. While their father and uncles were away on roundups and other business, Robert and Charles Sieben helped Sylvia care for the sheep. They also helped with the kitchen garden, chickens, and other livestock kept for the family. All family members were needed to keep the operation going, and women and children alike mended fences, rode out to find errant or lost livestock, and participated in the brandings and haying activities.

As Montana's population grew throughout the 1870s, it required improved infrastructure. A government road ran from Fort Shaw on the Sun River to Fort Logan on the Missouri River where Cascade, Montana, is located today, just north of the Chestnut community. There was an increasing demand for a river crossing, and between 1875 and 1876 the U.S. Army agreed to furnish a cable if local Chestnut Valley residents would build and operate their own ferry. Having grown up using Crandall's Ferry to cross Rock River in Illinois, the Sieben brothers were quick to say yes to the arrangement. They built the boat, secured the cable from the army, and operated the ferry for a short time. Soon they handed the operation over to a colorful trio of Nate Gibson, who lived in a dugout on the riverbank; Henry Zimmerman, who drowned when he fell off while crossing on a windy day; and Alvin Hodson, a neighboring rancher.

As Henry knew it would, the ferry opened up new economic opportunities for the Chestnut Valley. A village known simply as "The Ferry" soon sprang up on the east bank of the Missouri River. It was founded by George Steele, a merchant from Sun River, who seized the opportunity to open a dry goods store at the site. The little community soon consisted of the ferry house, a saloon, a restaurant, a rooming house, Steele's mercantile, and a cabin for the mercantile manager Thomas Gorham. The ferry itself was called the *Mayflower* for the "pilgrims" who crossed the water to their new homes. During low water, the remains of this boat may still be seen from the bridge that now stands in its place.[17]

The Ferry was a great benefit to locals and travelers alike. The Siebens no longer had to travel to Helena or Sun River to pick up mail or buy supplies. In 1880, a post office was established at The Ferry and residents

Before bridges, early settlers moved goods, animals, and people across the Missouri River by cable ferry. Henry would have used this St. Clair Ferry (pictured in 1888) near Cascade many times. Courtesy of the Montana Historical Society Library and Archives, 955-197.

named the small village Ulidia (it was later changed to Gorham for a brief spell and then to St. Clair).[18] A grocery store was established, and Steele's mercantile carried many necessary items including women's dresses, men's work clothes, Stetson hats, and boots (of which Henry was particularly fond). Travelers' needs were well accommodated. One early settler remembered that there was a keg of liquor next to the store. Mr. Gorham kept a lock on the keg's faucet but would give the key to anyone who asked for it. His clerks were not always so generous. One day a thirsty traveler sidled up to the clerk and asked for the key. The clerk handed him a wooden key, about two feet long and handmade. The stupefied man asked what it was, and the clerk replied, "That is the key to the river. Go help yourself."[19]

Of course, ferries were inefficient and seasonal, and within a decade they were replaced with more reliable steel and iron bridges. The first of these bridges to be constructed was the Missouri River Bridge at Fort Benton. By 1893, a new bridge spanned the Missouri River between The Ferry (now renamed St. Clair) and the new settlement of Cascade. Gradually, all business activity and many family homes moved from St. Clair to Cascade, and that same year the post office of St. Clair was discontinued.[20]

As the Chestnut Valley community grew and prospered, so did Henry Sieben's livestock operation. He and Leonard continued their cattle partnership throughout the 1870s, gradually increasing the herd and selling the beef each year in the growing urban centers of Helena and Fort Benton. They were soon expanding their stock to include horses and continued to help Jake as he attempted to make sheep a profitable component of their operation.

The three brothers were always ready to help each other, though, as evidenced by a story of one of Henry's buying trips. In the fall of 1876, Henry traveled eighty-eight miles to the southeast to White Sulphur Springs to purchase sheep for Jake's flock. After making the deal with Mr. C.W. Cook, Henry wrote home to advise that he was starting back, and asked Leonard to meet him at a stopping point called Beaver Flats. Henry spent the first night with the flock and a sheepdog at Fort Logan and went on to the flats but found no one to meet him. His letter was delayed, so Henry had to continue alone, keeping on until dark and camping on the ground. Henry later recalled that he had unsaddled his horse and settled down under a blanket with a small pile of dirt for a pillow. The pillow turned out to be an ant hill, and Henry soon found himself running to a creek to flush the hundreds of insects from his head and neck. With the flock now roused, Henry and the animals pressed on. Henry recalled that his sheepdog at the time was one of the best he ever had, and without him he would not have been able to guide the reluctant animals across the many creeks. He arrived at Hound Creek around two in the morning and found Leonard camped there with a grub wagon. Henry spotted his opportunity to get one over on his brother. He grabbed the gun that lay beside Leonard's hand, walked about ten feet away, let out a cry, and fired off the gun. Leonard leapt out of his blankets in terror before realizing it was Henry. His language turned the air blue, and Henry later admitted his brother should have killed him right there.[21]

By 1877, Leonard and Henry were the seventh-highest-paying taxpayers in the county, and thus some of the most eligible bachelors in the region. Until this point, the brothers seemed not to have had any serious romantic prospects. Their apparent disinterest is not unusual for the times, as their main focus had been in establishing financial security. By the end of the 1870s, Leonard and Henry had a sustainable business and a reliable crew on the ranch. This freed them up to travel for business (purchasing cattle and sheep, selling beef) and entertainment. They could now afford to travel and stay in Virginia City as well as Helena. Just a decade earlier, they were sleeping under wagons or pitching tents when they stayed overnight in these towns. Now they slept in fashionable hotels such as the International and the Cosmopolitan, which for many years were some of Helena's finest hotels that attracted all the movers and shakers of the era. Henry was often accompanied by his friend and fellow valley rancher, William C. Swett, on his trips to Helena.[22]

Local newspapers invariably took interest in their success. In early 1876, the *Benton Record* singled out Leonard in a piece titled "Bachelors of Sun River." The community had recently held a Leap Year Ball. The writer wryly suggested "a few of my bald-headed friends" were feeling neglected. Thus, the writer provided a witty report singling out the attire of a number of bachelors at the ball. Leonard is described as "black coat and vest; looked sheepish, but winked powerfully out of his left eye."[23] Henry and Jake must have been particularly amused with this description of their older brother.

That spring, a writer at the *Rocky Mountain Husbandman* visited the valley and wrote an insightful report on the activities and people in the area. He described the expanse of land, three miles wide at the Sieben's location, as well as the high-quality hay at their disposal. He referred to Leonard and Henry as the largest stockowners in the valley and noted their preparation to build a large two-story dwelling to house Jake and his family. He described the valley's residents as friendly and hospitable and touched on the fact the bachelors in the community encouraged immigration—especially women.[24]

By 1878, both Leonard and Henry were looking further afield to develop business opportunities as well as find love. Leonard left for Spring Hill, Illinois, in January to reunite with family and investigate romantic prospects. He left on the overland coach with another stock grower, J. L. Perkins of Birch Creek, for the "States" (what the residents of the western regions called the eastern portion of the country).

Leonard spent five months in Illinois. He found a wife, Sarah J. Hines, a native of the state. Sarah's family was also German. Her father, Henry Hines, was born in Germany, and his family immigrated to America when he was just three years old. Leonard and Sarah arrived in Montana in late May 1878. They soon welcomed a little girl, Olive, into their world.[25]

Henry was now the only Sieben bachelor, so in the fall of 1878 he followed Leonard's example and made his first journey home to Geneseo, Illinois, since he had left fourteen years prior. Henry spent the entirety of that winter out east. His intention may have been to find a bride, but the trip turned out to be primarily business focused. Henry made sure to keep abreast of economic and social developments in Helena while he was away. In January, he wrote to Ike Greenhood of Greenhood and Bohm Company Merchants requesting a three-month subscription of *The Helena Herald,* the earliest surviving letter belonging to Henry. As expected for an immigrant with little formal education, there are many misspellings, and traces of Henry's mother tongue are still evident in words like *mite* (might), *haf* (have), and *ben* (been).

It appears the Sieben brothers made regular and varying purchases from Greenhood and Bohm Company Merchants in Helena. In a letter dated March 6, 1879, Jake made a basic apparel order for a new member of the ranch crew. Jake bought the crew member a coat, pair of pants, and two pairs of cotton socks.[26]

On his return to Montana in spring of 1879, Henry stopped for a spell in Whitewater, Wisconsin. Whitewater was a prosperous railroad town at the time with flourishing local industries, including the manufacture of agricultural equipment and wagons as well as wheat growing. Henry bought a railcar load of Merino bucks, sixty-five head, to add to Jake's flock in the Chestnut Valley. He shipped the sheep by rail to Bismarck. Once there, he loaded them on the steamboat for Fort Benton for $2 ($60 today's value) per head freight. The *Husbandman* excitedly

Sharon Henry Co Ill
Jan 7th 1879

Mr Ike Greenhood

Sir please
Get the weekly Herald
send to me for Three month
and Charge the same to me
I would send to the
office direct but they mite
hesitate on the account of
the money wich I dont
want to send back
Oblige yours Truley
Henry Sieben

P.S. How is Buisness and
how is our affair tha we
talked about when I left

This is one of the few surviving letters written by Henry Sieben, which he wrote to Ike Greenhood in 1879. Courtesy of the Montana Historical Society Library and Archives, MC 130.

announced his return, declaring the Sieben brothers now had the finest flock in Meagher County.[27]

Back in the Chestnut Valley, Leonard was looking after his family and continuing in his efforts to develop Montana's infrastructure. Both he and Henry had been thrilled when, in 1870, the Fifth Territorial Legislature dealt with the inefficient and unpopular toll road system the brothers had navigated during their first few years as freighters. The legislature made the county commissioners responsible for maintaining the territory's road system and directed them to establish road districts and appoint road supervisors to upkeep them. Counties levied a road tax on property owners to pay for the construction of the roads. The counties also charged a poll tax to help maintain the roads. At $3 (approximately $90 today), this poll tax wasn't cheap. Those who couldn't pay it, however, had the option of working it off on road maintenance. In 1879, Meagher County appointed Leonard as road supervisor for Road District Number 8 to oversee its maintenance. Leonard would also use his "Fresno scraper," a horse-drawn machine he used to construct canals and ditches, for roadwork.[28]

While it was business as usual for Leonard, it was not the case for his wife, Sarah. Unlike Jake's wife, Sarah could not settle into her new home on the range. Leonard decided his time in the West had come to an end. He would return to Illinois to raise his family in an urban setting with all the amenities such a location brings. For the first time in their lives, Leonard's and Henry's paths were about to diverge.

Leonard would go on to purchase a farm in Phenix Township, Henry County, Illinois, where he would carve out a successful career in agriculture. He continued in his civic endeavors, and his honesty and natural leadership abilities earned him the trust of his neighbors, who elected him to the Office of the Assessor in 1884. He would later retire to Geneseo, Illinois, where his siblings resided.[29]

This was a formative moment in Henry's life. Henry had just turned thirty-three and, up until this point, Leonard had been by his side at every life-changing juncture. Together, they had survived the journey west, traveled the territory's dirt roads for miles and miles, and understood the dangerous beauty of the Montana Territory. They had observed and learned about market trends, had bet on themselves and the stock business, and had reached the decade's end as established stockmen. But the winds of change were propelling them on their own destinies.

Henry would now be solely responsible for the cattle operation and would no longer have his confidant to navigate the challenges ahead. But he had fallen under Montana's spell by this point. Henry was single, had built a network of business associates, and was still highly ambitious. After some reflection, Henry decided to stay, and he bought out Leonard's interest in their cattle business.

While Henry divested from Jake's sheep operation, Leonard retained a small interest for another ten years. Before Leonard's departure, Jake sold his flock to a recently arrived businessman, Paris Gibson, for $3.10 (approximately $100 today) a head and then purchased 5,400 more sheep from Red Bluff, California. This move made him one of the largest sheep-growers of the territory. Jake, like his brothers, took risks, but unlike Leonard and Henry, his risks didn't always pay off. One of Jake's recently purchased flocks proved to be very scabby, and he lost sixty-five percent of the herd the winter of 1879.[30]

On a sub-freezing day in December 1881, the Utah and Northern/ Union Pacific Railroad was about to finally reach the copper-rich town of Butte. This was the single most transformational economic development in the entire history of Montana. Equipment, capital, and people would begin to pour into the formerly primitive community. The next decade would bring new and bigger challenges and opportunities for Henry. The young man who couldn't stand to be idle would find himself more than busy. As he reminisced years later, it was at this jumping-off point that he decided from then on, "I paddled my own canoe."[31] ❖

Chapter 3

1880–1886

"THE RANGE WAS GETTING TO BE OVERSTOCKED"

As the new decade opened, Henry was among the most successful stockmen in Montana, as noted by the *Helena Weekly Herald:*

> Some of the prominent stock growers of Northern Montana are William C. Swett, Sieben Bros., Robert Coburn and J. Austin in the Missouri in the vicinity of Chestnut. All started a few years ago, now count their herds of horses, cattle and sheep by the hundreds and thousands.[1]

The same newspaper noted that favorable weather conditions during the winter of 1880 had resulted in very light losses in cattle and sheep: "Messrs. Swett, Sieben and other well-known stock-growers give their opinion that the loss in cattle during the present winter has not been more than 1%."[2]

That summer, under the column "Rambles of Our Traveling Man" for the *Rocky Mountain Husbandman*, one of the roving reporters known only as "Will" extolled the social and economic growth and potential of the Chestnut Valley:

> Letters were written and papers sent to far away friends who came and built homes, while one by one our bachelors have grown young, courageous, and skilled in the art of lass-(wo) oing, and have effected the hymenial tie. New, elegant and well-furnished residences have been reared in the front yards of their former cabins, farm fences joined to each other until they enclose a third of the valley, and the population increased

> nearly four-fold . . . the best locations along the river and foot hills have been taken, yet there is quite a large area of land between that is rich and level, and can be cultivated with ease, but is barren from settlement by the scarcity of water for irrigation. There is a probability, however, that in the near future this will be overcome by the building of a ditch from the river . . . This done, and the valley will treble its population quickly.[3]

On his way home, "Will" sought respite at a roundup camp on Hound Creek, located fifteen miles from Ulidia, where he met with thirty or more "cattle kings and herdsmen." He listed the principal owners of the herds who were in attendance: John H. Ming, Robert Coburn, R. T. Hill, Thomas Gorham, Kyle Price, H. Sieben, William Swett, John Morgan, and James Perkins. He described Ming as probably the largest owner, his herd numbering nearly 10,000, but the other gentlemen "count by the hundreds, many of the herds numbering between two and three thousand."[4] The Chestnut Valley was now a settled community with comfortable dwellings in place, fences erected between ranches, and fields where Jake Sieben's children could play among the abundant crop yields of wheat and oats.[5]

One interesting turn of events was the arrival of fifteen-year-old Frank Arnette aboard the *Far West* in Fort Benton on May 18, 1881. Frank was the son of Margaret Sieben Arnette—Henry's older sister. Margaret married George Arnette in 1857 at just fifteen years of age. They had purchased 160 acres from George's father in Loraine Township, Henry County, just south of where the Siebens lived in Whiteside County, Illinois. Margaret and George faced many challenges during the early years. They lost their home to fire during the Civil War, and in the summer of 1864, as Henry and Leonard arrived in Montana, they struggled to find men willing to work on their farm. With no other option available, Margaret would drive the horses of the reaper and George would bind the grain they had cut on their land. Fortunately, wheat prices advanced in price to $3 ($70 today's value) per bushel, and their young family of six children were able to get a good start in life. George would continue to purchase property until he became the owner of 1,300 acres in Henry County, Illinois, and 2,400 acres in Minnesota, thus becoming one of the most extensive landowners in the area. George also raised and handled livestock, specializing in Durham cattle. Margaret and George's son, Frank, did not travel west out of desperation. It is more likely that his uncle Leonard's recent return as a self-made man enticed young Frank to take his own shot at success in Montana. And so, the family made arrangements with Henry to send Frank west where he would learn to ranch under his uncle's care. Henry was thrilled to have an additional family member involved in the business in Montana.[6]

But it was not all sunshine and roses. While Henry's cattle operation continued to grow, Jake's sheep operation faltered. While the winter of 1880 had been so fruitful for Henry, Jake lost nearly fifty percent of his band of 5,000 sheep. He was devastated and perplexed by a new disease (likely a liver fluke infestation)[7] that was afflicting his flocks. He related their deaths as follows:

> The finest and best sheep die first. They become stupid, the head drooping, the herder finds it impossible to herd them. They lie down and cannot get up. They are heavy. First symptoms to death is 10–15 days. They have an effusion of yellow serum or water in their abdomen outside the bowels where it can't escape. Some sheep have up to 2 gallons of the serum.[8]

In another turn of unfortunate events, the following winter Jacob's wife, Sylvia, was the victim of a shocking incident on the family ranch. She was attacked by a cow as she stood outside her home gathering a bucket of water. Sylvia fought back and caught hold of the horns, which prevented her from being gored. But in her efforts to keep the animal away, she fell to the ground. The cow threw herself on Sylvia and didn't budge. When her two boys came outside to look for Sylvia, they startled the cow. She attempted to charge them, but they luckily escaped. The boys took their mother inside, and she was later taken to Fort Shaw for medical assistance. Local newspapers reported that Sylvia had sustained a broken collarbone and severe body bruising. Fortunately, she survived.[9]

As local and national promotion of the Chestnut Valley area increased in the early 1880s, so, too, did the number of stockmen settling on the range. Henry foresaw issues of overstocking in the area and began to look farther afield at new pastures for his stock to graze on. He observed that ranchers were pushing eastward down the Musselshell Valley in search of new range. One such rancher was his neighbor Robert "Bob" Coburn who had a ranch in the Chestnut Valley and had also settled on Flatwillow Creek. Henry's old associate from Virginia City, Granville Stuart, had recently partnered with businessmen Samuel Hauser and Andrew Davis to establish the famous DHS Ranch on the southeast flank of the Judith Mountains near Fort Maginnis.

Granville Stuart had combed eastern Montana by horseback in 1880 and had found mostly empty countryside. Stock were largely grazed on ranges of southwestern and west-central Montana at that point. In the far northern, eastern, and southeastern expanses of the territory, Native American lands were being consistently reduced, thus opening up vast new areas for stockmen from outside the territory to situate their herds.[10] Stuart was managing the DHS Ranch and seeking to increase their herds when he read about Henry's recent successes in newspapers. The updates encouraged him to write to Henry and inquire what was Henry's lowest price for stock. Granville offered to advance $1 ($30 today's value) a head and the balance when he received the cattle. There is no surviving documentation to clarify if Henry sold to Granville, but the letter succeeded in reestablishing a connection between the men. It was fortuitous timing for Henry as he was seeking new grazing land.

"Will," the *Husbandman's* roving reporter, had ended his 1880 exposé of the Chestnut Valley community with the following ominous remark about stock raising in the area:

> They have a fine and extensive grass range, and they manage to pasture it in the best possible manner. This is necessary, for

923

Henry Sieben Esq.
Chestnut. Meagher Co.
Mont.

Helena. Montana.
Jany 18th. 1880.

Dear Sir

I hear you have some Stock Cattle that you would probably sell. Please write me your very lowest price for all you have, delivered in the spring. I advancing you say one dollar a head now. And the balance to be paid when the cattle are received. Please let me hear from you at once.

Respectfully Yours.
Granville Stuart.

One of the earliest records we have of Henry Sieben's cattle business is this letter from Granville Stuart requesting to purchase cattle from him in January of 1880. Courtesy of the Montana Historical Society Library & Archives, MC 61.

> they fear that the increase in their herds will in a few years overtax the range and require a reduction of the cattle business or removal of their herds to obtain feed."[11]

Sure enough, by July 1881, Henry lost thirty percent of his herd during the frigid winter. His neighbors suffered similar losses. Henry attributed it to an overcrowded range more than any other cause.[12]

Fortunately for Henry, 1882 saw a rapid advance in the prices of both cattle and sheep. Some dealers held their herds at $23 ($700 today's value) a head with the promise of delivering them at the spring roundup, in comparison with the previous year when they sold for $18 and $20. Steers sold for $27 and $28 with some purchasers engaging them at $30.[13]

Henry had reason to be jubilant in the short-term, in any case. There were few cattle or sheep losses that winter; ranchers reported that herds were in as good condition as the previous fall; and the railroads had arrived in Butte and Billings, providing Montana's stockmen with the first dependable, year-round transportation source.

Henry and a fortunate handful of others were at the helm of this boom year. Since Leonard's departure, Henry had developed an informal partnership with his friend and fellow rancher, William Swett. That spring they sold 1,000 head of cattle at $30 a head—a record amount for that number of cattle in the territory. That is a sale worth over $700,000 dollars today. The herd included 700 four-year-olds and 300 three-year-olds. As *The River Press* commented: "Thirty thousand dollars is a nice little sum to realize in one year from the sale of the marketable cattle in a herd of three or four thousand!"[14]

Encouraged by this success, Henry started looking for new range. To maintain healthy herds and provide the quality beef that continued to yield significant—sometimes record-breaking—profits, he knew he needed to find less stocked and overgrazed land.

Through his correspondence with Granville Stuart and connections with other ranchers, Henry had heard favorable reports about Flatwillow, an area located 200 miles east of the Chestnut Valley. In his typical resourceful and pragmatic style, Henry decided to explore this available land and its potential for himself before making any big moves. The following excerpt is taken from a conversation between Henry and his son-in-law A.T. Hibbard in the 1930s, in which he reminisces on that solo trip on horseback across the territory:

> I left Chestnut valley the 10th of March on my way down to Flatwillow. Went from Chestnut to Shonkin and stayed all night with a man by the name of Joe Cobell. Got what information I could in regard to the Flatwillow country, and the next night I went to a place they called the "Big Sag" and visited a man by the name of Joe Lepley. The third night I went to Governor Brook's ranch (the T. C. Power ranch) and stayed all night with him and got what information I could get in regard to the country. The fourth day I went to Fort McGinnis. Granville Stuart was located there at that time. He was the manager of the Pioneer Cattle company and I got my directions from him to go to Flat-willow. There was a man by the name of Len McFarland, who was manager of the Montana Sheep company, located over there. I stayed four or five days with Mr. McFarland and then I went from there down to Flatwillow and picked out my location and started back home. The second night out I landed at McGinnis on my return trip. The third I got back to Governor Brooks', and then I left to make Blankenbaker's Sheep ranch on Box Elder, but I found the distance too great and had to camp out and hold my horse all night. It was dark and cold and stormy and it took me until 2:00 o'clock the next day to get to Blankenbaker's. After resting there for two days I came back to Chestnut valley and sold my ranch to Henry Austin.[15]

An article in *The Benton Weekly Record* in late March 1882 highlights that perhaps Henry didn't make the decision to move to Flatwillow as quickly as he remembered. On March 30, a few weeks after his return from Flatwillow, Henry was seen at the Choteau House in Fort Benton,

As roads improved, freighting businesses were able to replace oxen with horses, such as I. G. Baker's outfit pictured here in Fort Benton around 1885. Courtesy of the Montana Historical Society Library and Archives, 947-074.

a hotel owned and operated by a dapper Irishman by the name of Jere Sullivan. While there, Henry made it publicly known he was scouting for a new ranch. He was investigating areas on the Marias River, a tributary of the Missouri River that ran northwest of Fort Benton.[16]

Ranching required manpower and capital. Henry needed a new partner, and so upon his return to Chestnut Valley, he shared his enthusiasm for Flatwillow with fellow rancher Bob Coburn. At the time, Bob had two ranches in the Chestnut Valley and planned to expand and build a brick and stone residence in the area. He had established a small ranch on Flatwillow Creek a few years before in the area in which Henry was most interested.

Henry talked Bob into partnering and developing the ranch in Flatwillow. The two men didn't dally. They made arrangements for their Chestnut Valley crews to oversee the spring roundup of 1882 and traveled to Flatwillow with wagons and a team of oxen, mowing machines, and two men to locate their ranch. Few ranchers owned much of their range in the 1880s. Usually, they settled along rivers or streams and claimed contiguous rangeland by prior appropriation. Thus, Henry and Bob settled on a spot adjacent to Flatwillow Creek, just northeast from Len McFarland's sheep ranch on the Fort Maginnis range. Once the two hands were settled and had a plan in place to put up hay for the winter, Henry and Bob left them in early summer and returned to Chestnut Valley to tie up loose ends.

Henry sold his Chestnut Valley outfit to rancher Henry Austin and made arrangements for winter supplies at Ulidia. He bade farewell to Jake and his family and the people who made up the community he had come to call home. He joined Bob in driving their cattle to Flatwillow. They arrived at their new abode in the latter part of August in 1882.[17]

After several tiring and bumpy trips back and forth on the Old Carroll Road between Chestnut Valley and Flatwillow, Henry began settling into his new venture. The entire central section of Montana Territory, from the Sun River to Fort Benton, the Judith Basin, and the lower Musselshell, had large herds feeding on public domain. The ranchers located north of Yellowstone country in Meagher County included older, well-established operators like Granville Stuart, Conrad Kohrs, and James Fergus. At thirty-five, Henry was one of the youngest stockmen on what was known as the Fort Maginnis range.

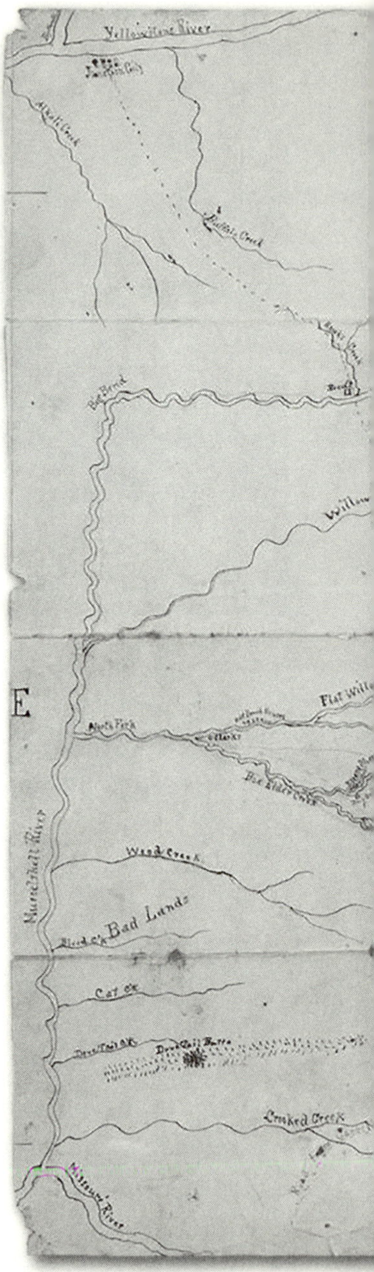

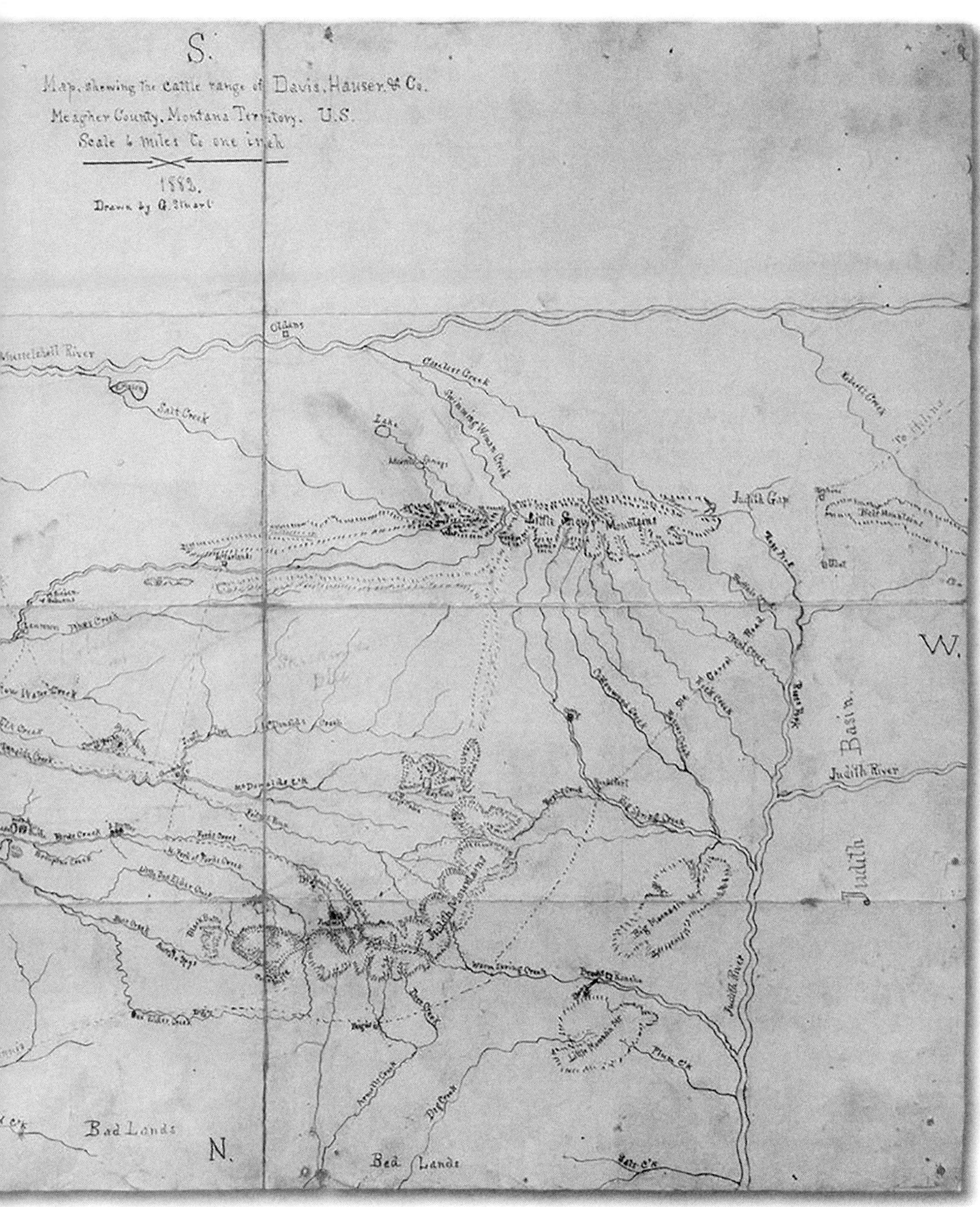

Granville Stuart's hand-drawn map showing the location of the Sieben and Coburn Ranch as well as neighboring ranches on the Fort Maginnis range in 1882. Courtesy of the Montana Historical Society Library and Archives, B37.

Henry learned that his neighboring ranchers were often in partnerships with local bankers and merchants, and they raised mostly shorthorn cattle. Unlike in Wyoming where there were armed conflicts over grazing rights, violent clashes between cattlemen and sheepmen did not occur in Montana. On the Fort Maginnis range, sheepmen such as Len McFarland were open to sharing the land and worked easily with cattlemen such as Henry Sieben and Bob Coburn, Granville Stuart, and James Fergus. The enormity of Montana's open range in the 1800s made accommodation of the two enterprises possible.

Henry and the surrounding ranchers were also getting increasingly anxious about another challenge—an invasion of corporate ranching operations. Many of these corporate ranchers were driving longhorns north from Texas, entering the Yellowstone drainage from the southeast in the hope of quick profits from minimal investments. On top of this, the managers of the new corporate ranches made no provisions for winter hay. All across the eastern two-thirds of the Montana Territory, large cattle and sheep corporate outfits were beginning to sprout like mushrooms, thriving on the free grass of the public domain.[18]

Henry and his stockmen neighbors gathered and quickly put together a plan to deter overcrowding of their range. They published weekly notices in the *Rocky Mountain Husbandman* stating the range in the Flatwillow area was fully stocked and "any stock growers bringing cattle to the said range will not be allowed to join us in our round ups nor to use any of our corrals."[19] The notice was signed by all the ranchers on the Fort Maginnis range.

Henry's next venture was waiting for him in hospitality. Native Americans had long known and used the hot springs situated on a tributary of the North Fork of the Smith River, just fifteen miles from Fort Logan. The springs were a natural draw for the ranchers in the area to help relieve the physical ailments that riding the range brought with it. James Brewer settled in the area in 1870 and was joined by Major R. C. Walker. Together they established "Brewer's Springs." They constructed dwellings, bathhouses, and stables and are credited with founding the town of White Sulphur Springs.

The local newspaper, the *Rocky Mountain Husbandman,* faithfully boosted the region and painted a rosy picture of the healing powers of the springs, which enabled the new owner, Dr. William Parberry, to sell the resort to a Helena-based company in 1883 for $80,000 (approximately $2.5 million today). Henry was part of that Helena-based company.

Armed with the cash he had made in his record-breaking sales the year before, Henry was ready to make this big business move. He had observed how other prominent ranchers such as John H. Ming, Thomas C. Power, Thomas Cruse, and Samuel Hauser had diversified their business portfolio to include investments not only in cattle but in banking, mining, railroads, and the arts. When Bob Coburn and a handful of other successful local businessmen began talking of the potential of a hot springs and hotel business in the up-and-coming town of White Sulphur Springs, Henry was primed to invest.

The purchase included nine acres of ground on which the hotel was situated and 1,000 town lots. Henry was one of the incorporators, purchasing 100 shares at $100 per share. Great Falls businessman and attorney Timothy E. Collins and banker Aaron Hershfield joined him in the venture. Dr. Parberry was included on the board of trustees along with Henry's ranching partner Bob Coburn and two other local businessmen. The *Husbandman* described the investors as "among the best and most enterprising of the citizens of Montana." Over the next decade, the paper would market the springs as "the Saratoga of the West."[20]

The group got to work on the property in spring of 1883, making extensive improvements to the hotel and bathhouses. Henry was invested in making the enterprise a success and became actively involved in the amelioration of the property and surrounding lots. In March, the *Husbandman* reported on Henry's plans to construct a one-story stone structure that would house John Connors's drug store and include a cellar.

Even as his ranching operations grew over the next few years, Henry remained engaged in the development of his business ventures at White Sulphur Springs. In spring of 1885, Henry left Flatwillow and traveled west to purchase cattle. Although prices were high and the purchasing trip turned out to be a bust, Henry turned his efforts to promoting the springs. On June 9, he wrote to Aaron Hershfield from the California House in Spokane Falls to share that he had been talking up their enterprise with several parties. Henry was getting questions about the composition of minerals in the water—something he was unsure of—and thus he requested Hershfield to send him a copy of the analysis. With this information, Henry was sure he could market the springs to people in the Spokane area and entice them to visit. After Henry's astute request, all the hotel's letterhead going forward would display a percentage analysis of the mineral content of the springs.[21]

Henry spent a significant amount of time at White Sulphur Springs in the mid-1880s. Over the years, he had forged a number of close friendships with other bachelors in the area, including rancher William C. Swett and John Lepley of Fort Benton. Lepley was also involved in White Sulphur Springs, so the pair availed of the healing waters, tended to business, and socialized. In a social update of fall 1883, the *Husbandman* described Henry and John Lepley as White Sulphur Springs society's most "gallant bachelors." They had spent their summer picnicking, fishing, picking berries, and going on sightseeing excursions and, most interestingly, had won many friends among the ladies of the "Saratoga." Romance had not been at the top of Henry's priorities in his early years. Henry's only goal during his initial years in the territory was to survive, earn money, and gather knowledge about running a business. While his brothers and friends one by one had married and settled down, Henry put off marriage. It is not clear how many, if any, romantic relationships Henry engaged in before the mid-1880s.

But love did bloom for a spell in White Sulphur Springs. Bob Coburn's wife, Mary, had a sister, Jeanette Morrow, who moved to White Sulphur Springs with the family. Henry and Jeanette soon struck up a close friendship. Jeanette's daughter, Pearl Leede Rhein, would later recall that her aunt Mary would often tease Jeanette about Henry, talking about the "dirt" she had on their relationship in the

LARGE FIRST CLASS SAMPLE ROOMS FOR COMMERCIAL MEN.

OFFICE OF

THE CALIFORNIA HOUSE

THE ONLY FIRST CLASS HOTEL IN THE CITY

W. C. GRAY, PROPRIETOR.

Spokane Falls, W. T., June 9th 1885

Mr Aaron Hershfield
Helena

Dear Sir

I haf ben talking to several parties about the White Sulpher Springs & they would like to know all the ingreadiens in ~~the~~ the watter & if you can send me a coppey of the analycies I probley could get several parties to go over there I haf not bought aney cattle they held then to hi for me. will start back as soo as i hear from hardy

yours Truley

Henry Sieben

In another rare letter, Henry Sieben wrote to Aaron Hershfield in 1885 inquiring about the mineral properties of the water at White Sulphur Springs. Courtesy of the Montana Historical Society Library and Archives, MC 115.

Henry Sieben was an early investor and promoter in the town that became White Sulphur Springs, Montana, pictured here in 1886. Courtesy of the Montana Historical Society Library and Archives, 951-670.

1880s and scolding her for not having married him when she had the chance. While the pairing did not last, Henry and Jeanette remained lifelong friends. Much later, when Henry lived with his family on Harrison Avenue in Helena, he would often stop by Jeanette's home on nearby Park Avenue on his way downtown. Pearl remembered how fondly her mother spoke of Henry. Jeanette counted Henry as one of her good friends. There was no bad blood, she said, life just had other plans.[22]

Henry's investment in White Sulphur Springs didn't slow down his expansion on the Fort Maginnis range. In 1882, the Northern Pacific Railroad reached Miles City, thus opening up the East Coast market to stockmen. From then on, Henry and his neighbors drove their cattle to Miles City every fall and then shipped them to Chicago from there. As 1883 approached, prices reached $40 ($1,200 today's value) a head for cattle, with Granville Stuart declaring that at Fort Maginnis, "we have the best range in the west."[23]

Henry followed a similar year-round schedule that he established in his years ranching in the Chestnut Valley. He traveled in the winter, returned in the spring to attend the roundup, traveled locally in the summer, and then located back on the range for the fall roundup and shipping cattle. While Henry continued traveling east, now that the railroads were well established in Montana, he also went west with his friend and fellow stockman John Lepley. In January 1884, they took the train from Butte to Ogden, Utah, where they boarded the Union Pacific to San Francisco and then made it farther south to Los Angeles where they remained until the spring.[24] Henry's direct involvement with the hot springs and hotel decreased as the needs of his cattle business and personal matters demanded more of his time in the mid-1880s. But he continued as a director of the White Sulphur Springs Association long after he left the area.

Some aspects of the American West remain unchanged to this day. Even in the late nineteenth century, weather and wildlife were hot topics. When Henry and Bob Coburn had arrived in Flatwillow in August of 1882, cattlemen were talking about the heat, fires, and smoke that filled the land. Bison no longer roamed the open range, so wolves were yet another headache for livestock owners. By 1885, *The Stockgrowers Journal* reported that ranchmen on the northern ranges were forced to use large quantities of poison to decrease the number of wolves. The method of distributing the poison is particularly notable: "The most efficient way of distributing the poison has been found to be to place it in the testicles of the calves castrated at the roundup and scatter them promiscuously over the range."[25]

Business prospects remained high in 1885, and that provided Henry with the opportunity to hone his skills as a cattle business promoter and capitalist. Stockmen were relieved that the winter of 1885 was neither long nor harsh, which resulted in minor loss of cattle. They crowed about the magnificent weather that fall, the quality of the grass, and, even though prices were down at the Chicago Stockyards, ranchers were optimistic they would make up for it the following year. Henry and Aaron Hershfield had established a good business partnership in their development of White Sulphur Springs, and it appears Henry built on that relationship to expand his cattle business ventures. Henry traveled to Chicago in the fall of 1885. He left for Billings with thirteen carloads of steers to bring to market. Once he reached the town, he wrote to Aaron to inquire about his bank in Chicago. This suggests Aaron had provided Henry with either capital or stock to expand his business that year.[26]

In December, Henry promoted the Montana cattle business. He traveled to Helena to meet with two men from Illinois who asked him to assist with "his knowledge of the country in selecting a location for a slaughterhouse."[27] These men, identified only as Hough and Dustin in the records, planned to erect ice houses that winter and a slaughterhouse in the spring. Henry was more than happy to show them potential sites for both.

But business wasn't completely smooth for Henry. Montana's district roundup associations were planning to introduce laws on mavericking—indiscriminately branding any stray calf that showed up—a practice that Henry had used to increase his herds. This incited Henry, who until this point was a behind-the-scenes player in such issues, to speak publicly. In the August 1885 edition of *The Stockgrowers Journal,* Henry argued that there were no maverick laws in Washington Territory—the man who got his rope on the animal first was the one that branded it. Consequently, cattle were worked all summer and good ropers were in strong demand. His argument fell on deaf ears—the roundup associations prohibited the use of branding irons at any time except during the regular roundups and declared that mavericks were the common property of the district associations. The mavericks would be sold to raise money for association expenses.[28] This is the first instance Henry engaged in a contentious issue in a public forum.

Another emerging headache for Henry and his neighboring ranchers was cattle rustling. For years, Montana stockmen had been petitioning to create a large, territory-wide organization to pursue and protect their interests. James Fergus was at the helm of leadership. He held a series of meetings in 1879 and organized the Montana Stockgrowers

Brands identified cattle ownership and helped prevent rustling on the open range. Henry Sieben held annual roundups and brandings, similar to the one pictured here on Little Pumpkin Creek in 1890.
Courtesy of the Montana Historical Society Library and Archives, 981-429

Association. It was confined mainly to western Montana and faltered in the early 1880s until thievery became an urgent issue again.

In the absence of bison on the plains, Native Americans had begun stealing livestock for food. Northern Montana stockmen formed the Shonkin Association, the territory's first regional cattlemen's organization, in July 1881. This covered the Shonkin, Highwood, Belt, and Arrow Creek districts. More than simply being a regional cattlemen's organization, their goal was to break up Native American camps south of the Missouri River and drive the Native Americans back to the north to their reservation.

Non-Native rustlers also easily stole stock on the unfenced open range. By the 1880s, cattle rustling had reached epidemic proportions in southeastern Montana and in the Judith Basin and Musselshell River areas where Henry ranched. Finding refuge in the Missouri Breaks, a motley assortment of unemployed whiskey traders, wolf hunters, woodchoppers, and trappers stole livestock from the range and took the animals across the Canadian border for sale.

At the 1883 legislature, Territorial Council President Granville Stuart tried to address the problem of thievery by proposing the creation of a Board of Stock Commissioners with the power to appoint subordinates to make arrests. It passed in the House and the Council but was vetoed by Governor John Crosby. He didn't think it was correct to introduce a general property tax to support the Stock Commissioners and was also worried about the considerable delegation of executive and legislative powers that would be given to the commissioners and their subordinates on the range.

Henry Sieben and his associates took a different tack, with Granville Stuart at the helm. Stuart held a roundup meeting at the DHS Ranch in May that year. Ranchers or their foremen on the Fort Maginnis range (there were now twelve outfits on the range) attended. While foremen attended in place of ranchers such as Bob Coburn, Conrad Kohrs, John Bielenberg, and Nelson J. Dovenspeck, Henry Sieben was present with his top hand, Horace Brewster. During the meeting, the ranchers decided to employ one man in each county as a detective whose duty it would be to track cattle rustlers and horse thieves and do all in his power to have them arrested and brought to trial.

Nearly every man present was also assigned a role at the roundup. Members elected Henry to two positions for the 1883 roundup. His first role was to tally all branded calves and make sure every owner was turning out seven bull calves for each 100 heifer calves. Fort Maginnis ranchers agreed upon this 7:100 ratio to ensure a healthy breeding population. Henry was also appointed to a committee on bulls and charged with inspecting them at corral. Old bulls were to be castrated. Castrating the old bulls not only meant they would be less aggressive and less likely to injure themselves or other cattle, it was also a way for ranchers to run the old bulls with the herd for a season and then sell them for a steer price rather than discounted as a bull.[29]

While Henry was east in the winter of 1883, newly arrived ranchers in the eastern portion of the territory formed a large organization of their own—the Eastern Montana Livestock Association at Miles City. They were also worried about Native American raids, and so James Fergus's Stockgrowers Association reorganized and began cooperating with the Eastern Montana Livestock Association. By April 1885, the two groups united to create the territory-wide Montana Stockgrowers Association. Cattlemen were now joined in one organization that would yield great economic and political power. Both Henry and Jake were members.

An 1884 Eastern Montana Livestock Association meeting in Miles City, which Henry attended, had "rustling" of livestock on the open range as the hot topic once again. A young, skinny, spectacled East Coaster by the name of Theodore Roosevelt was in attendance. Roosevelt first visited North Dakota and southeast Montana in 1883 to hunt bison, and his experiences of wrangling cattle, branding steers, and spending days in the saddle made a lasting impression on him. Reeling from the recent death of his wife and mother on the same day, Roosevelt returned to the region to seek solace in the rivers, streams, buttes, and hills, watching the movements of the cattle and horses. He purchased two ranches near the Montana border in North Dakota—the Elkhorn and Chimney Butte.

During this tumultuous meeting, Roosevelt came out strongly in favor of an all-out war against the rustlers. Granville Stuart stifled the proposal publicly, creating the impression the eastern Montana stockmen would take no action. He wanted to create absolute secrecy and avoid the publicity the planned action might attract. In the end, the group voted to take no action against the rustlers.

Word got back to the rustlers that the Stockgrowers would not be taking action, and they became more brazen in their thefts. After the spring roundup, a group of stockmen in central Montana banded together under Stuart's leadership. Stuart held a meeting at his ranch where he directed the operations of a group of reliable and tight-lipped men, later known as "Stuart's Stranglers." Like the Vigilantes in Virginia City Henry had encountered when he first arrived in Montana, these men felt driven to protect their interests on the open range.

The Stranglers gathered intelligence on the rustlers and prepared to strike. Stuart's Stranglers tracked down and killed at least fifteen men they suspected of rustling.

Vigilante justice continued in Powder River country, along the Little Missouri and Lower Yellowstone rivers. James Fergus justified the murders by declaring it a state of war on the range, but the stockmen were severely criticized for the murders. Neither Henry nor Jacob's names are included on any of the existing lists or in any recollections of those events. Henry never mentioned any physical involvement in the raids. But he did financially support Granville's action. On August 14, 1885, Granville wrote to Henry to inform him that he had paid a man by the name of Milton F. Marsh, a saloon keeper at Rocky Point on the Missouri River, to watch for thieves from October 1884 to May 1885. This was covered by the roundup dues paid by Henry and the other Fort Maginnis stockmen.[30]

Open-range cattlemen reached the peak of their power in 1885, the year they organized the Montana Stockgrowers Association. At the territorial legislature that year, the organization pursued the enactment of laws to protect their interests, and 1885 became known as the year of the "cowboy legislature." Legislators granted many favors to stockmen that year, including appointing a territorial veterinary surgeon and prohibiting branding except during the roundup season.[31]

But ranchers still faced difficulties that could never be fully mastered. Natural and man-caused prairie fires continued to destroy their herds. Wolves and coyotes continued to take a heavy toll. Partnerships and family-operated ranches such as Henry's were becoming a thing of the past.

Henry maintained a cool head throughout these tumultuous events and continued to partner with other ranchers in pursuit of long-term security. In spring of 1886, he, Joseph Conrad of Fort Benton, and his old friend William C. Swett spent time in Oregon where they purchased 11,000 head of cattle. That fall, Henry and the Fort Shaw Cattle Company shipped 287 steers from Helena to Chicago (the only shipment from the area that year) and sixteen carloads of cattle from Billings to Chicago. Prices for cattle had dipped, but Henry was still making sharp business decisions and investments.[32]

In his usual pattern, Henry was east during the winter of 1886. Word reached Montana in December that on the seventh of that month Henry had married Miss Alberta Gordon in a well-attended ceremony at the bride's home in Whitewater, Wisconsin. Since his first stop at the railroad town in the late 1870s to purchase sheep, Henry had been returning to Whitewater to pursue business matters. Alberta's father, John Gordon, was a successful manufacturer of wagon components, and he and Henry became good friends and often visited when Henry was in town. Henry soon got to know John Gordon's daughter, Alberta.

Alberta Gordon shortly before her marriage to Henry Sieben in 1886. Courtesy of the Hibbard family private collection.

Perhaps it's not surprising they were drawn to one another. Like Henry, Alberta grew up in farmland areas and enjoyed the outdoors. Henry was a successful bachelor who could offer Alberta security and a standard of living she was accustomed to. Both wanted children. Where Henry was reserved, Alberta was a social creature and loved the arts. They would complement each other well in Montana society.

The newlyweds arrived in Helena on December 23, 1886. They stayed at the Grand Central Hotel to receive friends and bask in the celebration. But Henry couldn't stay in his bride's company for too long. Ceaseless storms and record low temperatures were hitting Montana and decimating herds. The "Hard Winter of 1886–1887" had arrived. While Alberta sought out a permanent home for them in Helena, Henry returned to Flatwillow to see for himself what he could do to keep his business afloat.[33] ◈

Chapter 4

1886–1892

"IN THE HANDS OF THE ELEMENTS"

After twenty years on the open range, Henry was finally beginning to enjoy the fruits of his labor. His ranch and crew were flourishing, and he found the wife he'd been hoping for. Then the Hard Winter of 1886 to 1887 brought that progress to a halt for Henry and Montana's stock industry. But all Henry needed was another opportunity. It appeared with the expansion of railroads and the federal government's growing control over and seizing of Native American lands. Through his own grit and smarts, Henry understood winning had little to do with the cards he was dealt and more to do with how he played them.

A small community sprang up around Henry's ranch on Flatwillow Creek in those early years on the Fort Maginnis range. A general store was in operation from 1880, a post office was soon opened, and then locals established a bank and saloon. In 1883, German immigrant and cattle tycoon Conrad Kohrs, who would become one of Henry's dearest friends, bought out A.J. and Irvin Davis of the DHS Ranch for the princely sum of $400,000 (nearly $10 million today). For this eyewatering price, Kohrs acquired cattle, horses, buildings—everything belonging to the operation, which he renamed the Pioneer Cattle Company. Kohrs's ranch manager, Granville Stuart, was at the heart of the local ranching community on the Fort Maginnis range. As ranching families grew, Stuart provided a log schoolhouse to educate children during the winter months. For anyone wishing to develop their intellectual interests, Granville opened up the doors to his enormous library that contained, to the amazement of his neighbors, 3,000 volumes. At the James Fergus ranch on Armells Creek, locals could also access another well-stocked and diverse library.[1]

While social and environmental factors varied from year to year, one constant was Henry's skill at employing top hands and crew to ensure his operation thrived. Jim Spurgeon, whose father was a foreman for Granville Stuart's DHS Ranch, declared Henry "was probably the best ranch operator in this state and other states. Of course, he had the knack of hiring good men that stayed with him. He had foremen that stayed with him for years and years and years. Run his outfit and run them good. That was his success which was something to be able to do."[2]

Henry's top hand was "the well-known bronco buster"[3] Horace Brewster. Horace was born in Cleveland, Ohio, on January 9, 1855. His family emigrated west, first landing in Colorado and then making their way to Montana. They took the Bozeman Trail to Virginia City in the fall of 1864, just a couple of months after the Sieben brothers arrived at the mining town. As a young man, Horace followed a similar path to the Sieben brothers. He hired out to the Diamond R freighting company in the early 1870s and then turned his attention to the growing cattle business. Horace earned his stripes working for Bob Coburn for a short period, then for ranchers and Helena stockyard owners Louis Stadler and Louis Kaufman before returning to work for Bob Coburn and Henry at Flatwillow in 1883. Brewster gave artist Charlie Russell his first cowpuncher job in 1882. Brewster related a colorful memory of Russell, describing him as "the queerest looking object he had ever seen. His hat had a large brim but no crown and one leg of his leather trousers was tucked in his boot and the other dangled out."[4]

Horace's knowledge of the cattle business and the psychology of range cattle and cowboys was instrumental in helping Henry successfully grow his business at Flatwillow. He oversaw the laborious work of shipping Henry's cattle from Custer, a small town on the Northern Pacific Railroad. Custer was 120 miles southeast of the ranch. Granville Stuart described cattle on these drives as "wild as antelope and it required eternal vigilance to keep them from stampeding and running all the fat off. The slightest unusual sight or sound would start them off pell mell."[5] Henry entrusted Horace to receive cattle he purchased on business trips nationwide. Henry would notify Horace to send an outfit to some point on the railroad. These men would unload the cattle and trail them back to the ranch.

Horace also managed a team of wild but loyal cowboys or "cowpunchers" at Flatwillow. By the mid-1880s, with 600,000 cattle on the range, cowboys were an institution. Henry hired "dyed in the wool" cowboys who had been born and raised on open ranges, isolated from everything but cattle, and so they knew and understood the habits of range cattle as no one else could know them. Granville Stuart described the cowboys on the Fort Maginnis range as wearing the best clothes they could buy and taking great pride in their personal appearance and trappings. They would pay $25 (approximately $800 today) for a pair of made-to-order riding boots when the best store boots in Helena were $10 ($300) a pair. Their trappings consisted of a fine saddle, silver mounted bridle, pearl-handled six shooter, latest model cartridge belt with silver buckle, silver spurs, a fancy quirt with silver mountings, a riata (lariat) sometimes made of rawhide, a pair of leather chaps, and a fancy hatband often made from the dressed skin of a diamondback rattlesnake. Since this species of rattlesnake is not native to Montana, it appears that clothing stores were importing this specific hat to the territory. A cowboy's hat preference was the expensive stiff-brimmed, light, felt type, and they wore brilliantly colored silk handkerchiefs knotted about their necks, light-colored shirts, and exquisitely fitted high-heeled riding boots. Henry didn't lose any sleep on what cowboys wore as long as they got their job done and were honest, loyal, hardworking, and most importantly, kind to his livestock.[6]

Henry had an instinctive love of animals that set a powerful example for his employees. Of course, protecting and managing his stock with care made good economic sense, but Henry carried a hatred of the mistreatment of stock from his freighting days. He detested bullwhips that could rip chunks of hide from the backs of heavily laden oxen. According to his daughter, Margaret Sieben Hibbard, Henry once took a whip away from a heavy-handed driver and destroyed it on the spot. On Henry's ranch, Horace Brewster and his hands understood the standing order against any mistreatment of stock. It is not surprising, then, that Sieben's stock had a reputation of arriving at markets in top condition.[7]

Henry was riding this wave of the great open-range boom that was mounting steadily through the mid-1880s until a series of unfortunate events brought it all to a grinding halt. Local Montana promoters, eager to lure outside capital, were painting a rosy picture of the profits to be made in ranching. Eastern and foreign capital began pouring into the lucrative livestock industry. For instance, in the summer of 1882, the Nebraska-based Carpenter and Robertson outfit brought 3,000 head to graze by Rosebud Creek, and the Niobrara Cattle Co. drove 10,000 cattle into the Powder River Valley. The Concord Cattle Company of New Hampshire settled on the Tongue River. The Hash Knife operation, perhaps the first Texas enterprise north of the Black Hills, based itself at the head of the Little Missouri River. By 1883, they had moved northward to the Montana-Dakota territorial boundary and were soon joined by other Texas outfits such as the 777 and the Mill Iron. It wasn't long before more Texas investors, like the XIT and the Matador Land and Cattle Co., also moved their business to Montana. Because of these increased numbers of ranches and livestock on the range, feed was becoming scarce and the ranges crowded.[8]

Henry and established Montana ranchers had little enthusiasm for the "Texas invasion." Bob Coburn reported the longhorns that were being driven in as "all horn and bushy tails" and inferior to the shorthorn stock that he and his fellow "old-time" Montanans ran in western and central Montana.[9] Coburn, Sieben, and others who used graded bulls and took pride in their stock feared that the imported low-quality longhorns would overcrowd the range and endanger their quality-bred herds. They were nervous that this influx of cattle would decrease beef prices and the availability of good grass.

Tensions also flared over the question of a "national cattle trail." Texans and other southern operators petitioned the federal government to put aside a corridor of land they could use to move their cattle from Texas to the northern ranges. Henry and his colleagues argued it would overcrowd the range and introduce longhorn-carried diseases such as the Texas Fever. The national cattle trail never materialized, but long drives continued to move cattle into southeastern Montana until well into the 1890s.

The growth of the livestock business on the frontier not only attracted national investors; word spread overseas. Some of the foreigners who turned up were known as "remittance men"—wealthy and adventurous youngsters who lived mainly off their families' money. But others were serious about the cattle business, like French stockman Pierre Wibaux, who built a large and successful operation in the Beaver Valley along the Montana-Dakota line. English and Scottish investors were the most common foreign buyers.[10]

This set of circumstances created a division between Henry and other established ranchers and the newcomers. Historian Michael Malone described Montana-based cattlemen as "she stockmen." They used the ranges for breeding purposes, while the newcomers tended to be "steer men," who brought cattle from Texas for maturing on the northern grasslands. They differed in other ways, too. The cowboy poet Teddy Blue Abbott, who worked for Granville Stuart and married one of his daughters, noted that Montana-based owners showed more concern for their men and provided them with better food and shelter.[11]

But it was business as usual for Henry in the fall of 1885. He headed east, likely to join Granville Stuart at the National Cattle Growers' Association meeting in Chicago on November 17 and 18, 1885. Stuart was Montana's delegate, and he devoted his energies to securing governmental policy on quarantining animals to prevent disease spread and to having Native American lands further reduced and opened to settlers. Both of Stuart's proposals were adopted, and the latter decision, in particular, would be of critical benefit to Henry as well as many other Montana stockmen in the challenging decade ahead. In another advancement for the stock industry, at the Montana Stockgrowers Association meeting in Miles City on April 2, members decided to form a committee charged with consulting with the people of St. Paul, Minnesota, about the possibility of establishing stockyards and a cattle market. Their goal was to provide northern stockmen with an alternative and more accessible shipping location. They succeeded and, in the fall of 1885, St. Paul's stockyards were completed and ready to receive cattle.[12]

The optimism permeating among Montana's stockmen in 1885 evaporated with the catastrophic winter of 1886. As Henry traveled to purchase cattle that spring, ranchers on the Fort Maginnis range reported significant cattle losses caused by poisonous plants. The plants made their appearance because of a particularly dry spring. Drought persisted through the summer and fall. While Granville Stuart didn't identify the plant species, he described them as "being drouth resisting they come up early, grow luxuriantly and are the first green things to appear in the spring and the cattle will eat them."[13] When Henry returned that summer, he noted that short grass was dry and parched, and that streams and water holes had dried up. To his chagrin, he observed stockmen were still bringing in cattle from Washington and Oregon and the herds from the South were also coming in undiminished numbers. Added to the drought was the heat, with temperatures of 100 to 110 degrees Fahrenheit for days at a time. Then came hot winds that licked up every drop of moisture and shriveled the grass.

After urgent consultation with Conrad Kohrs and Granville Stuart of the Pioneer Cattle Co., Henry and Bob Coburn decided to drive some of their cattle north of the Missouri River. Kohrs had secured a lease of 100,000 acres in the Cypress Hills in Canada and wanted to drive cattle to that location but Stuart disagreed. He believed the area was lacking shelter and was too far north to benefit from the warm chinook winds. Conrad conceded and the two cattlemen decided to reduce their herd as much as possible by shipping to market all the cattle fit for beef and gathering the bulls and feeding them at the home ranches. In the end, they moved 5,000 head across the Missouri River to the foot of the Little Rockies. Henry moved 3,000 head to the same area. Granville Stuart's foreman, G.P. Burnett, gathered and moved their herd while Horace Brewster and Henry's young nephew, Frank Arnette, took charge of the Sieben cattle.

It was an arduous cattle drive north. The crews moved a mixed herd, which is always hard, as young cattle move quickly and old cows and calves slowly. The hot weather continued, and the creeks and waterholes ran dry. Henry lost a large number of his cattle in quicksand when they crossed the Missouri River at Rocky Point, though the remaining herd finally reached its destination in good condition. There were heavy shipments of beef to the markets that fall, which helped relieve the overstocked range. Henry shipped 287 steers from Helena to Chicago and sixteen carloads of cattle from Billings to Chicago. The prices for cattle had dipped, but Henry bet on selling at a lower cost now rather than keeping the cattle for another winter. His sharp business instincts would prove crucial at this point. He held out hope for rains that fall and left for the East Coast, leaving Frank Arnette to oversee the Sieben cattle.[14]

The fall of 1886 did not bring the much-needed rains, and there were ominous signs of a severe winter ahead. Granville Stuart described how wild geese, ducks, and other birds started their migration south earlier that year. The range cattle even seemed to take on a heavier, shaggier coat of hair. Snowy owls descended on the range from the Arctic and into the Judith Basin. Native Americans exclaimed "Heap Cold,"[15] recalling a terrible experience in the long past that still lingered in their memory. The first severe storm hit in November. The cattle north of the Missouri, being unaccustomed to the new range, drifted badly and kept working their way back to the river. On December 5, 1886, another storm hit. Granville Stuart was in Chicago on business but as soon as word reached him, he rushed home. He took the train to Custer and made the 120-mile journey to the ranch via stagecoach in a blinding blizzard.

As the series of catastrophic storms engulfed Montana, Henry was becoming increasingly anxious and distracted in Whitewater, Wisconsin. He had spent the fall with Alberta Gordon and her family in Whitewater but was eager to return to Montana with his bride so that he could be closer to the events that were unfolding. When the couple arrived in the territory days before Christmas 1886, Henry had no fixed abode. His crew had moved his cattle north the previous spring, leaving the Flatwillow Ranch empty. Even if Henry had wanted to settle there with Alberta, the severe weather made it impossible. Instead, the couple chose Helena as their future home. Henry found temporary accommodations on Benton Avenue in what his daughter Margaret later described as "a rooming and boarding house and it was supposed to be the nicest place here you could live in the early days."[16] Helena had been the territorial capital for over a decade. Other prominent stockmen such as T.C. Power, John T. Murphy, and Thomas Cruse were settling in the town. Henry decided that Helena's future was a sure bet. Henry had also learned that the isolation of ranch life could be difficult for women, and he was not willing to gamble on Alberta's happiness.

While Alberta and Henry settled into their new life in Helena, winter storms continued to ravage the territory. In mid-January 1887, a ten-day storm aroused Henry's fears for his cattle and men. He had received reports that their cattle had been drifting before the storm and that even fat, young steers were freezing to death along the trails. The Pioneer Cattle Co. lost fifty percent of their herd in the storm. Smaller, less severe storms arrived in February, but cattle could no longer withstand them.

Henry had seen really bad winters before the Hard Winter of 1886 to 1887. He came through those winters in reasonably good shape thanks, in part, to an abundance of grass and feed and cattle that were well acclimated to northern winters. In the early days on the range, ranchers put up winter hay, but by 1886, things were different. Cattle ranges were overgrazed. A market glut and falling beef prices in 1885 to 1886 produced a carryover of many steers that otherwise would have been marketed in the fall. And cattle and sheep had been pouring into the territory in larger and larger numbers. Many of the trail cattle, especially those from the South, arrived late in the autumn in poor condition to face the winter.

Sieben's first visual of the disaster was likely a sketch drawn by Charlie Russell. Russell was working at the O-H Ranch in the Judith Basin in the winter of 1886 to 1887. The ranch foreman received a letter from the owners, Henry's friends and fellow German immigrants, Louis Stadler and Louis Kaufman, asking how the cattle herd had weathered the storms. In reply, the foreman sent them a sketch that Russell had drawn of a gaunt steer being watched by wolves under a gray winter sky. Russell gave the sketch the haunting title *Waiting for a Chinook.* Stadler and Kaufman showed the drawing to friends and business acquaintances, one of whom was very likely Henry Sieben. Moved by how well the small sketch captured the realities of the harsh winter, it was published in newspapers across the country. After this, Russell began to receive commissions for new work. Russell later painted a more detailed version of the scene, which became one of his best-known works, *The Last of 5000.*[17]

When a chinook wind known as "Gentle Annie" finally arrived later in the spring to melt the snows, cattlemen looked on in horror at the bloated carcasses of their once-great herds that lay scattered across the landscape. The ranges were tragic, and for Henry and most ranchers it was a wrenching, emotional experience. Frank Arnette, having spent the long winter overseeing Henry's operations in the Little Rockies area, informed his uncle he was leaving. He couldn't stomach any more death and hardship and decided "to make some independent ventures" instead. Granville Stuart also hung up his riding boots: "A business that had been fascinating to me before, suddenly became distasteful. I wanted no more of it. I never wanted to own again an animal that I could not feed and shelter."[18]

Stuart was not the only rancher affected so. Henry suffered huge losses, as did many others. Perhaps 362,000 head of cattle perished that winter—sixty percent of the territory's beef population. At Henry's best estimate, he lost seventy-five percent of his cattle. He was devastated and could not have imagined a more precarious manner in which to begin marital life. Henry had spent twenty years in Montana territory, working patiently to acquire a sense of financial security. Henry had finally felt confident he could offer stability and comfort to a wife and start a family. In one horrible winter, that security disappeared.

The large Montana cattle outfits were the heaviest financial losers that winter because they had borrowed large sums of money at high rates of interest. The remaining cattle after the disastrous winter barely paid their debts. Eastern men who invested large sums of money closed out the remnants of their herds and quit. Granville Stuart aptly declared "this was the death knell to the range cattle business on anything like the scale it had been run on before."[19] The boom atmosphere evaporated.[20]

Naturally frugal, Henry resisted fast money opportunities. From his first years in Montana when he chose to freight instead of mine, to his decision to move his herd from an overgrazed Chestnut Valley to Flatwillow, over and over he displayed calculation and long-term vision in his business decisions. After the Hard Winter of 1886 to 1887 Henry took the opportunity to take a step back, assess the situation, and look for the economic opportunities that inevitably present themselves after any disaster.

Recovery came surprisingly soon for Henry and a like-minded cohort. As Eastern investors closed out the remnants of their herds, Henry was able to buy their cattle at low prices. The following winter of 1887 to 1888 was mild, and the spring brought a high number of healthy calves. A combination of ample rainfall and understocking brought the range back quickly. The losses of 1887 had increased beef prices. The combination of good weather and high sales returns meant that Henry and other ranchers with financial reserves, intelligence, and perseverance began to prosper.

It wasn't always every man for himself during these hard years for the stock industry. Henry's friend, Conrad Kohrs, lost sixty-six percent of his herd during the winter of 1886 to 1887, but with the help of a generous friend, he wasn't down for long. A.J. Davis, from whom Kohrs bought the DHS Ranch five years earlier, sent for him. Davis was based in Butte at the time, and upon hearing of Kohrs's losses, Davis offered Kohrs $100,000 on the spot without any security. Kohrs remarked that "the confidence of such a friend added to my courage."[21] He didn't accept the offer at that moment, but Kohrs made use of the funds the following year to purchase cattle. Davis's help would ultimately be a springboard from which Kohrs would soar to new heights of success.[22]

Henry had a similar strong reputation among friends and business associates. A fellow rancher in Wolf Creek, Brian O'Connell, remarked,

"He was a gentleman. . . . Oh he thought the world of everybody. Everybody respected Mr. Sieben . . . I would I think, I would like to be like him."[23] Henry may also have received a helping hand from a friend or friends with financial reserves, but he never documented it. One thing we can be sure of is that this time of financial need greatly influenced Henry's activities later in life when he would informally help others who found themselves in difficult financial situations.

In January of 1888, both Kohrs and Sieben began what would be a parallel and supportive journey in steadily rebuilding their stock operations. By 1891, both men along with Bob Coburn and M.E. Milner owned five large cattle outfits in Chouteau County. Together, these businessmen were some of the largest taxpayers in the county, paying taxes on $334,320 of property (nearly $11 million today) to the county.[24]

Railroad magnate James J. Hill had just completed the Great Northern Railway, which stretched from Minnesota across North Dakota and Montana and into Washington. The route became known as the Hi-line because it was the northernmost transcontinental route in the United States. It opened up northern Montana and transformed the opportunities available to ranchers in the area. The railroad companies had been pressuring Congress to open up Native American lands in Montana since the early 1880s so that they could expand their lines. The Great Northern Railway needed permission to cross Assiniboine, Gros Ventre, and Blackfeet reservation lands. Stockmen were also advocating for the reduction in reservation sizes. In a comment that revealed the mindset of most white settlers of the time, Granville Stuart stated in 1885 that the immense reservations should be thrown open to "actual settlers."[25]

Tribal leaders resisted the idea of giving up more land, but their people were suffering. The bison were gone, and miners had destroyed many of the places where they had traditionally harvested important foods. In the end, the tribes agreed to sell the government seventeen million acres of land—including the sacred Sweetgrass Hills region—for $1.5 million (approximately $48.5 million today). The 1887 Agreement, again, reduced the land reserved for the Blackfeet, which had stretched across almost two-thirds of eastern Montana, to a relatively small area between the Continental Divide and the headwaters of the Marias River. The Agreement resulted in the creation of three reduced reservations—the Blackfeet, Fort Belknap, and Fort Peck reservations. With vast new grazing areas now available north of the Missouri River, Sieben and Kohrs concentrated their efforts there. They would keep their herds together in this area for the next five years.[26]

In January 1888, Henry traveled to Payette, Wyoming, to purchase cattle with Conrad Kohrs. The two men looked the field over but made no purchases. After this initial investigation, Henry increased his herds in 1888 and 1889. There is no known record of Henry's purchases, but Kohrs's account of his activities during this time sheds light on how and where Henry may have purchased cattle. In the spring of 1888, Kohrs traveled to Boise, this time with a foreman, Dick Williams. He purchased 9,000 steers and shipped them to Big Sandy and Bowdoin, stations on the Great Northern line. Through 1889, Kohrs continued to buy stock in Idaho as communities there were not shipping east. He would ship the cattle to Butte and then load them on the Northern Pacific to Helena, transferring there to the Great Northern and unloading at Bowdoin, a station seven miles east of Malta. Those in poor condition he sent to the ranges, and the balance were sent on to the Chicago Stockyards. They netted him a profit of $15 ($500 today's value) per head.

The weather for the next couple of years was in Henry's and Conrad's favor. Winters were mild with little snow, and there was an abundance of grass on the prairie as the range was no longer overstocked. The Hard Winter of 1886 to 1887 had taught everyone the value of winter feed and shelter for calves and weak cows. Like most ranchers, Henry and Conrad also provided for more hay acreage. Statewide, there was an astonishing increase in hay acreage from 56,000 acres in 1880 to more than 700,000 acres in 1900. By December 1889, Henry had a healthy herd with significant enough numbers to warrant him stopping in Fort Benton, on a journey back from Chicago with Alberta, to consult with Chouteau County officials over assessment of his cattle.[27]

Bob Coburn also grazed his herds in Chouteau County. However, there appears to have been a falling out between Sieben and his once close friend and partner. From the mid-1890s onwards, Henry does not mention Bob, and after 1893 they never ranched in the same vicinity again. There is no mention of Henry in Bob's biography, written by his son Walt Coburn. The details of the falling out are unknown, but Henry's daughter, Margaret, would later confirm that Henry "didn't think much of him." She elaborated that "Father got to know him and he didn't admire him at all. I don't know how they got together."[28]

Until this point, Henry had invested most of his money and time in ranching on the open range. He had dabbled in property at White Sulphur Springs and had even purchased and sold land in the Chestnut Valley. From the 1890s onwards, however, Henry turned his attention to buying and selling land. Interestingly, in 1891, an issue came to light involving a piece of land Henry had sold to neighboring Chestnut Valley rancher C.H. Austin ten years prior. Austin never recorded a patent for the land after he purchased it. So, legally he had no title for the property. This meant Sieben could have taken possession of the land anytime in the interim. The *Great Falls Tribune* brought the story to light to reveal that 500 or more patents had still not been recorded in Cascade County. The journalist's goal was to remind landowners to record their patents and avoid potential litigation. Henry did not pursue the reacquisition of the land.[29]

While Henry's inclination was to focus on cattle and land to diversify his business portfolio, his young, handsome, and entrepreneurial nephew Frank Arnette had piqued Henry's interest in mining. Since Frank left the open range after the Hard Winter of 1886 to 1887, he had been speculating in mining in the White Sulphur Springs area. It is hardly surprising the young man was interested in gold. The arrival of railroads in Montana brought unprecedented growth to the territory's mining industry.

Frank Arnette focused his efforts on the booming mining town of Castle, close to White Sulphur Springs. The town derived its name from its location at the base of the Castle Mountains. Rich deposits of lead and silver brought miners to the area beginning in 1882, and the town grew up around a single cabin in 1887. As silver prices soared, Castle's population grew to 2,000 residents, and numerous businesses, including fourteen saloons and seven brothels, sprang into existence. Into this atmosphere came a character who had lived in Virginia City at the same time as Henry all those years ago—Martha Jane Canary, better known as Calamity Jane. After having lived a "wildlife" in the boomtown of Deadwood, South Dakota, for several years, she tried for a short time to live an "honest" life and decided to open a restaurant in Castle. Her business failed and she soon returned to Deadwood.[30]

The future looked bright for Castle in the late 1880s and Henry, who had always been generous to family, spotted a golden opportunity. During the Constitutional Convention just a year earlier, delegates protected the special tax status granted to the powerful mining industry. Delegates called for mines to be taxed only on the value of the original mining claim. Most original mining claims cost only $5, even ones that produced millions of dollars of copper or silver. Since Henry's ranching operations were paying most of the state's expenses, he decided to profit from the mining deal. He partnered with Frank, forming a real estate company called Sieben & Arnette. In 1890, the firm purchased four mining claims that also contained log cabins. In 1891, the Golden Messenger Mining and Milling Company came up for sale at public auction outside the courthouse in White Sulphur Springs. Sieben and Arnette were the highest bidders, putting $3,635 (over $110,000 today) on the line. The purchase included the Golden Messenger quartz lode mining claim as well as the Little Dandy quartz lode mining claim. The mines were located in the Belt Mining District, Meagher County.[31]

Unfortunately for Henry and Frank, this investment failed. Congress repealed the Sherman Silver Purchase Act of 1890, which had been put in place to prevent the further depletion of the government's gold reserves. This resulted in the Silver Panic of 1893. By the mid-1890s, Castle residents had moved on. Frank lost all of his capital in the business venture. The experience soured his interest in mining, and Frank returned to ranching—now a safer bet in his eyes. Meanwhile, it appears that Henry held on to the Golden Messenger and Little Dandy quartz lode mines for another decade at least. He filed for the mining patents in 1897 and, according to former business associate Brian O'Connell and Henry's daughter Margaret, he enjoyed solid returns from this investment, which later encouraged him to invest in mines in Rimini.[32]

Henry was working as hard as he ever had, but his personal life now also required his attention. Henry's marriage to Alberta was expanding his once monocular vision of life. Alberta brought a levity, warmth, and security to Henry's world that had been missing. After their first apartment, they found a home at 512 Madison Avenue on the affluent west side of town and welcomed their first daughter, Berneice, on December 26, 1890. The Siebens turned out to be a perfect fit for Helena society. For the first time in his life, Henry joined social clubs. He eased into the new routine and found he enjoyed socializing with other entrepreneurial members at the Helena Rod and Gun Club. His friends here included horse owner Harvey Barbour, drugstore owner Henry Parchen, newspaperman A.J. Fisk, and orchard owner James Perkins. Henry also joined the King Solomon Masonic Lodge Number 9 in 1892, but his tenure as a mason proved short-lived. There is no record of Henry as a member after that year, and his daughter Margaret would later confirm that he was a mason but he "didn't take it any more seriously than Alfred [son-in-law] did."[33]

Throughout the late 1880s, Helena continued its process of refinement as it emerged from its wild mining town days and settled into serving as Montana's capital city. Henry could now scarcely remember the crooked path of Last Chance Gulch, weaving between mining claims, tents, and saloons. Helena's origins as a chaotic gold camp were now becoming a distant memory. Since its establishment as territorial capital in 1875 and the arrival of the Northern Pacific Railroad in 1883, downtown buildings in a rich variety of architectural styles arose and streetcars transported its residents around town. Women were the heart of the glamorous entertaining. They dressed beautifully and often had their gowns made in Chicago or in New York. Alberta was social and outgoing and thrived in high society Helena. Margaret recalled the wonderful collection of gowns her mother owned. She also described Helena women as "entertaining beautifully" when she was a child.[34]

Alberta established herself as a charming host in Helena. She held regular afternoon gatherings with some of the most well-known women in Helena, including Mrs. Mary Kleinschmidt (wife of banker Theodore Kleinschmidt), Mrs. Margaret Cruse (wife of miner and banker Thomas Cruse), and Mrs. Edna Hedges (wife of miner and attorney Cornelius Hedges). At her Christmas entertainment on December 11, 1892, Alberta hosted thirty women. The gatherings were convivial occasions with Alberta telling the local newspaper that "fancy work" was the excuse to get together but "other things may have been more alluring." Alberta was a gifted seamstress and entered her work into a Blue-Ribbon Day competition at the Helena fairgrounds in 1894. She came home laden with trophies—taking first prizes for her buffet scarf, doilies, her embroidered flannel skirt, infant shawl, and lunch cloths.[35] She also played golf, a sport Henry never appears to have enjoyed. Margaret remembered her mother wearing a cape for her golf outings and that she had a plaid bag for her clubs. In a humorous anecdote, Margaret recalled that Alberta was a member at one of the first golf courses in Helena that had "great big concrete circles . . . about twelve feet in diameter with a little hole in the middle. Those were the greens for the golf course. Concrete, can you imagine playing that way and I don't think many people know about that!"[36]

Montana had a coming-out party of its own in 1889 with the long-awaited transition to statehood. Montana could now control its own funds and residents could elect their own governor, judges, and state officers. A constitutional convention convened in Helena on July 4, 1889. Voters approved the resultant plan of government on October 1 of that year. There was an effort to have a women's suffrage clause included in the state constitution (at this point women could only vote on school board elections and on tax issues). In a wry anecdote, Conrad Kohrs, one of the men elected to the convention, recalled that women presented those who voted in favor of the bill with bouquets and those who opposed it with thistles. Conrad didn't disclose whether he voted for or against the clause, but it didn't pass. Montana women would have to wait until 1914 to win the right to vote. One of the constitution's provisions called for the electorate to select the new state capital. The Lewis and Clark County Courthouse in Helena had housed the territorial government since 1875, and delegates thought it fitting to leave the choice to the people before constructing a more ornate capitol building. Even though Butte was more populous in 1890 with 23,000 residents compared to Helena's 13,834, Helenans were confident that their community would remain the capital.[37]

The contest was highly competitive. Several communities made strong cases: Paris Gibson entered Great Falls in the race, Marcus Daly backed Anaconda, copper king William A. Clark put Helena forward, and rancher and businessman Nelson Story extolled Bozeman's promising future. The communities of Deer Lodge and Boulder also made their case. As election day approached, an uptick in corruption tainted the contest. Helena and Anaconda backers were accused of bribing newspapers for endorsements. In the end, Helena won the vote.

Henry would certainly have supported Helena's bid for the capital city, but it is not known if he exerted his money or influence in the capital fight. However, for the first time on record, he did get involved in civic affairs. In March 1889, Henry was elected as a delegate for the Democratic Convention, which would nominate candidates for mayor, city treasurer, and police magistrate. He was elected from the fifth ward along with other well-known male citizens including rancher Daniel Flowerce, school administrator S.C. Gilpatrick, rancher John T. Murphy, and businessman Thomas Cruse. The same year, Jake ran an unsuccessful campaign for Republican Cascade County commissioner.[38] Henry was very deliberate in every decision he made, and it is noteworthy he declared himself a Democrat (if only for a short period of time).

In the late 1880s, promises were made to ensure Montana would be admitted as a U.S. state. Conrad Kohrs alleged that mine owner George Hearst promised the U.S. Senate that if Montana's bid were to come to fruition, it would mean two more Democratic senators. To fulfill his promise, he wrote to Marcus Daly asking him to spare no expense in making Montana a Democratic state. Perhaps Kohrs influenced Henry's political leanings at the time. In 1888, William A.

Clark secured the Democratic nomination as delegate to Congress. The nomination, in a territory famed for its Democratic leanings, should have secured his election. When the votes were tallied, however, Clark had lost by more than 5,000 votes to a lesser-known Republican named Thomas H. Carter. Clark had suffered a humiliating defeat, and he put the blame on his rival Marcus Daly. Clark, who was a Protestant Scot, had been openly nativist in his campaign—to the point of scheduling a large fundraising political rally with a beef, lamb, and pork barbecue in Anaconda on a Friday. The meat-heavy event enraged Irish Catholic Marcus Daly as well as the Irish Catholic community at large in Butte. In retaliation for the insult, Butte's "safe" Irish/Democratic wards went overwhelmingly for Carter, the Catholic son of Irish immigrants.[39]

Sieben's fidelity to William A. Clark and the Democratic party waned in the late 1890s. By that time, Henry found his more "natural" home in the Republican Party—the party of favor for most Montana Stockgrowers Association members. Henry's switching of allegiances indicates an aversion to the corrupt political practices of leading Democrats such as William A. Clark and Marcus Daly. Although Henry was not as vocal about politics as other leading businessmen in the state, it seems he, too, played a part in the tribal aspect to the way the political game was played in Montana.[40]

Henry's business ventures continued to grow in the early 1890s. In the spring of 1892, local butchers suffered a meat shortage. Two businesses, Chartier based in Butte and Stadler & Kaufman (owned by Henry's friends and ranchers Louis Stadler and Louis Kaufman) in Helena accompanied Conrad Kohrs to Malta to look over his and Henry's cattle. The butchers were so pleased that Kohrs and Sieben sold large trainloads of beef to Helena and Butte that year. The cows brought $45 a head ($1,500 today's value) and the steers $65 ($2,200 today's value). Later that summer, Henry shipped fourteen carloads of cattle from Malta. All of this shows that Henry's methodical approach to rebuilding his enterprise had worked. But he took none of his current good fortune for granted. Instead, he kept a close eye on the extraordinary events unfolding in neighboring Wyoming. Henry was worried the conflict could extend into Montana and potentially upend Montana ranchers' work to rebuild their herds and businesses.

A range fight, known as the Johnson County War, that had begun in 1889 came to a violent culmination in Wyoming in 1892. The battle between large cattle ranchers and small farmers in Johnson County, Wyoming, would influence Henry and his wealthy stock grower associates' actions in the ensuing years. Similar to Montana, in the early days of Wyoming, most of the land was in public domain, which was open to stock raising as an open range and farmlands for homesteading. Large numbers of cattle were turned loose on the open range by ranches. However, as more and more homesteaders, called "grangers," moved into Wyoming in the 1880s, competition for land and water enveloped the state, and the large cattle companies began monopolizing large areas of the open range to prevent homesteaders from using it. The uneasy relationship between the wealthier ranchers and the smaller settlers became worse after the Hard Winter of 1886 to 1887. To protect what remained, large cattle owners in Wyoming reacted with a catch-all allegation of rustling against their competition. Hostilities worsened when the Wyoming legislature passed the Maverick Act, which stated that all unbranded cattle in the open range automatically belonged to the large ranchers.[41]

The Johnson County War began when big cattle companies started ruthlessly persecuting alleged rustlers in the area. The Wyoming Stock Growers Association (WSGA), which represented the state's large cattle companies, decided to employ an agency of detectives to investigate cases of cattle theft from its members' holdings. On July 20, 1889, one of those detectives, George Henderson, accused a local rancher, Ella Watson, of stealing cattle from a larger stock grower, Albert Bothwell. The cattlemen sent riders to capture Ella and her partner, Jim Averell. Both of them were subsequently lynched. The gruesome act was one of the rare cases in which a woman was lynched. The *Cheyenne Daily Sun* printed sensational newspaper articles immediately after the lynchings portraying Watson as a prostitute who accepted cattle for her favors, and she was given the nickname "Cattle Kate." It was later discovered that an employee of one of the Cheyenne dailies owned by a powerful cattle owner had written those articles about Ella Watson. It was later proven that Ella had legally taken up a homestead claim, bought a brand for her cattle, signed a political petition, and applied for a marriage license. She was a woman who, just like Henry Sieben and their cattle ranching peers, wanted to own land and have security. But because she had homesteaded in the middle of the cattlemen's customary range and refused to sell her land to Albert Bothwell, she was murdered.

Over the next couple of years, employees of the WSGA declared war on alleged rustlers. On April 5, 1892, fifty-two armed men traveled north from Cheyenne toward Buffalo, the Johnson County seat. Their mission was to hang seventy men. The "invaders," as they became known, included some of the most powerful cattlemen in Wyoming, their top employees, and twenty-three hired guns. The invaders got word that "rustlers" were holed up in a cabin at a local ranch. They surrounded the cabin, eventually torching it and killing an identified "rustler," Nate Champion, who had been elected president of an association formed by small ranchers. By then, locals had been alerted, and men from all over the area rushed to confront the invaders. A posse that eventually grew to 400 people surrounded them. Over three days, the group slowly closed in on the invaders. In the nick of time, Wyoming Governor Amos Barber telegraphed President Benjamin Harrison in Washington, D.C. President Harrison called on soldiers from nearby Fort McKinney to suppress the "insurrection" and arrest the invaders. The powerful cattle ranchers were later protected by a friendly judicial system. The vigilante killings were highly effective as a deterrent to rustling, but, as in the case of the "Stuart's Stranglers" vigilantism in central Montana in the 1880s, the stockmen were severely criticized for their arbitrary killings. Cattle rustling in Montana in the late 1800s was an ever present headache for Henry and other large stockowners. They likely knew many of the cattle operators in Wyoming who were involved in the war and identified with their issues. Henry's actions in just a couple of years indicate he studied the infamous events in the neighboring state, analyzing what worked and what didn't. The events in Wyoming would be a template for implementing a solution for rustling in Montana.[42]

As the 1890s rolled on, Henry's ambitions to continue growing his operations remained strong. His attention had been fixated on potential opportunities in eastern Montana for the past few years. He noted that land for the Assiniboine had been further reduced, thus opening up new grazing lands to stockmen. He observed that the Great Northern Railway provided shipping points all along the Hi-line, which benefited ranchers including his brother, Jake, who was successfully ranching near Glasgow. He had also been tracking Pierre Wibaux's success in running one of the largest spreads in the state. Henry's business senses tingled; he wanted some of the eastern Montana pie. All he needed was a capable partner who could also see the opportunity and manage a ranch on the ground. That partner came in the guise of Wyoming rancher P. O. Brewster in 1893.[43] ◈

Chapter 5

1893–1897

"SLOWLY AND QUIETLY"

The early 1890s was a shaky economic period in Montana as well as across the nation. The Panic of 1893 (a four-year-long economic depression in the United States), severe weather, and over-grazing combined to create potential disaster for the cattlemen. Never one to shrink from challenging circumstances, Henry navigated the instability by hedging his bets on a ranch in Culbertson, a small, remote town on the eastern edge of Montana. While others may have balked at making such a move, Henry understood that the area offered large amounts of land for the taking and was a shipping point on the Great Northern Railway. Once again, he saw potential where others did not. Within a handful of years, Henry was running one of the largest spreads in the region. He found the experience of operating a ranch so far from home quite difficult, but he proactively tackled the challenges that arose. Henry helped establish the Northern Montana Roundup Association, which aimed to eliminate cattle rustling, a huge headache for area stockmen. Through his work with the organization, Henry helped effect long-term change for Montana's stock industry.

The year 1892 to 1893 was challenging for ranchers in the West. Due to the intense cold, many ranchers lost substantial numbers of their herds. Conrad Kohrs lost fifty percent of the yearlings he shipped that fall. Furthermore, the fall market of 1892 was a bust, with many cattlemen barely recouping the cost of shipping stock. It was also getting harder to provide quality grass for cattle. Each rancher wanted to expand his or her own herd. There was no authority to determine when there were more cows and sheep feeding in a region than the grassland could sustain. Henry, Conrad Kohrs, and Bob Coburn were becoming

When Henry Sieben and his partner, Paul Brewster, arrived in Culbertson in 1893, it was a rough and tumble town full of cowboys and saloons. Courtesy of the Montana Historical Society Library & Archives, 946-593.

anxious about the increasing number of cattle grazing on the rangeland near the Little Rockies.

As the stock industry navigated these events, the Panic of 1893 devastated the nation's economy. Banks closed and millions of ordinary people lost their life savings. The Panic became even worse in Montana when the federal government decided to stop minting silver coins that fall. When the government stopped buying millions of ounces of silver for coins, Montana's silver mines closed. Silver towns like Castle, Wickes, Granite, and Elkhorn became ghost towns overnight. After 1893, silver came to be for the most part a mere byproduct of large-scale copper mining at Butte. Within a few months, nearly one-third of Montana's 60,000 workers lost their jobs.

With both stock and mining investments losing money, Henry had to pivot. That opportunity arose in spring 1893 when Conrad Kohrs decided to move the DHS operation's herds, which included Sieben's and Bob Coburn's cattle, to a ranch he owned at Rim Rocks just northwest of Shelby at the foot of the Sweet Grass Hills. Kohrs gave his ranch manager, Jim Spurgeon, the task of trailing the cattle to Rim Rocks and hired Henry's nephew, Frank Arnette, to receive the cattle at the ranch. Henry agreed to send his cattle and calves with Kohrs's herd, but he was also itching to restart his own ranching operation. He took the plunge and began rebuilding his own cattle enterprise, his first since the Hard Winter of 1886 to 1887, at Culbertson. This was not an impulsive reaction on Henry's part. It was the culmination of years of observation and research on the growth and potential of eastern Montana. Henry's ability to think several steps ahead once again ensured he had a plan in place he could implement when needed. Henry always endeavored to turn a crisis into an opportunity.[1]

Henry's daughter, Margaret, remembered: "He was deliberate, he didn't ever run or hurry. He did things slowly and quietly, but he got them done always and they were done right."[2] This methodical approach served Henry well. Since his cattle and calves were going northwest to Shelby with the DHS Ranch, Henry needed to ship his steers east. He knew this endeavor would require most of his time and energy in the spring and summer of 1893. With that in mind and having just endured another harsh winter, Alberta decided to take Berneice to Whitewater, Wisconsin, to spend the summer months with her parents and siblings. Henry used the time to start up a new operation with a fresh business partner, P.O. Brewster.[3]

Paul O. Brewster of Cheyenne, Wyoming, was a successful rancher, described by the *Chinook Opinion* as the "prince of cattlemen."[4] He owned a ranch in Nebraska and was the treasurer of the Warbonnett Livestock Company in Cheyenne. In 1892, the same year that the Johnson County War came to a violent head, Brewster left Wyoming for Montana. He purchased B.E. Brewster's share in a multi-partner ranching operation in north-central Montana. The ranch was referred to in the *Chinook Opinion* as the Mellick & Brewster, or B.E. Brewster Trus. Ranch. They used the historic **UΩ** brand. It seems like a strange coincidence that both men had the same surname, but there is no evidence they were related. Paul Brewster brought in 6,000 head of cattle from Idaho but, like Henry, he settled in Helena with his family. Brewster's wife,

Within just a few years of Sieben's arrival, Culbertson had become a bustling and respectable supply center, as shown here around 1905. Courtesy of the Montana Historical Society Library & Archives, 946-590.

Jessie Brewster, sang at various public programs around town and was described as having "one of the sweetest soprano voices ever heard in Helena."[5] Brewster was an experienced cattleman, and with mining interests on the wane, the timing was right for both men to collaborate on a new venture in Culbertson.[6]

Culbertson in 1893 was not for the faint of heart. On a trip to the town in the late 1890s, a local told cowboy Jim Spurgeon that they were "going to a hell of a place when you go down to Culbertson."[7] The town was created in June 1887 with the arrival of the St. Paul, Minneapolis & Manitoba Railway, later known as the Great Northern Railway. It was named after American Fur Company trader Major Alexander Culbertson, who in 1839 took over as factor (highest-ranking officer) at Fort Union, twenty-three miles to the east. Culbertson married Natawista Iksana, known as Medicine Snake Woman, at the fort. Natawista was a peacemaker and interpreter and played a key role in helping establish treaties and navigate negotiations between American and British traders with Blackfoot tribes.[8] The ranchers of the 1890s helped Culbertson flourish. During the cattle industry boom, thirteen saloons lined the three-block-long main street, providing diversion twenty-four hours a day for thirsty cowboys. Culbertson served as the shipping point for area ranchers and homesteaders located from East Redwater Creek to the Canadian border. By the time Sieben and Brewster shipped their cattle to Culbertson and turned them loose on Muddy Creek, just west of town, there were a number of ranches already up and running. The Day Ranch ran a large operation on the Missouri River, the Star Ranch was situated twelve miles east of Culbertson on the river bottom, and the John Manning Ranch was located fifteen miles northwest of Culbertson. Sieben and Brewster established their rangeland on the Missouri River about nine miles south of Culbertson.[9]

Since Sieben and Brewster could not control rangeland they did not own, they set their sights on holding acreage without owning it. These experienced businessmen understood that ranchers who controlled water sources controlled the land around them. According to Frank B. McCann, a Culbertson local who would later acquire the Diamond Ranch, cattlemen "were fighting on water all the time. All the ranches were . . . they didn't have to own the land but they better own the water hole. That was the big deal."[10] Henry began buying up several small ranches with a water source as well as filing his own homestead claims enabling him to control thousands of acres of grazing land.

Sieben and Brewster also got creative with acquiring land. Once they hired their crew, they had some of their cowhands file homestead claims on choice bottomlands with the understanding that when the men improved on it, they would sell to Henry and Paul O. Brewster. Even though filing fraudulent homestead entries was technically illegal, it was common practice among ranchers at the time. Henry's former partner, Bob Coburn, located all of his Circle C cowpunchers on the choice bottomlands along the creeks with various springs and water resources within a twenty-five-mile radius on all sides of the home ranch. Sieben and Brewster also had their crew "squat" on what they chose as their "accustomed range" close to the Missouri River and protect it as best they could. For the most part this worked, but it wasn't foolproof. In one incident, some of their crew squatted on a location and even built a couple of log houses only to find out local Oswald Peterson and his brother had already homesteaded on the site. The crew had to promptly dismantle and move their buildings about a mile north. However, these tactics proved fruitful in general, and Henry ultimately acquired 1,600 acres of deeded land and ten sections of land under state lease. By 1897, Henry had the largest number of cattle in the area.[11]

Sieben and Brewster ran their cattle north and west of the Missouri River. In the first year, they added to the steers Henry moved from the Little Rockies by purchasing 800 head of polled Angus cattle (born without horns) and 2,100 head of one- and two-year-olds. Henry paid $18 ($600 today's value) a head for the cattle, and they netted him $66.50 ($2,000 today's value). The sale of these cattle provided him with a substantial profit early on. Sieben and Brewster's herds ran alongside Muddy Creek all the way north to Poplar Creek on the Canadian border. They had a couple of thousand head of cattle in 1893 to 1894, but considering that in most semi-arid areas it took forty acres to feed a cow for a year, they needed 40,000 acres of land to survive.[12] The sparsely populated open range in eastern Montana provided that land for Sieben and Brewster. Henry continued to use the diamond brand he and his brother, Leonard, had acquired in the Chestnut Valley all those years ago. They branded on the left ribs for cattle, reversed and on the left shoulder for horses. By the end of the decade, Henry and his partners would name their operation the Diamond Ranch.

For the first time, Henry was also invested in raising and breaking horses for sale. He observed there was money to be made on horses in this area and he dove into the market. For example, Frank B. McCann's father, who ranched in the Culbertson area, would trail horses to towns along the Hi-line and sell or trade them. Frank estimated a horse was worth $150 ($5,000 today's value) and a cow was worth $0.03 ($1 today's value) a pound. So, for the sale of a single horse, Frank's father would receive cash as well as three or four head of cattle. Frank recalled that during the 1890s, Henry had 200 to 300 horses he would sell to cowboys from Culbertson all the way west to Chinook. Not only did Henry make a profit from selling horses, Margaret also recalled that her father was particularly fond of the animal: "Father was a wonderful horseman and he spoke quietly and gently to horses and they just loved him too."[13]

Since Sieben and Brewster themselves were based in Helena, their ranch crew members were responsible for establishing the Culbertson ranch headquarters. The team built log houses and constructed a windmill as well as an ice-house. They cut ice out of the Missouri River and placed it all around the building. The ice-house interior contained a chopping block where they cut up their beef and hung it inside. The team cut hay from 100 acres to winter the stock because, as Henry put it, "one experience like Flatwillow was enough."[14] Henry spared little expense on his employees. He kept all his ranches supplied with good food for the hands, and he hired mechanics to keep equipment in

Sieben's operation near Culbertson was known as the Diamond Ranch (for his first registered brand). Here, some of his ranch hands gather in the Diamond bunkhouse for a game of cards in 1905. Courtesy of the Montana Historical Society Library & Archives, 946-504.

constant repair and prevent shutdowns while broken gear was carried to distant blacksmiths or harness-makers. He insisted that supplies and equipment be maintained and well cared for. These were courtesies and conveniences, but they also made economic sense.

Both Sieben and Brewster had young families in Helena, but for the first few years it appears Paul O. Brewster spent lengthy periods of time at the ranch overseeing day-to-day operations. Henry's trips to Culbertson amounted to a handful of times a year. Both he and Brewster needed a strong, capable, and reliable foreman to run the ranch. They found their trusted hire in Texas cowboy Nolan Armstrong. Armstrong was an experienced cow puncher and a bachelor who was willing to live at the main ranch and oversee day-to-day operations. Armstrong hired Pat Nacey, who had worked as a troubleshooter for neighboring sheep outfits. Nacey did not board at the ranch headquarters; he homesteaded on Muddy Creek and worked for himself as well as Sieben and Brewster. Nacey would later become the first sheriff of Roosevelt County. Sieben and Brewster were particularly grateful that they had a trusted team in place when cattle went astray and drifted too far north.[15]

Henry had to make last-minute trips of 465 miles from Helena to Culbertson when problems on the ranch arose. One particularly rainy year, in approximately 1895, there was an abundance of mosquitoes disturbing the cattle. The prevailing winds in the Culbertson area come from the northwest, so the cattle drifted into the wind as it blew the mosquitoes off their skin. The cattle traveled as far north as Canada, and it wasn't long before the provincial governor ordered Henry to gather his stock. Henry immediately dropped business in Helena, jumped on the next train, and arrived at the Culbertson ranch to pick up Armstrong, Nacey, and a wagon before heading north to round up his cattle. However, when the men crossed the border, there was so much grass that Henry and his crew decided to leave the cattle where they were. Conrad Kohrs experienced a similar incident and later explained he had struck a monetary deal with the Canadian provincial governor to have his cattle released. After that, the governor treated them with great consideration. It is possible Henry reached a similar agreement with Canadian authorities.

The winter of 1896 was severe, and Henry was getting nervous about the condition of the cattle in Canada. He was determined to ensure he never again would lose seventy-five percent of his cattle as happened in the Hard Winter of 1886 to 1887. So, Henry left his young family for a second time that year and traveled to Culbertson in the dead of winter. He rode with Armstrong and Nacey as well as a pack outfit until they found the cattle in Redstone, an area close to the Canadian border. The cattle were weathering the storms just fine, and the trip was for nothing. This wasn't the end of Henry's last-minute grueling trips to Culbertson in search of cattle, though. When the ranch crew put a shipment of young steers, described as "wild dogies" (cowboy parlance for motherless calves) on Muddy Creek in July of 1895, the cattle fled the minute they were unloaded and stampeded into Canada and North Dakota. Once again, Henry caught a train from Helena, stopping at the ranch only for a buckboard before heading north to hunt the cattle. He failed to locate them. Then he sent Armstrong and Nacey with a crew and packhorses. They failed, too. Finally, Armstrong took a round-up wagon and some riders into South Dakota and Canada, where they rode from May until November before locating all the cattle. Rustlers had branded 140 head of cattle. Henry was furious. Henry would never have imagined stealing from others. Henry was determined to prevent further incidents of rustling.[16]

By the mid-1890s, Henry had nearly thirty years of experience in the stock industry. He had blossomed from a scrappy German teenager hauling freight in Montana Territory into a respected and experienced rancher and businessman. Henry dressed accordingly. His daughter Margaret recalled he "never owned a pair of cowboy boots." Instead, "he wore his little old black shoes with the little heels . . . and the shirt and then a vest . . . and a little hat, probably was a Stetson, but it was a little business hat. A little felt hat." Henry's attire mirrored his outlook. Margaret remembered: "He never had a cowboy hat and he never had cowboy boots and he never was a cowboy . . . he was a stockman."

She described Henry as a serious looking man, but "he was fun and he was jolly and he had a sparkle. He was a very genial person, but he wasn't a flabberer . . . he just was honest and he was what he was."[17]

This earned trust and respect that Henry now commanded stood him in good stead when he decided to help build an organization that would protect the interests of northern Montana stockmen. In April 1895, Henry gathered with cattlemen of northern and northeastern Montana as well as railroad representatives in Chinook. Chinook was one of the most important cattle shipping points along the Great Northern in Montana, with thousands of cattle loaded at the station that year alone. It was a fitting meeting place for the leaders of the stock industry to gather and talk about problems that were affecting their businesses. They discussed issues like the wolf problem and shorter beef roundups.

The leaders understood the power of gathering to collaborate on their common goals and brainstorm on industry problems. They decided to unite and formally establish an organization called the Northern Montana Roundup Association that would better protect their stock interests along the Great Northern Railway. A committee that included Henry's two good friends, Conrad Kohrs and Louis Kaufman, was tasked with drafting resolutions to regulate beef shipments and establish the price for stock killed in railroad accidents. Those present elected Sieben to the executive committee along with ranchers such as M.E. Milner of the Square Butte outfit, John Survant of Malta, and Louis Kaufman. Henry's partner, Paul O. Brewster, was elected as secretary, and Daniel Floweree and Bob Coburn also joined as members of the fledgling organization. There was an energy to the meeting; a movement was beginning. Newspapers in the region dedicated substantial column space to reporting on the gathering.[18]

Three months later in July 1895, the organization members met in Fort Benton to declare their chief purpose in organizing—to put an end to cattle rustling. Those present, including stockmen representing twelve local roundup associations in Cascade, Chouteau, Teton, and Valley counties, acknowledged rustling was increasing rapidly and changing in nature. Henry and Paul O. Brewster knew from their recent experience in Culbertson that rustlers were no longer happy to pick mavericks off the range. Chairman M.E. Milner rose and spoke to the crowd alleging that rustlers were taking calves from cows, altering brands on young stock, and slaughtering mature beeves and selling the meat in towns and mining camps. He spoke on behalf of those present to share their dissatisfaction with what he called the "lackluster laws" in place to protect their property. Milner grumbled about the mountains of evidence needed to secure a conviction when thievery occurred and was highly critical of the county officers assigned with protecting stock, arguing that they were not up to scratch for the job. This account was similar to the declarations made by Wyoming's stock growers in 1889 before they organized and financed their invasion. The noteworthy meeting was, once again, widely covered by local newspapers. Like their Wyoming counterparts, the Montana cattlemen were painting themselves as victims, with little to no support. Their only recourse was to take drastic action to protect their property.

Remarkably, in response to Milner's speech, stock growers openly declared that rustling would be most effectively dealt with if they implemented "the summary methods prevailing in the [18]80s" (i.e., vigilante justice). They concluded they should suppress the problem according to the law but pronounced that, should this prove inadequate, "resort must be had to methods that have proved effective in the past."[19] There is no doubt Milner's speech was a thinly veiled threat to lawmakers in Helena to provide appropriate protection for ranchers' stock. Rancher S.S. Hobson moved to have Milner's address made available in the meeting's minutes, and Henry seconded the motion. *The River Press* printed Milner's speech in their following issue. Word spread like wildfire and the public took note. The stock growers had forcefully placed the ball in the hands of Montana's elected officials.

At the organization's fall meeting in Great Falls in December 1895, it was clear the Roundup Association's urgent strategy had worked like a charm. Worried that circumstances would result in scenes like those in Johnson County just a few years earlier, the state's lawmakers decided that police would assist stockmen in prosecuting cattle rustlers. During the Roundup Association's meeting, members publicly thanked Cascade County, as well as the general public, for having made it possible for stockowners to receive the same degree of protection for their property that was accorded to other classes of property. They specifically named Sheriff Dwyer and the Cascade County Attorney for vigorously prosecuting cattle thieves in the area. The members reflected on a job well done.[20]

Secure in the knowledge that he had done his best to establish an organization that would better protect his stock, Henry turned his attention, once again, to personal as well as other business interests. While 1895 marked a turning point in the organization of Montana's stock industry, it was also a life-changing year for Henry and Alberta. The couple were now well-to-do residents of Montana's capital city, and they enjoyed being at the center of Helena's social scene. In 1893, Henry had been elected a member of the city's premiere social club, the Montana Club. A group of Helena's elites founded the club in March 1885 "for gentlemen only," organizing for "literary, mutual improvement, and social purposes."[21] This membership brought status for Henry among Helena's

Henry Sieben, seen here at approximately forty-three years of age in 1890, was becoming a respectable business and family man with a base of operations in Helena. Courtesy of the Montana Historical Society Library & Archives, PAc, 76-30 F09.

elite and provided him ample opportunities to socialize with other prosperous men in the town. Members built a beautiful seven-story building on the corner of Sixth and Fuller Avenue in 1893, the same year Henry joined.

Conveniently, just a couple of years later, Henry found a new home for his family just east of the club in the heart of town at 221 East Sixth Avenue. The attractive brick duplex with two-story bay windows, granite sills, decorative brickwork, corbelled cornice, and open front porch was built in 1890 and located in the prosperous Courthouse Square neighborhood. It accommodated two families and was especially convenient for the Siebens' neighbor, the Honorable Henry N. Blake, an attorney and district judge. The distinguished residence was one of the district's best examples of the Italianate-style urban row house. The Siebens' neighbors across the street were the William Chessman family. The Chessman's romantic Queen Anne–style mansion would later serve as the official residence of Montana's governors until 1959. William Chessman was a California "49er" who, like Henry, came to Montana in the mid-1860s. Chessman settled in Helena in 1865 and since that time had acquired mining interests, developed real estate, and was a key player in the development of Helena's early water system. The buildings in the courthouse area demonstrated the architectural exuberance of the period when Helena earned the nickname "Queen City of the Rockies."[22]

The Siebens settled into their new Helena home in the upper-class neighborhood and, on March 20, 1895, Henry and Alberta welcomed a second daughter, Margaret Sieben. With a growing family and an increasingly diverse business portfolio, Henry spent most of Margaret's infancy traveling to tend to his cattle operations in central and eastern Montana and attend meetings of the Northern Montana Roundup Association. Alberta took on the role of primary caretaker for their two young daughters in Helena. Alberta had hired help for the children, and she was fortunate to have a wide social circle and support network of friends. But without familial support in town and Henry on the road, it was at times a challenging and lonely experience. However, for Henry this was a pivotal time to take advantage of opportunities that were presenting themselves to provide further financial security and the home of his dreams for his young family. As Margaret later recalled: "He loved his wife, he loved his home, he loved his children and his family, that was the heart of his existence . . . and you know his whole idea when he was working so hard and getting his cattle together, then sheep, was to have enough money to build a nice home for his family."[23]

Throughout the mid-1890s, Henry continued to grow his real estate portfolio. In summer 1895, Henry was still a director and stockholder of the White Sulphur Springs Association in Meagher County. The following winter, Henry decided to expand his real estate interests in Cascade County. In February of 1896, Henry made several trips to Great Falls where he now had "extensive interests in Cascade County."[24] Most of those property interests were centered in Cascade and the Chestnut Valley area where he still maintained strong ties. In 1894, Henry had purchased land from his former Chestnut Valley neighbor, Rufus J. Hardy, for $5,000. In February 1895, T. L. Gorham, one of Chestnut Valley's first residents and the proprietor of Steele's Store, passed away. Gorham had platted the town of Cascade and owned a lot of the property in the area. With an ear always to the ground, Henry saw the potential of the town of Cascade. It was now a stop on the Great Northern Railway, businesses were flourishing in the town, and it was even in the running to become county seat. Upon Gorham's death, Henry made an offer of $800 to the administrator of his estate to purchase ninety of Gorham's lots in Cascade. Henry was now heavily involved in stock raising, mining, and real estate.[25]

To protect his financial interests, Henry made sure to regularly attend organizational meetings. In April of 1896, Henry was on the road again, this time to Miles City for a gathering to celebrate the twelfth anniversary of the Montana Stockgrowers Association. The list of those in attendance was a who's who of the state's cattle business, many of whom were Henry's close associates. Henry was delighted to see his brother, Jake, and his former Chestnut Valley neighbor, C.H. Austin. He was also reacquainted with Thomas Clary—the man to whom he and brother Leonard sold their freighting outfit all those years ago. There was time for Henry to reminisce with his Flatwillow neighbors, H.P. Brooks and James Fergus, and to socialize with longtime friends like Conrad Kohrs and T.C. Power. The meeting also provided the opportunity to make new acquaintances, including one particularly fortuitous encounter with Thomas A. Grimes with whom he would later build a partnership. There is no doubt that Henry's roots now ran deep in Montana. He was no longer the wiry upstart. He was an established and connected power player.[26]

From the amiable environment of the stock grower's meeting in Miles City, Henry traveled to Chinook for the second annual meeting of the Northern Montana Roundup Association. Issues of wolving and cattle thievery were once again at the forefront of the members' minds. The following language used by members to describe livestock issues captures their shared non-Native viewpoint of the world: "ensure the speedy removal of the Cree Indians and half-breeds to their own country, and also to have the bounty on wolves increased."[27] The stockmen's perspective reflected government policies on Montana's reservations. The prevailing thoughts were that the best way for Native Americans to adjust to a rapidly changing world was to give up their tribal traditions and live like Euro-Americans. But even on their reservations, Native Americans had little autonomy. Each reservation had an agent who managed the tribes' limited budget and controlled how the money was spent. He also set the rules for the reservation, and he could arrest people or withhold food rations if they broke those rules. The tribes owned their land, yet agents had almost complete control over life on the reservation. The solutions for cattle thievery and wolves would, as they had since Henry first arrived in Montana, come at the sacrifice of the Indigenous peoples' land. There is a sentimental tone to the meeting with a journalist later reporting:

> Among those present was many a bluff old pioneer, who had crossed the plains with a "bull team", and who since, has become rich in the cattle business. And now these men, representing every state, and almost every country, and whose adventures,

> vicissitudes and hairbreadth escapes, in this wild western country would make a thrilling romance, have done Chinook the honor of choosing it as their meeting place.[28]

While the language is grandiose, the reader can sense the nostalgic atmosphere of the gathering.[29]

In the meantime, the stock industry continued to grow. In 1896, The *Rocky Mountain Husbandman* estimated that 30,000 head of cattle, mostly from Idaho, Utah, and Oregon, would graze in the Milk River country in northeastern Montana as cattlemen increased their herds. For example, Conrad Kohrs was planning to add 8,000 cattle, Bob Coburn was bringing in 4,000 head of cattle, Jake Sieben wanted to add 1,000 head, and Paul Brewster would add 2,500. Half of Sieben's and Brewster's stock arrived in Montana the following month. They unloaded two trainloads of two-year-old steers from Milford, Utah, at the Fort Benton stockyards and planned to turn them loose on Muddy Creek near Culbertson. Overcrowding was a constant worry for Henry, but he was relieved he had made the decision to locate his ranch in remote country farther east than most of his peers' operations.

Once Henry completed beef shipments in summer 1896, he turned his attention to finances. Despite his growing affluence, Henry was a man who always kept a sharp eye on his money, a practice instilled from his humble beginnings. In August 1896, Henry traveled to Glasgow to solicit a reduction in tax assessments of his and Brewster's cattle. In this case, Sieben and Brewster appeared before the Board of Equalization in Glasgow with affidavits regarding their cattle ranging in Valley County. Sieben claimed he should only be assessed on 500 head of cattle while Brewster insisted his total number of cattle was 900. The Board reconsidered their earlier assessment and reduced the number of cattle to be taxed. The Board ordered Henry be assessed for 700 head of stock cattle and Paul Brewster for 1,400 head. While it wasn't the amount Henry hoped, his trip east still provided a reduction in taxes. Henry always tried to instill this frugal approach to business in his partners and later in his descendants.[30]

At the end of a busy 1896, members of the Northern Montana Roundup Association met at stockman W.G. Preuitt's office in Helena. Those present included Henry, Paul Brewster, W.K. Floweree, and Bob Coburn. The organization's attorney, J.W. Tattan, was present to report on prosecutions of cattle rustlers, but the main concern of the group was a familiar foe—Mother Nature. The ranges were buried in snow from a storm that had raged for the past week. They needed a chinook like that of 1882 to remove the snow before a freeze set in.[31]

Luck was in the cattlemen's favor. The new year of 1897 brought the much-wished-for chinook and Henry enjoyed a prosperous year. It began with a court case win against a cattle rustler at the ranch in Culbertson. A man by the name of John Boyd was accused of killing a steer belonging to Sieben and Brewster. Sheriff Kyle and Stock Inspector Thomas Dunn traveled to the ranch to arrest the man, and they fined Boyd $100. Henry was pleased with the result and the effectiveness of cattle prosecutions since the establishment of the Northern Montana Roundup Association. On top of that, the DHS Ranch continued to run Sieben's cattle and make regular shipments of stock. The Diamond Ranch was becoming one of the largest ranches in eastern Montana, and Henry's real estate portfolio was growing. The years of hard work that Henry had put into reestablishing his businesses had been a success.

However, Henry's long and frequent absences took a toll on the family. Alberta spent most of 1896 to 1897 as the sole caregiver for their two young children, and she was worried about the effects the relentless travel was having on Henry's health. As Henry approached his fiftieth birthday, he paused to reflect on his long-term personal life. His brother Jake had just built a large five-room residence on his farm about three miles from Cascade, and it likely influenced Henry to build. He decided it was time to build his family the home of their dreams. The idea of physically putting down roots in Montana's capital city likely appealed to Henry. Margaret recalled that when Helena stockmen such as Mr. MacNamara and T.C. Power had successfully established their ranches, they soon built beautiful homes for their wives and children in the city and "the best was none too good."[32] Henry eyed a corner lot available at 520 Harrison Avenue, across from former Senator T.C. Power's home, on Helena's fashionable westside. He would purchase it in 1898 and hire Howard Pew, a Helena contractor and carpenter originally from New York, to build his home.

In the meantime, Henry and Alberta decided to take an extended family vacation in 1897 to Hot Springs, Arkansas, a favorite spot of his friend Conrad Kohrs. Newspaper reports indicated they intended to be out of town for a year so they could spend summer and fall with Alberta's family in Wisconsin. While Henry would return that summer to attend to business affairs, the few months of restful vacation with his family brought Henry clarity on what he wanted to create for them. The family photo of Henry, Alberta, and their two daughters on donkeys reveals that a governess may have accompanied the Siebens on their vacation. Due to Henry's frequent absences, Alberta likely had hired help in their home.[33]

The Sieben family on holiday in Arkansas in 1897. From left: Henry, Margaret, unidentified woman (possibly a governess), Alberta, and Berneice. Courtesy of the Montana Historical Society Library & Archives, PAc 76-030 F08.

Henry's younger brother, Jake, had proven to be a thoughtful businessman and confidante to Henry over the last decade, and the pair were once again partnering on a number of profitable adventures. Jake had successfully invested in Cascade County real estate during the 1890s and won a bid to provide a new building for the Cascade County offices in Great Falls. In February of 1897, Governor Smith established a board of stock commissioners and appointed Jake to represent Cascade County. Henry was immensely proud of his younger brother, who had grown from the naïve young sheep man in the Chestnut Valley into a successful businessman with a steady head on his shoulders. In summer of 1897, Henry, Conrad Kohrs, and a handful of other stockmen hired Jake to spend the season in Chicago inspecting brands of cattle for purchase. Jake did well and took advantage of his time in the Windy City to develop his own sheep interests.[34]

Jake was riding the wave of the sheep industry, which had been expanding through the 1890s. In August of 1897, representing a syndicate of western wool growers, Jake closed a deal with owners of bottomlands in Trempeleau, a shipping point in Wisconsin. He acquired 500 acres to build a sheep ranch in the small town that would be a fattening and resting point for sheep shipped from the West. Jake planned to construct buildings and accommodations that would shelter up to 50,000 sheep. Animals unloaded from cars at the Trempeleau station would be placed in good condition before being shipped to eastern markets. Not for the first time, Henry took note of his brother's innovative approach to business. In 1897, the sheep population in Montana was in the millions, making it the nation's number one wool-growing state. With this new sheep depot in Trempeleau, Henry now began to consider reinvesting in the sheep market—something he would never have thought after his experience in the Chestnut Valley twenty years earlier. But Henry was always open to change for a favorable prospect.[35]

Meanwhile, the cattle business was up and down. Drought was a worrying factor for all Montana stockmen, and Henry drew public attention to it in the *Daily River Press,* stating it was "becoming a cause for serious alarm."[36] Stockowners in the Culbertson area were not only shipping beef cattle, they were also sending a much larger proportion than usual of their cows and young stock with them in case the drought continued.

Overgrazing continued to plague the growing cattle industry. After five years, the DHS Ranch decided to leave Shelby for this reason and Conrad Kohrs began shipping his steers out. Jim Spurgeon recollected that his father, then manager of the DHS Ranch, shipped a trainload of three-, four-, and five-year-old steers from Shelby to the Chicago market every two weeks in the summer of 1897. The younger steers were shipped to a new range near Saco in northeastern Montana. Frank Arnette had recently been made the Oregon and Idaho buyer for the DHS Ranch. On one of his trips, he bought some stock of his own and, with Henry's blessing, Frank shipped them to Culbertson to run on Henry's range. Margaret recalled that Henry "thought of Frank more as a son,"[37] and with five years of ranching and buying experience under his belt, Henry felt Frank was ready for new and larger responsibilities.[38]

Henry hired Frank as foreman of the Diamond Ranch in Culbertson. Paul Brewster soon retired, and it appears he returned to Cheyenne and continued to oversee his stock interests in Nebraska. Before he left, Brewster sold his one-third interest in the ranch to Augusta cattleman and county commissioner Elizur Beach. Henry and Frank Arnette held the other two-thirds. With the Diamond Ranch in Arnette's capable hands, Henry turned his attention to his two young daughters and building a new home in Helena. Henry began to slowly and intentionally create a legacy that would remain in his family for generations to come.[39] ❖

By 1900, Henry and Alberta Sieben were well-established members of Helena society. Courtesy of the Montana Historical Society Library & Archives, PAc 78-51.03.

Chapter 6

1898–1906

"A MODEST MARCH TO AFFLUENCE"

As a new century dawned, Henry was growing in stature and importance in the civic, social, and economic life of Montana. Inspired by Alberta's example, Henry joined a legion of Montana progressives in their efforts to improve the quality of life for residents of the new state. He encouraged the next generation, mentoring family members and providing them with the opportunity to succeed as long as they displayed a commitment to hard work. As Henry's business interests expanded and diversified in the early 1900s, he relearned the timeless lesson that the only constant in life was change

By the time the Siebens rang in the New Year of 1898, Henry had expanded his business interests to include an impressive real estate portfolio. A property ledger in Henry's private collection dating from 1898 to 1916 reveals he owned and rented commercial and residential properties in Helena and Great Falls.[1] Henry owned and rented at least one lot in Great Falls and had incomc from what appeared to be several commercial rentals on the site. In Helena, Henry added to his investments by purchasing and renting at least two residential houses in Helena. He refurbished a home at 518 Harrison Avenue, adjacent to his own home, in 1898 that he would later generously give to Alberta's sister, Florence, after her wedding to Fred Kessler in 1902. In addition to that home, Henry owned a property at 613 Hemlock (later renamed Power) Street, which he typically rented out. While his home was under construction during 1898 to 1899, Henry moved his family into that property so he could oversee the work of contractor Howard Pew while the house was under construction.[2]

But it was into his own home at 520 Harrison Avenue Henry poured his soul and his pocket in 1898. Henry did not typically engage in extravagant displays of wealth but spared no expense with his home at 520 Harrison Avenue. On July 19, 1898, *The Helena Herald* reported that Henry bought the south corner property on Harrison Avenue. The journalist declared Henry was "about to begin the erection of an elegant residence which they estimated would cost about $18,000 (over $665,000 today)."[3] Howard Pew, a Helena contractor and carpenter who had built several homes on Helena's westside, won the contract. Henry's daybook ledgers titled "1898 Sieben Residence" provides a brief glimpse into Howard's management of the construction project.

On the first page of the otherwise empty ledger exists a half page entry. The content of the note suggests the author was the general contractor for the construction of Henry's new home as well as the refurbishment of the house next door at 518 Harrison Avenue. Therefore, one assumes the author was Howard Pew. Howard began the text stating he started work today, September 30, 1898, on the old Harrison house taking out the "cistin" [*sic*] and putting in plumbing. He also staked out the foundation for the new house for Henry. "I will take charge of all the work and look after buying material, bidding contracts and supervising all the work for Henry at a commission of .10% of the overall cost of the work." Four days later, Howard hired a contractor, Jake Kunz, to excavate earth at a cost of 45 cents per yard and 80 cents ($17 and $30 today's value) for rock. Based on Margaret's following recollection, one senses Howard was likely too busy overseeing the project to keep a regular update of events.[4]

Margaret's memory of the construction of her family home is not only humorous, it illustrates the industriousness of the site's workers:

> Well . . . I was just three when we were living in that house and I would go over and watch the bricklayers and the stone masons and the carpenters working and it was just great for me. I can remember that. [I knew] the daughter of the man who was laying bricks or putting the stone foundation in, he was busy and I was trying to talk to him and he wouldn't listen to me. I would say hello and he wouldn't look at me and I finally

> said why won't you say hello and that just broke him down. He laughed . . . and he told his wife about it and he told his daughter about it and [later] his daughter worked at the Union Bank when Alfred [Margaret's husband] was president of it and she told me about it. So, these little simple things that happened, isn't it funny how just little things like that live. He finally said hello and we became good friends.[5]

Henry employed one of the most talented architects of the time, Charles S. Haire, to design his new home. Haire's firm, Link and Haire Associates, provided plans for a variety of Montana jails, courthouses, schools, and state buildings. In Helena, Haire put the plans together for the First Unitarian Church (now the Grand Street Theater) and the Algeria Shrine Temple (now the Civic Center) as well as other residential homes on the westside. Henry's documentation indicates he spent nearly $700 (over $20,000 today's value) for Haire's services between 1898 and 1900. Henry hired all local contractors to build his home including the Northwestern Stone Company for the stone material, Anton M. Holter for the hardware, Kessler Brickyard for the bricks, and Helena Light Company for the gas connections. Local contractors including E.W. Fiske, W.G. Bennett, Henry Schimpf, and John Sturrock completed tasks including plumbing, plastering, woodworking, painting, stonecutting, building fences, building a barn, and providing electricity. Henry and Alberta focused on details that enhanced the elegance of the home, spending $104.50 ($4,000 today's value) on cornices for the library, parlor, and hall. The total cost of the project, including installation of Kessler brick for the sidewalk in 1902, came to $18,479 ($662,702 today's value). While Henry had splurged on certain features and in hiring a renowned architect, true to his detailed and frugal nature, he still managed to close out the project on budget.[6]

Once completed, the three-story red brick home was an architectural jewel. Haire's design offered a curved porch, offset entry, and multiple bay windows, which enhanced the asymmetry required of the Queen Anne style. The interior was finished with finely crafted cherry,

As Henry's wealth and influence grew, he built a family home to reflect his new circumstances. Here we see Alberta and Berneice Sieben in a carriage in front of their home at 520 Harrison Avenue in Helena. Courtesy of the Hibbard and Baucus family private collection.

walnut, birdseye maple, and oak. The walls of the hallways were covered with embossed leather. Once the family moved in, Alberta spent many years methodically decorating the interior with the finest furnishings. She selected Arabian curtains for the dining room, green silk curtains for the library, oil paintings, a mahogany clock, linens, a range, and volumes of works by authors such as Shakespeare, Dickens, and Twain as well as lectures by the American traveler and photographer, Burton Holmes. Alberta even purchased volumes of George Eliot's works for their daughter Berneice. The contents of the Sieben library suggest that, although Henry never seemed entirely comfortable with his own literacy skills, he and Alberta encouraged their daughters to read widely. To run the household, Henry and Alberta hired a team that Alberta oversaw. She hired a woman for $30 (approximately $1,000 today) a month to cook, serve the meals, and do the laundry by hand. A caterer, Hilma Gardner, came in when the Siebens entertained. Sadie Ford did the fine linens at her home over T.C. Power's carriage house. Her husband was the coachman for Power. Calvin Parker waxed the floors, washed the windows, mowed the lawn, and helped in the garden. Susan Higgins, a seamstress, was brought in for a week during the spring and fall to alter the family's clothes.

Leonard Sieben's daughter, Ruth Sieben Hagelin, later recalled the beautiful interior details: "I remember the little gold chairs in the parlor and another thing I remember is the box they had with the pounded brass or copper or it was brass around, that they kept the wood in for the fireplace."[7] Every item down to the number of salad forks, their cost and type ("cinq fleurs") was recorded in Henry's property ledger. The total spent on house furnishings amounted to $9,568.47, an eye-watering $319,000 sum today. Margaret aptly described the ornate residence: "It's one of the show places today. Someone was talking to me about it just the other day and they went through the house, and they couldn't get over the woodwork and how beautifully it was finished, and it was. Every detail was just perfect."[8]

Now fully established in Helena society, Henry and Alberta frequented parties at the homes of their upper-class westside neighbors. In January 1899, the Siebens attended a New Year open house hosted by Thomas Cruse and his niece, Miss Cruse, who lived just northeast of them in the neighborhood. The *Helena Evening Herald* reported that members of the legislature and other prominent citizens of the city and state were lavishly entertained. Those in attendance included Senator Thomas C. Power, Colonel Wilbur Fisk Sanders, Justice W.T. Pigott, and rancher Percy Kennett.[9] It is no coincidence Henry was in the company of so many politicians. He was eyeing a seat in the Montana House of Representatives for himself. Until now, Henry had only participated on the fringes of political life in Montana. However, the impending 1899 legislative session resurrected the William A. Clark and Marcus Daly feud. At the time, U.S. senators were selected by state legislatures rather than by popular vote. William A. Clark was determined to be Montana's choice, allegedly without regard to cost or morals. Henry was troubled by the influence Clark exerted and the dirty tricks he had up his sleeve. Henry was not alone in his concerns. Both locally

The new Sieben home at 520 Harrison Avenue in Helena boasted a music room (above), a ballroom (not pictured), and a grand staircase and landing (below). Courtesy of the Montana Historical Society Library & Archives, PAc, 78-51.09 (music room) and PAc, 78-51.10 (stairs).

and nationally, a movement demanding change in America's social and political systems was growing.[10]

Like many Americans, Henry became increasingly concerned with mounting social problems, and he took up the cause of reform between 1900 and 1916. The Progressive Era reformers identified a range of social problems including corporate abuses, the exploitation of women and children, traffic in alcohol, and political corruption. Most progressives were middle-class Americans who believed the "system" could be made to work properly with only a few changes. They believed that what America needed was direct democracy—placing power directly in the hands of the people. In Montana, residents such as Henry had watched in anger while millionaires such as William A. Clark and Marcus Daly had gained control of the party nominating conventions over the last decade. Progressives began favoring the direct primary system of nominating candidates for public office. A direct primary law would curb political corruption by allowing the voters to nominate party candidates by secret ballot in special primary elections. By the early 1900s, public opinion in Montana supported such a system. The 1906 Montana legislature enacted a local option system of direct primary nominations. That experiment proved unworkable but finally, using the new initiative method, the citizens of Montana approved a statewide direct primary law in the election of 1912.[11]

In 1898, however, these reforms were still years away from realization. Henry, swept up in the progressive movement of the time, tried his hand at direct democracy and ran for a Republican seat in Montana's 1899 legislature. On September 23, 1898, Republicans gathered for the party's Lewis and Clark County convention. They nominated Henry for the legislative ticket in the House of Representatives.[12] His fellow Republican candidates for Lewis and Clark County included other well-established businessmen such as superintendent of Kessler Brickworks Charles H. Bray, grocer R.C. Wallace, attorney F.E. Stranahan, fellow rancher J.L.B. Mayer, and Marysville businessman Charles Watson. The *Helena Evening Herald* published a summary of the Republican candidates stating, "they need no introduction to the old settlers of the country and the *Herald* only mentions them now for the benefit of those who have become voters here in the last decade."[13] The paper's profile of Henry Sieben highlights his quiet determination and success as well as his commitment to Helena:

> Henry Sieben is a stock man who has so quietly attended to his affairs, enjoyed his prosperity that few, except old settlers, appreciate his modest march to affluence. He moved to Helena some years ago from northern Montana and is now testifying to his confidence in the capital city by erecting a comfortable residence which will be finished in the coming year.[14]

Voting began on November 7, and by November 10 it was clear there had been a Democratic landslide. Democrats ended up taking everything in Lewis and Clark County except for the positions of county assessor and county surveyor.[15] In fact, one of the elected Democrats was W.G. Bennett—the man painting and wallpapering Henry's new residence. In typical Henry style, his actions in response to this defeat spoke louder than his words ever could. He never ran for public office again.

From the day the legislature convened on January 2, 1899, rumors were rife about William A. Clark's corrupt tactics to win the Senate seat he so avidly desired. Reports that Clark's agents were bribing legislators became so widespread that lawmakers referred the matter to the Committee on Privileges and Election for investigation. The community of Helena, which was loyal to Clark, appeared to accept bribery as necessary. One journalist called Helena "a city hysterical with guilt and greed."[16] On January 28, 1899, the Montana legislature elected William A. Clark to the United States Senate. Helena put on another gala celebration for Clark, who reputedly spent $30,000 (approximately $1 million today) on champagne. But Clark's victory was not complete. On April 23, 1900, after hearing extensive testimony from ninety-six witnesses, the Committee on Privileges and Election returned a report unanimously concluding that Clark was not entitled to his seat. Before the Senate could remove him, Clark resigned his office. Governor

Robert Burns Smith appointed sheep rancher and businessman Paris Gibson in his place. Gibson served from 1901 to 1905. Henry must have been disgusted. Observers across the nation watched in amazement and horror at the events unfolding. Montana, it seemed, had been thoroughly debauched by mining money.

The 1900 election campaign marked a turning point in the "War of the Copper Kings." Marcus Daly died in November 1900, and the Montana legislature, without Daly's influence at work, quietly sent William A. Clark to serve his term in the United Sates Senate from 1901 to 1907. When his term ended, Clark did not seek reelection, but for the rest of his life he was known as "Senator Clark."[17]

Henry continued his quest for reform but from this point forward he focused on improving public life and morality from the sidelines. During the opening decade of the twentieth century, Montana progressives endeavored to improve public life, public health, and public morality through direct action. At the state level, they aimed to limit the power of large corporations, especially the Amalgamated Copper Company. They pushed an impressive number of reforms through the legislature, including laws that expanded popular participation in government, laws that protected workers (such as mine safety and compensation), and laws that protected the public (such as railroad regulation, pure food and drug legislation, milk and meat inspection, and the creation of a state board of health). At the local level, cities like Billings, Butte, Helena, Missoula, and Great Falls produced civic clubs and citizens' leagues that concentrated on beautifying their towns and cleaning up government by hiring professional city managers and electing city commissions.[18]

Helena was rapidly changing. In 1888, shortly after Henry and Alberta had arrived, the population stood at 3,624 residents, and by 1900 it had tripled to 10,770. The marital status of residents had changed dramatically over time, too. When Henry first frequented the mining camp in 1870, just twenty-two percent of the population was married. That percentage had increased to forty-five percent in 1880, and by the time Henry and Alberta lived at 520 Harrison Avenue in 1900, fifty-seven percent of Helena's population was married. With more families invested in making Helena their permanent home, the demand for public amenities, better health, and governmental services increased. Henry did not shy away from actively participating in improving his adopted city.[19]

During the summer of 1898, Henry established himself as a voice of civic affairs in Helena. In June, he focused on testifying on behalf of ranchers Louis Stadler and Louis Kaufman. Henry had navigated the Hard Winter of 1886 to 1887 alongside Stadler and Kaufman, and the men had become good friends in Helena. He had no problem supporting them in a case brought against them by Helena Water and Electric Power Company. Henry agreed with his friends that they were being swindled in the sale of their ranch to the company, and he was eager to publicly share his opinion. A commission had recently awarded Stadler and Kaufman $20 ($750 today's value) an acre for the property. The ranchers did not feel the assessment was sufficient or fair. They put a number of cattlemen on the stand to prove to the jury that the value of the land was considerably more than the commission's appraisal. Ranchers such as Andrew Thompson, Jesse I. Phelps, John Owens, and Henry Sieben swore the ranch was worth at least $40-$50 ($1,500-$1,800 today's value) an acre. A week later, the jury decided in favor of Stadler and Kaufman that the market value of their land was worth more than the commission had previously decided upon. Once again, Henry was making a public stand against what he perceived to be corrupt practices.[20]

In August, Henry continued his contributions to civic life in Helena by putting his name to a petition, signed by other leading businessmen, that focused on improving public health in Helena. The petitioners wrote to the Helena City Council stating that a water supply was of vital importance to the present and future of Helena. The businessmen advised that the city council procure the necessary capital without creating debt. They recommended contracting with a responsible water company and working with a high-quality water source. The *Montana Record Herald* published the petition in its August 28, 1898, edition and named all the petitioners including Henry's friends and business magnates L. Hershfield, H.M. Parchen, William Wheeler, W.G. Preuett, A. Kleinschmidt, Nick Kessler, H.H. Guthrie, C.W. Cannon, A.J. Seligman, A.M. Holter, and C.A. Broadwater. The astute businessmen accurately predicted the trouble ahead. The city council would endure seventeen years of conflict with the Helena Waterworks Company before city voters agreed to build a new water plant. In 1911, the organization agreed to sell its water system to the city for $400,000 (approximately $13 million today).[21]

The following year, in June 1899, Henry again actively participated in Helena's civic affairs by publicly petitioning the city council. This time he urged councilors to improve Helena's beauty and stature by providing an appropriately elaborate site for the construction of a federal building. Petitioners encouraged councilors to allow Helena residents to vote on the city's proposal to purchase the remaining portion of the block where the federal building would be erected. The petitioners argued that purchasing the entire block for the government building would ensure a "splendid site for the structure." The Renaissance Revival-style federal building was completed in 1904 on a large and prominent site at 316 North Park Avenue, just as Henry and the other petitioners had wished. This building has had a long and distinguished life of use in Helena. On its opening, the building housed the federal court, U.S. Marshals Service, and post office. In 1931, the city built two prominent but unadorned side wings and a rear addition, which reflected the expanding role of the federal government. In 1978, the City of Helena and Lewis and Clark County jointly acquired the building, which remains an important center of government today.[22]

Inspired by her husband's progressive action in public matters, Alberta joined Henry in what would be the couple's lifelong support of local causes that benefited the improvement of local society and the needs of the vulnerable. They both became active members of the Helena Improvement Society. In 1907, Randall J. Cordon, secretary of the Helena Civic Club, summarized the goals not only of his organization but of the Helena Improvement Society and progressives in general: "Better schools, better churches, better public buildings, better playgrounds, better public service, better support of disinterested public officials, unsightly billboards abolished, cleaner streets and alleys, better enforcement of all laws and city ordinances."[23] Henry and Alberta threw themselves into supporting the work of the Helena Improvement Society in the early 1900s. Henry was a life member of the society that had 265 members in 1902. He contributed $25 (nearly $1,000 today's value) annually, and Alberta served on the executive committee that organized an annual fundraising ball held at the auditorium. All proceeds from the Society's work went to the improvement of Helena as a place to live for its residents. Between 1898 and 1902, the organization succeeded in improving the Hawthorne Elementary School grounds (the elementary school Berneice and Margaret attended), the high school grounds, and the public library. In the fall of 1900, Alberta decided to serve on the advisory committee for Associated Charities in Helena. The group provided clothing and other necessities such as coal and food for those who were unable to provide for themselves.[24]

As Helena came into its own as a settled capital city in the early 1900s, Henry and Alberta were becoming key social and economic movers. They joined many of their peers as committed members of the First Unitarian Society, which initially met weekly at the G.A.R. Hall in downtown Helena. Henry was a trustee of the Society and Alberta served on organizing committees for different events. Although Henry had been raised Catholic, there are no records to suggest he practiced that faith in Montana. Helena's branch of the First Unitarian Society was founded in the early 1890s and focused on community, fellowship, and helping those in need. Their progressive pastor Reverend Brown brought the most recent ideas on religious thought for discussion at mass each week. The progressive ideology of the church was certainly a better fit for Henry's mindset than Catholicism, which is rooted in tradition.[25]

The couple also ensured the church's permanence in Helena by helping establish a beautiful new building for the congregation on Park Avenue. In 1901, the Society paid for the site. Henry, wholesaler Edward I. Goodkind, and sheep rancher A.K. Prescott each donated $500 (approximately $18,500 today) to help with construction. The Society worked with Charles S. Haire, the architect for Henry's home, to design what is the only known example of Haire's work in the Richardsonian Romanesque style. Public-spirited Unitarians believed churches should serve the community. They planned the building to function as a public auditorium and theater as well as a church. Furthermore, the church organized a Sunday school, a ladies society, and a free kindergarten. Alberta served on the organizing committee for benefits to raise money for the worthy cause of offering a free kindergarten that would encourage Helena's mothers to work outside the home if they so wished.[26]

Henry and Alberta's involvement with the church further cemented them in Helena's social life. The Society attracted many of the town's conscientious and philanthropic society members. Margaret recalled the Sieben family found a supportive and tight-knit social community in this church. Margaret remembered attending church and Sunday school and afterwards the parents would drive their surreys (door-less, four-wheeled carriages popular in the early twentieth century) and the children would ride horses to Jackson Creek, near present-day Montana City, for picnics. Margaret recalled that "father was great as a camp cook cause he'd been out, you know, doing that since he was in Montana. And he probably did it for years you know. Well, he did do it beautifully, but that's a job. There must have been about twenty of us, you know different families would go after church. That's what we'd do on Sundays in the fall."[27]

While firmly establishing himself and his family as respectable members of Helena's affluent westside, Henry still had agricultural enterprises to manage.[28] Throughout the opening decade of the 1900s, Henry continued to visit Culbertson, making the trip at least three times a year, to check on business at the Diamond Ranch. He left the day-to-day operations, however, in the hands of his nephew, Frank Arnette. Fortunately for Frank, conditions and profits for Montana's stockmen soared during the late 1890s and early 1900s. The weather was in ranchers' favor with few cattle losses reported. As a result, the *Chicago Drovers Journal* reported in 1899 that figures for cattle sales were higher than any year in the past twenty-two years except for four years: 1882, 1884, 1888, and 1891.

Under Frank's management in the early years, the Diamond Ranch thrived and grew. One local rancher, F.B. McCann, recalled that Arnette was running close to 10,000 cattle all the way north to the Canadian border between the Muddy River and the Poplar River. The expansion of cattle was a result of purchases and investments Henry made in the early 1900s. Henry's ledger and pocketbooks from that time period reveal that in addition to their Diamond Ranch interests, he and Frank Arnette had cattle interests in Cascade, Lewis and Clark, and Valley counties. These investments saw steady profits year upon year in the early 1900s. Henry also purchased a neighboring ranch and brand in Culbertson, the Star Ranch (and star brand). Frank Arnette oversaw the Diamond and Star Ranch operations and ran all these cattle together north of Culbertson.

Buyers paid good prices for the Diamond Ranch cattle at the Chicago Stockyards. Henry's brother Jake was once again appointed to Montana's Board of Stock Commissioners in 1899. This meant that Jake was in Chicago every fall to protect the interests of Montana's stockmen during shipping season. Having a close ally in Chicago meant that neither Henry nor Frank had to be there every time they shipped stock. In August 1899, Frank sent two carloads of Henry's cattle to Chicago. The first load of 101 cattle had an average weight of 1,295 pounds and sold at $4.75 ($180 today's value) per head. The second load contained forty-six cattle weighing an average of 1,340 pounds and sold at $4.65 ($175 today's value) per head. In September of that year, Henry shipped ten carloads of steers from Fort Buford to the Chicago markets. Henry's sole surviving ledger that records cattle accounts during this period indicates the Diamond Ranch made increasing profits on cattle between 1898 and 1906. In 1905, the Diamond made $46,238.25 (approximately $1.6 million today's value) in profit. Frank was establishing himself as a capable foreman, and to date Henry's bet on his nephew was more than paying off.[29]

Not only was Frank thriving professionally, he was also making Culbertson a home, and Henry was thrilled to observe Frank putting down roots in the area. In 1900, Frank married Dr. Alma Brockman, the local dentist. Alma had graduated from Western Dental College in Kansas City, Missouri, in 1899 and met Frank while on a professional trip as the pioneer dentist at Culbertson. She was a member of the first class to take the state board dental examination in Montana and served as eastern Valley County's first resident dentist. The couple soon welcomed two daughters, Rowene and Wilma. Margaret recalled visiting the Diamond Ranch with her father as a child and being "very impressed to see a dental chair and to have a woman being the dentist because that was an unusual thing . . . she had her office just off of the living room [of the ranch house]."[30]

Of course, it wasn't all plain sailing for Frank at Culbertson. The severe weather and the relentless demands of managing one of the largest cattle operations in remote territory was often challenging. Rancher F.B. McCann recalled Frank was more than capable to rise to the challenge of managing the enormous herd of cattle. He described Frank as a skilled roper who always made sure to ride a decent horse. McCann recalled that Frank lost a thumb when dallying, which is when a cowboy winds the lasso rope around his horse's saddle horn when roping. If the move wasn't executed correctly, it could severely injure the cowboy's fingers or hand. McCann revealed his father lost a thumb, too, and stated that most old ranchers lost their thumb in dallying. It seems to have been a fate Henry fortunately escaped.[31]

Wherever possible, Henry's preference was always to partner or include family members in business operations, so in 1898, Alberta's younger brother, Merrill Gordon, joined Frank at the Diamond Ranch. The Siebens had visited the Gordon home in Whitewater, Wisconsin, while on vacation the previous year. Merrill was just eighteen years of age, bored, and looking for adventure. Henry undoubtedly understood that wanderlust when he saw it. However, he didn't believe in handing anything to anyone on a silver plate. If Merrill was committed to making a go of it in Montana, Henry wanted him to cut his teeth in rural Montana just as Henry had done all those years ago. According to Merrill's daughter, Peggy Gordon Lestz, Merrill went straight to

Culbertson to work under the watchful eye of Frank Arnette. Peggy remembered that it wasn't long before the realities of cold winters in isolated Culbertson kicked in for Merrill: "And it was cold. He didn't care for it there. I think it was the coldness that he hated most although they have plenty of cold in Wisconsin but they don't have those sweeping winds that you would get there." Merrill's daily routine at the ranch consisted of a six-mile daily trek with a four-horse team for hay in twenty degrees Fahrenheit below zero weather. Apparently, Merrill's only comments to his family on his time in Culbertson were to describe how cold and miserable he was, "that was about all he ever said about it. He thought it was rather very bleak." Merrill's son, John, later recalled his father told tales of digging out a shed filled with 400 cattle after a severe blizzard. The shed was filled to the eaves with snow, but the cattle survived, stiff but unharmed. John reflected that, like Henry, Merrill was not a Westerner, but he grew to be one. Having persevered through a few years of Montana initiation in Culbertson, Henry took Merrill further under his wing, providing work for Merrill at his other ranches and helping him purchase land of his own.[33]

While Henry's nephew Frank managed the day-to-day affairs at the Diamond Ranch, the crew understood who the boss was. Henry's pocketbooks from the years 1898 to 1906 reveal he frequently traveled to Culbertson to either help with animal, equipment, or crew issues that had arisen or to just check in with his ranch crew. Henry's visit to the ranch in the new year of 1900 was an exception. The year had rung in with a literal bang for the Diamond Ranch crew. Henry's trusted foreman, Texas cowboy Nolan Armstrong, was killed in a shootout in downtown Culbertson. Jim Spurgeon, a neighboring rancher whose father was a foreman for the DHS Ranch, described Armstrong as a "harmless fellow and a hell of a nice fellow everybody tells me, but when he got drunk and left town he would always put his six-shooter up in the air and shoot up the town as he left."[34] It appears that is exactly what Nolan Armstrong did on the night of January 21, 1900. Unfortunately for Armstrong, the town had just passed an ordinance to reform Culbertson. The night Armstrong chose to shoot up the town, a deputy sheriff and brand inspector were also in the vicinity. Spurgeon claimed that the officers were "gonna kill Nolan Armstrong if he shot up the town that night and so sure enough they did." Newspaper reports claimed cowboys were shooting up the town, and when Deputy Sheriff John P. Eder attempted to arrest Armstrong, he shot at the sheriff with a six-shooter, the bullet passing through the sheriff's hat. Eder returned fire with a double-barreled shotgun, killing Armstrong instantly. Eder then fired the other barrel into a crowd of eight men who were firing at him.[35] The last shot hit another cowboy, Tommie Reid, in his face. Deputy Sheriff Eder was later acquitted of the charge of murder, and newspaper reports declared that the citizens of Valley County were relieved with the decision as it demonstrated that Montana's laws "and the officers who execute them will be upheld."[36]

While Henry had seen and heard of many similar events during his time in Virginia City and across the open range, Montana had changed and grown up in the intervening years. It was now a state, and there were many large corporate entities, especially railroad companies, interested in promoting a squeaky-clean image of Montana to encourage immigration. The "wild and woolly" days were gone. Henry was furious about Armstrong's death. Not only had he lost a trusted foreman, but the event also highlighted the unruly behavior of his crew. It appears Henry reprimanded Frank and the crew, and there were no further reports of disorderly behavior at the ranch. Henry needed his manager and crew focused on the difficult task at hand: running thousands of cattle on the open range.

As much as possible, Henry oversaw operations from his residence at 520 Harrison Avenue in Helena. Henry had a "den"—Margaret shared that he never called it an "office"—on the northeast corner of the second floor of his newly built home. The den had lots of big windows and natural light. The centerpiece was the big rolltop desk in the den. Margaret recalled that every day he would "go up there and spend the morning there and do his book work."[37] However, Henry continued to develop his cattle business interests by traveling to Utah and Texas to purchase cattle and attend conventions. He frequently made trips to the stockyards at St. Paul and Chicago in the early 1900s. Leonard Sieben's daughter, Ruth Sieben Hagelin, remembered that while he was east, Henry would visit their family nearly every other year in Geneseo.[38]

With an eye always to opportunity, in the early 1900s Henry decided to once again expand his business interests, this time by investing in Montana's financial industry. The heart of that industry lay in Helena. The town had survived after the placer gold played out in the late 1870s and population declined, because pioneer entrepreneurs had made it a financial center. Nine banks were organized in Helena by 1890, many by his good friends L.H. Hershfield, Charles A. Broadwater, T.C. Power, and Thomas Cruse, and were equipped to handle "dust," which was the prime medium of exchange. Although Henry had minimal formal education, he had incredible business acumen, and his enormous commercial success illustrated his expansive knowledge of the financial markets. Henry dipped his toes into banking, first as a director of the Kalispell First National Bank and later taking up positions at Helena's American National Bank and Union Trust Bank. Margaret believed the bank officers sought the shrewd businessman's advice on the livestock business and "they couldn't have talked to anyone that was more knowledgeable than father about it. It had been his life for years right here . . . and I'm sure he wasn't one to just go and just talk to them and take their time. I'm sure he was doing something constructive while he was at the bank." After a spell at the bank (Margaret didn't believe he had an office there), Henry would walk to the Montana Club to visit with his old ranching friends and fellow business magnates. Margaret recalled the friends liked to chat over poker games that they called "sluff." Margaret remembered the rules involved to "draw six cards and discard five and I think that was the type of poker they played. They never played for money, the loser would buy the drinks." Henry was not an excessive drinker, returning home each evening by dinnertime. Later in the evenings, Henry sat in a big green chair in the south window of their home to read, think, or reflect on potential business ventures. Margaret's following recollection illustrates Henry's thoughtful, quiet, and deliberate nature that ensured his long-term success: "I can see father sitting there, he would sit there and read, or sit there and he wasn't reading, and mother would say now don't disturb your father. Well, I said why he's not reading. He is thinking and you mustn't disturb him. And he would, he would read and then he would just sit there and think . . . and he was thinking too. Kind of figuring out things."[39]

Henry remained an active member of the executive committee for the Northern Montana Roundup Association during the first years of the 1900s. Members were satisfied with the continued work of the association's inspectors in arresting and convicting cattle rustlers on the range. In fact, the inspectors' work directly and positively impacted Henry's operations at the Diamond Ranch. In November of 1898, a man by the name of Joseph Hackney stole horses from the ranch, but thanks to the efforts of the Northern Montana Roundup Association, Hackney was soon arrested and convicted of the robbery in the Valley County District Court. Hackney was sentenced to one year in the Deer Lodge Penitentiary.

While efforts to prevent cattle rustling were working, Henry and the wider ranching community became increasingly concerned about gray wolves. In the stockmen's eyes, wolves were becoming an expensive menace, as they killed substantial numbers of livestock. At the annual meeting of 1898, members called for the extermination of the animal. They lobbied the incoming 1899 legislature on the matter and state officials amended the bounty law. This was a big relief for Henry. He and his ranching peers correctly guessed that the amendment would lead to the destruction of the gray wolves in Montana. Gray wolves were essentially extirpated from Montana and the rest of the western United States in the early 1900s.[40]

While Montana's stockmen could influence issues such as rustling and predators, adverse weather would always remain outside of their control. In March 1903, Henry Sieben and John M. Boardman of the Pioneer Cattle Co., Conrad Kohrs's son-in-law, aired their concerns about the severe weather and heavy losses on Montana's northern ranges. They spoke to the *Montana Record-Herald* from a meeting of the Cattle Raiser Association in Texas. Boardman stated that the severe losses expected that year, coupled with the railroad's increase in freight prices, meant that northwestern ranchers were reluctant to pay last year's prices for cattle, which Southerners insisted upon. Just a few days later, Henry arrived in Chicago where he debunked claims that stockmen's accounts of cattle losses were exaggerated. Henry claimed the story was misrepresented and instead shared "a sad story of starvation and cold in Valley County."[41] Henry stated he was providing additional feed for about forty percent of his stock in hopes it would reduce the number of cattle fatalities that year. But he was worried. Henry had visited the Diamond Ranch before traveling east and noted that stock in Valley County were in poor condition. His foreman reported they had two months of cold with below zero temperatures without a single thaw. Henry's cattle were dying. He counted twenty-five head dead the day he visited. Henry declared that "with the exception of 1893, it is the most severe winter northwestern cattlemen have experienced since 1886." Not only was Henry frustrated and concerned about the cold temperatures, he declared that railroad interests were sending out "colored winter reports from the northwestern range, the purpose to encourage immigration regardless of the misery that it might bring people traveling here." Henry was clearly irked with the beginning of what would be a sustained and years-long rosy campaign promotion of Montana to out-of-staters by corporate interests.[42]

It seems stockmen did not exaggerate the severe conditions in northern Montana in 1903. Culbertson rancher F.B. McCann recalled the severe losses the Diamond Ranch suffered and painted a harrowing scene that was eerily reminiscent of Henry's experience in 1886:

> They lost an awful lot. The winter . . . the big tough winter. But there was no fences. The railroad didn't have a fence and the cattle came across to go to the Diamond, from north to south and went with the wind and blizzard, and there were cattle stuck in the snow drift all the way through. Frank Arnette got a bunch of Indians to skin these out and he wanted the hide but they could have the meat because he didn't want to

> have any Indian or anybody else to have the Diamond brand. He [Frank] lost those cattle. He lost how many I don't know, but he lost a lot of cattle.[43]

Henry and Frank stuck with their operation, and Henry made numerous trips to the ranch to support his nephew and his crew. They were still making profits in 1904 and 1905, but the experience of another hard winter so far from his home began to take a toll on Henry. He began to see the benefit of refocusing his business in central Montana.[44]

As the twentieth century dawned, both Henry and Alberta flourished in their new home on the westside of Helena. Margaret recalled, "Mother and father had many happy years there . . . they had a group of friends and would do a lot of things together and they would entertain together."[45] Their home's location enabled Henry to walk his two daughters to Hawthorne Elementary School, just one block away. Margaret fondly reminisced about those years: "He loved his daughters and was just wonderful to us . . . he was a wonderful father. My, I was proud when I could walk through the Hawthorne School yard with him and let all my friends see how nice my father was." Despite the tremendous business pressure Henry was under, he began to loosen up in social settings and enjoy his life with Alberta. As their two daughters grew older, the couple began joining more organizations and, with encouragement from Alberta, Henry even began to attend society dances. In 1901, he attended regular classes at a new dancing club in Helena.

The couple then showcased their skills at some of the many social dances that were held in the capital city over the next few years. They were members of the local Elks Lodge and regularly attended the group's Charity Ball along with other local leaders from Helena, Butte, Anaconda, and Great Falls. In 1904, the Siebens participated in fun events to celebrate Leap Year in Helena. In April of that year, society ladies hosted a Leap Year Dance at Electric Hall in honor of the men of the city. The *Montana Record-Herald* wrote a humorous account of the evening commenting on the men's appearance and demeanor.

Just a month later, Helena's society men, including Henry, threw a ball at Harmony Hall to return the favor.[46]

Alberta found her own niche in Helena as one of the leading society ladies of the early 1900s. Margaret depicted her mother's warm personality, describing her as follows: "My mother, Alberta, was the oldest of the Gordon girls and just a lovely, delightful, darling person and very lovely to look at."[47] Alberta opened up the Sieben home to host some of the social highlights of the calendar year. Her younger sister, Florence, who had recently relocated to Helena, often cohosted with her elder sister. In May 1901, Alberta and Florence hosted a lavish luncheon at the Sieben home. The *Montana Record-Herald* described the white lilacs that formed the centerpiece, which were held in a basket of ferns, tied with a graceful pink ribbon. It was during this time that Florence met Frederick Kessler, the son of Nicholas Kessler who founded the Kessler Brewery and Western Clay Manufacturing Company. Fred helped manage the various enterprises and, given his father's and Henry's long history as pioneers in Helena, it is not surprising he was a good friend of Henry and Alberta's.

In July of 1902, the Siebens hosted a dinner at their home to celebrate Florence and Fred's engagement. Florence and Fred married at the First Unitarian Church, the first wedding the building hosted. As Alberta's and Florence's parents had both recently passed, Henry stood in to give the bride away, and the Siebens hosted a reception at their home that evening. The newlyweds would move into the home next door to the Sieben family, the one that Henry had built for them, until they moved to a house at the brewery later that decade. Florence and Fred had two daughters, Helen and Louise, and Margaret fondly recalled wheeling Helen around in her baby buggy next door.[48]

Alberta's social skills and love of entertaining firmly established the Sieben family as prominent leaders in the community. She was particularly fond of card parties and would regularly attend or host get-togethers to play Sixty-Three, Cavendish, and whist. In one edition of the *Montana Record-Herald* on January 9, 1904, the Society section of the paper placed Alberta at four different gatherings in Helena in one week alone. The society pages of the newspaper regularly reported on the local gatherings and included descriptions of the host's lavish décor, sumptuous food, and fine prizes (which Alberta often won) including vases, wares, and even silk stockings.

Alberta's get-togethers were elaborate. Her card parties often attracted 100 guests, bringing together Helena's leading society members at the Sieben home. Alberta entertained guests on the third floor or, in good weather, on the veranda: "They would have afternoon parties that they called parties alfresco ... they would write notes inviting their friends to come and the children would have to deliver the notes to the families. I can remember going around giving the notes to the people who were invited to come."[49] Guests included Mary and Anton M. Holter; Augusta and Conrad Kohrs, who had recently relocated from Deer Lodge to Helena; Minnie Babcock and E.C. Babcock, the proprietor of an elegant gentlemen's furnishings business; Lily Toole and Governor J. K. Toole; as well as Julie Broadwater and Adelaide Child, wife of Harry W. Child. These prominent Helena women are captured in a colorful photograph taken at a luncheon given by Julie Broadwater circa 1903 or 1904. The visual brings to life the women, including Alberta Sieben, who moved the needle for civic and social causes in early-day Helena. Alberta never publicly addressed her political views, but in 1902 she attended a talk given by Carrie Chapman Catt, a well-known speaker on equal suffrage. This suggests Alberta and her social circle supported women's suffrage, and one imagines they supported Jeannette Rankin's efforts a decade later to secure women's right to vote in Montana.[50]

While Henry's family featured often and prominently on the society pages of the *Montana-Record Herald*, it seems his brother Jake and his wife, Sylvia, led a quieter life on their ranch in Cascade. Pioneer rancher Frank Sterling's description of the Sieben brothers suggests that, while the two brothers had much in common professionally, they may have deviated in their personal approach: "[Henry] was a very good businessman. I would have to say he was a much better businessman than his brother I always thought. That's my personal opinion you know.

By 1903, Alberta Sieben had become an integral member of Helena society women, as seen here (second row, third from left) at a luncheon at the Broadwater Hotel in Helena. Courtesy of the Hibbard family private collection

Because he was the leader between the two men, I would say that. Jake was . . . he was a good worker, but he liked to drink a little bit . . . but they were both good men, good honest men and hard workers."[51]

In 1902, Jake suffered two life-changing and devastating blows. Wildfires that spread from Saco to Culbertson and north from the Great Northern to the Canadian border destroyed millions of acres of prairie land, decimating Jake's holdings in the area. In a newspaper report that October, rancher M.E. Milner stated that Jake was the most affected of the large cattlemen and would have to find new range.[52] On a trip to Glasgow later that fall to sort his business affairs, Jake suffered a stroke. Upon hearing the news, Henry's and Jake's elder sister, Margaret, traveled to Cascade to care for him. In December 1904, Jake and Sylvia visited Geneseo to spend Christmas with his family. Leonard's daughter, Ruth Sieben Hagelin, remembered him dying at their family home. She recalled, "[I] just remember he was a nice uncle. But we put a bed in the parlor for him because he got sick at our house and he died there."[53] Newspapers around the state shared the news of Jake's death at the age of just fifty-three, describing him as a pioneer and "one of the best known cattlemen" in the state. Sylvia settled Jake's business affairs and "considerable estate"[54] and moved to San Diego with her daughter-in-law, Edna, and her grandson, Robert.[55]

Jake's death greatly shocked brothers Leonard and Henry. Leonard's first impulse was to travel to Montana with his family. He wanted to see Henry and experience, once again, the land that the three Sieben brothers had made home thirty years before. Ruth recalled she traveled by "Pullman" (railroad sleeping car) with her father to Montana. They happened to be seated across from Mary and T.C. Power on the train. When the Powers figured out who Leonard was, they invited him to visit while he was in town. Henry brought Leonard and his family out to Cascade and to the Chestnut Valley where they visited with their old friend C.H. Austin. Ruth recalled they visited the cabin where her mother, Sarah, had lived for just a year before returning to Illinois with Leonard. As they reminisced about their early years and adventures in Chestnut Valley, Leonard and Henry recalled how their cattle would always drift away back into the mountains behind the valley and the brothers would have to saddle up their horses and look for them. The funny thing was they always found their cattle in the same place, close to where Middle Creek Dam now stands. Henry called it "Hole in the Wall" and remembered he had once declared if he ever got enough money to buy a ranch of his own and if property was available, he would purchase it. After spending time reflecting on their youthful days in the valley, the Siebens visited Jake's widow, Sylvia, and her son, Charles, on their ranch in Cascade. Ruth laughingly remembered that, to Leonard and Henry's horror, Charles brought the two Sieben families on a carriage ride through Great Falls' red-light district. The family reunion may have brought some needed closure to the brothers' grief while also instilling in Henry a renewed interest in the land east of the Chestnut Valley.[56] ◈

Chapter 7

1898–1915

"A SYSTEMATIC AND CAREFUL MAN OF BUSINESS"

Opportunity allowed Henry Sieben to purchase two ranches he long had his eye on—the Mitchell Place north of Helena and the Adel Ranch in the Chestnut Valley area. This move brought his life journey full circle. He dove back into the sheep industry, strategically whittled back his cattle operations, and left northeastern Montana for good. Fortune favored Henry's bold endeavors for a time. The weather and economy boosted his efforts and, for the first time, the women in Henry's family got a seat at his business table.

On September 15, 1898, the *Independent-Record* announced that Martin and Eliza Mitchell had transferred their ranch thirty-five miles northwest of Helena to Henry Sieben and Thomas A. Grimes. The outright sale was made for $15,000 (approximately $500,000 today). With this purchase, Henry and his partner acquired a ranch at the mouth of the Little Prickly Pear Canyon that was made up of 1,600 deeded acres and 375 square miles of open range.[1] Henry knew this to be one of the oldest and most historic spreads in the area. Malcolm Clarke settled there in 1864 to run a stage stop for travelers along the Benton Road. Henry and Leonard had driven countless wagons full of freight and journeyed across this land some thirty years previously. After Clarke's murder, his family had buried him behind his home on the ranch, where he still lies today.[2] What a kick Leonard must have gotten when he learned Henry had purchased the Mitchell Place. Neither brother would have ever dreamed they would someday have the good fortune of owning lands they once traversed by foot and by wagon.

The cabin at Henry's ranch, known as the Mitchell Place near Wolf Creek, was far less stately than his new home in Helena, but it became much beloved by the family (Thomas Grimes cabin, ca. 1900). Courtesy of the Hibbard family private collection.

Once Sieben and Grimes completed the purchase of the Mitchell Place in 1898, they divided roles and responsibilities. The partners' personalities complemented each other perfectly. Thomas Grimes was known as a cantankerous character who did not get along well with his neighbors, but he was suited to ranch life and content to live at headquarters to oversee day-to-day operations. This left Henry to oversee finances, maintain partnerships, join organizations, and advocate for ranchers' interests from Helena. A neighboring rancher, Brian O'Connell, described Thomas Grimes as difficult to work with.[3] Nick Hilger, whose father, Joe, owned an adjacent ranch, agreed, noting that Grimes could get "pretty ornery once in a while and Dad would go to Sieben and . . . Sieben would straighten him out."[4]

The partners used the historic buildings on the Mitchell Ranch and then built new structures to accommodate their needs. Several of Malcolm Clarke's historic cabins were still standing and in good condition. The cabins were a series of log rooms that contained a stove and a door and were likely used as accommodations for passengers on the stage stop. Thomas Grimes decided to build his cabin on the Benton Road that traversed their property. Mail was picked up from the ranch house porch, bagged in a large white bag, and hung on a special hook system for the railway mail car on a passing train to pick up.[5] Sieben and Grimes built a stone spring house, which contained a milk separator and rows of large milk cans, in the quaking aspen grove across Benton Road from the horse barn. A trough from the adjacent spring held cold water that kept the milk fresh.[6]

Sieben and Grimes intended to run some cattle at the Mitchell Place, but their primary goal was to partake in Montana's expanding sheep industry. Once the partners added to the necessary structures at the ranch, they pastured half of the thirty carloads of steers Henry had ordered from Oregon in 1897. The other fifteen carloads were sent to the Culbertson Ranch. Thomas Grimes had years of experience running cattle in the Judith Basin roundup, but he was also a knowledgeable sheep man. After nearly twenty years of cattle ranching in central and northeastern Montana, Henry was ready to take another gamble on the sheep business. Many other stockmen who had formerly specialized in cattle were now heavily investing in sheep, such as Henry's former partner, Bob Coburn, and his younger brother, Jake Sieben.

By the time Sieben and Grimes took over the Mitchell Ranch, the sheep industry had come of age in Montana. The sheep population expanded throughout the 1890s, and by 1900 it stood at roughly six million head. Henry, as usual, was aware of what was going on; one foreman later recalled: "Henry did not like to work with sheep at all . . . because he was just not a sheep man, but at that time sheep was the big business and Mr. Sieben was a businessman."[7] Henry was convinced that with his and Thomas Grimes's combined experience, they could make their mark on the sheep industry.

As Henry predicted, over the next few years, he and Thomas Grimes made a substantial profit from the sheep industry. In July 1904, 500,000 pounds of Montana wool was sold at the local wool exchange in Great Falls. Bidding from East Coast buyers such as Barraclough and Thayer was pushed to the limit, and sales were so high that the exchange closed early that year. Sieben and Grimes sold 65,000 pounds of wool at just over 16 cents (approximately $5 today) per pound. The following year, sales of wool doubled during the exchange in Great Falls. In May of 1905, more than one million pounds of wool was sold at the exchange. All sales were under advance contract, and buyers paid prices of 20 or 21 cents (approximately $7 today) per pound. At that exchange, Sieben and Grimes sold 100,000 pounds of wool, making them an incredible $21,000 dollars ($730,000 today's value) that season. In the space of just a few years, the partners turned the Mitchell Place into one of the largest sheep operations in the state.[8]

The relative proximity of the Mitchell Place to Helena meant that for the first time, Henry could involve his family in his ranching operation. By the early 1900s, Henry's daughter Berneice was a teenager and his younger daughter, Margaret, was finishing elementary school. They were growing into capable and curious young women. Henry was determined to provide them with the formal educational opportunities he was never afforded, but he also intended to share his knowledge and passion for ranching, animals, and his crew with his daughters. In Henry's mind, the first step toward that goal was to ensure they had good horses.

The Sieben family's ranch life was very different from their town life, as shown by a young Berneice Sieben on her horse "Doctor" at the house on Harrison Avenue in Helena. Courtesy of the Hibbard and Baucus family private collection.

Margaret described her father as a great horseman, remembering that "he knew good horse flesh."[9] Henry's peers respected his judgment of horses and often sought his advice when purchasing certain breeds. When Henry believed it was time for Berneice and Margaret to own and ride five-gaited horses (horses with five types of gaits—walk, trot, canter, rack, slow gait), he went to Mexico, Missouri, to purchase American Saddlebreds for his daughters and a driving horse for Alberta's carriage. At the time, Mexico, Missouri, was noted as the "Saddlebred Horse Capital of the World." Margaret related that when several of Henry's friends discovered the purpose of Henry's trip, they asked him to purchase horses for them, too. One such friend was Nick Gould, vice-president of T.C. Power's American National Bank. He asked Henry to select a driving horse for him. Charles Kessler requested Henry purchase three or four teams of large powerful horses, likely Clydesdales or Belgian Draught horses, that could haul his brewery wagons. Henry made enough horse purchases to fill a railroad car, and Margaret remembered it as "quite something" when the beautiful horses were unloaded in Helena. Berneice and Margaret were thrilled with their horses. Berneice excitedly named her horse "Doctor" and Margaret called hers "Cricket."

From approximately 1903 onwards, the Sieben family spent their summers at the Mitchell place. Henry and Alberta made the trip from Helena in a fringed surrey that was pulled by their driving horse, Molly. Berneice and Margaret rode behind the surrey on Doctor and Cricket. Margaret recalled that the backseat of the surrey was packed with the family's summer clothes and a gray-and-white plaid shawl covered the clothing for protection against dust. To break up the five-hour, twenty-five mile journey, the Siebens regularly stopped and had lunch at the Gehring Ranch on Lincoln Road. Bartholomew Gehring was born in Germany and raised in Illinois before coming to Helena in 1865 where he raised cattle. Bartholomew and his wife, Jane, had developed a successful, mixed farming operation along the Helena-Fort Benton Road, and to attract customers they placed a trough by the road where passersby could water their stock while purchasing chickens, dairy products, berries, apples, potatoes, and other garden produce. It was the perfect respite for the Siebens and their animals as they journeyed to and from the Mitchell Place. As they neared the ranch, Henry always cautioned Berneice and Margaret not to run their horses as they were tired by that point, but the girls humorously defied their father. Against Henry's wishes, they galloped to the ranch as fast as they could, delighted to have reached their destination.[10]

Berneice and Margaret were four years apart in age, and Berneice often viewed her younger sister as little more than a nuisance. Alta Sanders, niece of Wilbur Fisk Sanders, knew the Sieben sisters well. She described the physical differences between the siblings, describing Margaret as having blond hair that blew in the wind, similar to her mother Alberta, while Berneice was darker like Henry, with brown eyes and olive skin. While Margaret was still a child, Berneice was a young teen and regularly attended lavish picnics and parties at the Broadwater Natatorium or at the homes of her society friends, many of whom were the children of Henry and Alberta's friends. The young women's get-togethers were often featured on the society pages of the *Montana-Record Herald*. Margaret recalled that at one formal event at the Babcock home, Alberta had instructed Berneice on what to say and how to act as she walked down the receiving line. However, when Alberta and Berneice got to Mrs. Babcock, Berneice shook her hand and said, "I am so happy to come Mrs Bobcack." Berneice's innocent blunder of mispronouncing the lady's name broke the ice and ended the formality. When Berneice's friends visited the Sieben home, the group retreated to a room on the third floor, burned incense, and enjoyed some tea. Margaret was tasked with making fudge, lemonade, or tea for Berneice and her friends. It was not until Margaret reached high school that the two sisters grew closer. But when they vacationed on the ranch, outside the confines of Helena society, the pair got along quite well.[11]

During their ranch vacations, the Siebens stayed in a wood-floored tent pitched near the stone spring house, with a lean-to for a kitchen and dining room. Henry's property ledger indicates he called their summer abode the "bungalow." From 1905 to 1908, Henry purchased materials to outfit their accommodation. His purchases included large

12'x13' army tents, screens, a 16'x18' awning, three iron beds, springs, mattresses, dining furniture, and silverware. To appease both daughters, Henry and Alberta allowed them to each have one friend stay with them. Margaret recalled that she and Berneice each had a double bed and that her friend, Mary Longmaid, would stay with her. Henry and Alberta slept on the other side of the curtain.

Because Henry raised his daughters to share his love of horses, he taught them to care for theirs with a gentle firmness. Henry dealt with horses in a quiet manner. He did not wear boots with spurs to kick his horses, and he refused to whoop and holler while riding. By watching their father, Berneice and Margaret learned to do the same. One night, shortly after the family had arrived for their summer sojourn at the Mitchell Place, they were awakened by a ruckus in the barn. Henry recognized it as Margaret's horse, Cricket, and shocked Margaret by telling her she must light a lantern, get dressed, and go down to the barn to take care of the animal. Margaret described her heart sinking, but she followed her father's orders and walked down the dark lane to the barn. Sure enough, she found Cricket with one foot in the manger and the other over the halter rope. Margaret untangled and soothed her horse and recalled she "felt so proud to think I could take care of my own horse and I went skipping back under the stars at 2:30 in the morning to tell Father that I had taken care of my horse." Margaret attributed that lesson to her lifelong love of riding, which she continued well into her eighties.[12]

With business expansion, better defined laws, and an influx of other ranchers to the Prickly Pear Valley, Sieben and Grimes were involved in numerous legal battles involving the Mitchell Place property in the early 1900s. Ever since the Hard Winter of 1886 to 1887, stockmen such as Henry understood the days of the open range were numbered. Not only had the disaster taught them the value of harvesting hay for winter feed, they also realized the need for fencing. Of course, fencing also required decisions about whose responsibility it was to build and maintain fences that separated hayfields from the open range. In 1887, two years before statehood, the Montana territorial legislature passed a law declaring that the stockman who separated the hayfield from the public domain would have the responsibility of fencing to exclude all free-roaming livestock. But fencing property didn't just separate hay from livestock. As homesteaders began arriving in Montana to farm, established cattlemen began to fence off larger tracts of land with barbed wire to try to prevent potential homesteaders' claims.

By 1887, nearly 250,000 acres of public domain in Montana had been illegally enclosed with barbed wire. In fact, the production of barbed wire in the United States tripled between 1880 and 1890, and this increased output had been unrolled in Montana. Federal reaction was prompt. Land office attorneys flooded into federal courts with complaints. President Grover Cleveland ordered every foot of fence torn down. Stockmen were angry and humiliated. The cattle kings' actions to protect access to the rangelands and water also infuriated many homesteaders. All too often, large ranch owners not only fenced the property over which they claimed ownership but also property they considered public land. Some homesteaders retaliated by cutting the barbed wire of the fenced areas to give their livestock access to the land. This started a widespread series of conflicts, known as the Fence Cutting Wars, that spread across the American West.[13]

When Henry acquired the Mitchell Place in 1898, he began, in what appears to be the first time in his ranching career, fencing in portions of his property. And, therefore, Sieben and Grimes soon found themselves embroiled in a court case. In 1901, the partners applied to the District Court for an injunction to restrain Lewis and Clark County commissioners from tearing down the fence that ran across a number of their sections, most of which they owned, some of which they leased from the state. They alleged the land was valuable for pasture only, and the fence was necessary to prevent stock from running loose on the range. The situation escalated, and in 1905, U.S. attorney Carl Rasch filed a case in the U.S. Court charging Sieben and Grimes with unlawfully fencing public lands in Lewis and Clark County. Rasch argued the fences prevented and obstructed others from entering and/or settling the public land. Sieben and Grimes lost the case and removed the fences. However, the most well-known of Henry's legal cases that focused on this open range doctrine of ranchers fencing out neighbors' animals on their property was the *Herrin v. Sieben* case.[14]

In 1911, neighboring rancher Holly J. Herrin filed a suit in the District Court against Sieben and Grimes alleging the defendants repeatedly pastured bands totaling 5,000 sheep on land he had bought from the Northern Pacific Railroad. Herrin claimed that when Sieben and Grimes drove their sheep to public pastures in the area five miles south of Wolf Creek, they wrongfully crossed Herrin's land. Herrin argued that the sheep destroyed the grass and herbage and requested $2,000 ($65,000 today's value) in damages. The jury ruled in Holly J. Herrin's favor, awarding him $1,200 ($40,000 today's value) in damages and $100 ($3,000 today's value) in exemplary damages to deter others from repeating the act that led to the lawsuit. Herrin was also granted his request for a permanent injunction to prevent Sieben and Grimes from trespassing. Henry and Thomas Grimes decided to appeal the ruling. A year later, the Montana Supreme Court modified the lower court's rulings.

In an opinion written by Henry's friend and neighbor Chief Justice Theodore Brantley, the justices cut the District Court's award in half. They acknowledged that while Sieben and Grimes's sheep had caused "depasturing," this did not result in permanent damage. Regarding the injunction, the Supreme Court ordered the District Court to find a way for Sieben and Grimes to cross Herrin's property to reach the public grazing land they customarily were entitled to use.

The judgment in the *Herrin v. Sieben* case was full of contradictions. It awarded Herrin damages for Sieben and Grimes's trespass and concluded that even though Herrin's land was not "inclosed," Sieben should have made himself aware of property lines. But the court also ruled that Sieben and Grimes had the right to access public land that was only accessible by crossing Herrin's land. The problems addressed in the ruling went all the way back to the 1864 Northern Pacific Charter. For each mile of rail the Northern Pacific (NP) completed in connecting the East and West Coast, the company received incentives, including forty-six million acres of federal real estate stretching from Duluth to Bismarck to Oregon. The NP was awarded every other section, usually the odd-numbered sections in townships within a forty-mile corridor on either side of its railroad tracks. In order to pay the line's construction costs, the company sold this land east of the Missouri River for $4 ($80 today's value) an acre and west of the river for up to $2.60 ($50 today's value) an acre.

The resulting checkerboard pattern of ownership caused the legal issue between Herrin and Sieben and Grimes. Sieben and Grimes owned sections next to Herrin's land and the government's land. Because it was impossible to access the public lands without crossing some part of the odd-numbered sections, the United States reserved an understood "easement by necessity." It operated in the interests of the government and, in this case, of citizens such as Sieben and Grimes who wanted to enter the public land for grazing. Over time, other justices disagreed with the ruling, reversing and reinstating the doctrine of easement by necessity. Amid the landmark case, Sieben and Grimes found themselves embroiled in other property issues surrounding the question of water rights.[15]

Water had always been and would always be a top priority for ranchers in Montana. In 1903, Henry, along with ranchers Benjamin D. Phillips and Henry Liston, brought an appeal case to the Montana Supreme Court, enlisting Joseph. K. Toole as their attorney. Sieben et al. alleged that Henry's former partner, Bob Coburn, and his son, William Coburn, had diverted 2,000 inches of Warm Springs Creek north of Lewistown in Chouteau County. They sought a perpetual injunction to restrain the Coburns from continuing with the diversion. Chief Justice Theodore Brantley ruled in favor of the Coburns, stating they had given appropriate notice about the water diversion and were entitled to use it for the agricultural purposes they had outlined. Sieben lost the case.

In 1906, Henry was involved in another legal dispute over water rights when neighboring rancher Susanna Hilger sought damages of $1,000 ($35,000 today's value) from Sieben and Grimes at the Mitchell Place and two other local property owners, Chris Zabel and Richard

Cooper, for the alleged wrongful diversion of waters at Tow Head Creek. Hilger claimed that Sieben and the other ranchers had diverted the water for their own use when the natural flow served to irrigate the Hilger ranch's lands. Susanna Hilger also sought an injunction to prevent the defendants from further alleged diversion. The judge ruled in favor of Hilger. Sieben and the other defendants appealed, and the case ended up in the Montana Supreme Court in 1909 with the judge ruling in favor of a retrial. Susanna Hilger died before the retrial process began. While Henry did not welcome the time and money he spent on the cases, he knew it was part and parcel of the changing landscape. And as always, he was ready to adapt and to fight.[16]

Henry also became embroiled in a murder case involving one of his ranch crew at the Mitchell Place. On New Year's Day 1905, Sieben and Grimes's sheepherder, Jesse Liefer, was involved in an altercation with neighboring sheepherder Theodore Grimaud. The two men's bands of sheep became mixed up on a portion of disputed range near the Mitchell Place. Liefer alleged Grimaud advanced on him with a heavy stick, struck him, and continued to advance, so Liefer drew his gun and shot Grimaud in self-defense. Thomas Grimes and Henry Sieben both took the stand to testify to Liefer's character. Scenes during the short two-day trial became heated when Thomas Grimes and a witness, C.H. Wood, got into a scuffle outside the judge's courtroom. Liefer was found guilty and sentenced to ten years in prison. Throughout the trial, Henry stood by his crew man and paid his legal fees. His actions deliberately illustrated to Liefer and his crews at Mitchell Place and the Diamond Ranch that he had his employees' backs.[17]

Though circumstances were often challenging, business was profitable at the Mitchell Place, and Henry's interest and influence in the sheep industry continued to expand in the early 1900s. Henry cemented his commitment to the sheep business when he decided to help organize to protect sheep ranching interests just as he had in the early days of the cattle business. The inspiration to organize came about in 1905 when Henry and other woolgrowers witnessed the Wyoming Woolgrowers Association's success in ensuring eastern buyers paid more

Having arrived in Montana nearly penniless, Henry Sieben was careful to maintain an image as a successful businessman, and he was nearly always photographed in a suit and tie. Here, Henry takes stock of a pen full of his sheep at the Mitchell Place (later Sieben Ranch). Courtesy of the Hibbard family private collection.

for Wyoming wool than any other state. In the fall of 1906, Henry got to work, meeting with other prominent woolgrowers across the state to petition Governor Joseph. K. Toole to call a meeting of the state's sheep men. The goal was to form a state organization that would be affiliated with the National Woolgrowers organization. In October 1906, the group filed articles of incorporation for the Montana Woolgrowers Commission Company. The organization's headquarters were in Helena and all stock was owned by members. Henry was appointed as a director of the organization. The group's aim was to enable sheep men to deal directly with eastern manufacturers, thus ensuring woolgrowers would secure the fair market price for their wool. Sieben maintained his strong ties with the cattle business during these years but made strategic decisions to scale back his interest in that endeavor.[18]

During the time he was helping form the Montana Woolgrowers Commission Company, he also traveled to Utah and Texas to purchase cattle and attend cattle conventions. In the fall of 1905 and 1906, Henry traveled to Culbertson to assist Frank with the roundup and shipment of cattle, and in 1907 they shipped eleven cars of cattle to Chicago. But Henry later recalled that within four years of locating at Culbertson, economic, agricultural, and social changes were taking hold, and with a large influx of newcomers, the cattle business became less profitable.[19]

Unprecedented numbers of homesteaders began moving to the plains of east-central Montana during the early 1900s in the great land rush sometimes called the Second Homestead Boom. This semi-arid region had seemed hopelessly dry to frontier farmers in the nineteenth century. They were also deterred from settling in Montana when they learned about the lack of railroad connections, the enormous Native American reservations, and the huge open-range livestock operations. Instead, they headed to the inviting grass-filled valleys of the Rockies and the Pacific Coast. It was only after 1900 with the advent of new land policies, new farming technology, advancements in methods, and new land promotions, that homesteaders placed their bets on Montana.

The Newlands Reclamation Act passed by Congress in 1902 was an early warning to Henry Sieben that Montana's remote eastern plains would soon face unprecedented change. That law committed the federal government to building large-scale irrigation projects throughout the arid West. Montana and Great Plains promoters argued that once the Missouri and its tributaries were dammed and diverted, "the deserts could be made to blossom."[20] For a time in the early 1900s, reclamation seemed to be the key to success. Between 1904 and 1906, construction began on several large federal reclamation developments: the Huntley Project east of Billings, the Lower Yellowstone Project along the Montana-Dakota state line, the Milk River Project in the Diamond Ranch's area of the state in northern Montana, and the Sun River Project west of Great Falls. These projects were a huge benefit to the state, but they still left most of Montana's vast lands un-watered. Agricultural boosters abandoned their hopes of turning the semi-arid western plains into an irrigated "garden" and turned instead to the promise of dry farming.[21]

Dry farming is practiced without irrigation in regions of scanty precipitation. By the early twentieth century, experienced farmers in semi-arid regions such as Utah and eastern Washington and some pioneers in Montana had developed different methods of moisture-conserving tillage. They let their lands lie in summer fallow every other year, and they worked the ground intensively to retain soil moisture. Henry's business associate, Paris Gibson, in neighboring Great Falls had long been an advocate of dry farming. Gibson believed that his own farm operation had proved as early as the 1880s that dry farming could work in Montana. Farther east, Henry's entrepreneurial nephew, Frank Arnette, was one of the most successful early pioneers in dry land farming. Frank routinely broke up some of the sod on the Diamond Ranch in order to raise hay for winter feed. One season his oat crops could not be harvested green enough for hay because of wet weather, and the grain matured before it was cut. Frank decided to thresh the grain, and the yield was approximately seventy-five bushels to the acre. Frank and Henry concluded that the eastern plains were much better adapted for farming than they had thought. That remarkable oat yield encouraged Frank to incorporate crop growing into the Diamond Ranch's operations. He successfully tried his hand at sowing alfalfa and corn and established a farming enterprise on the ranch that comprised 1,000 acres. Frank's early success strengthened Henry's belief that it wouldn't be long before farmers would arrive in droves to Culbertson on one of James Hill's trains.[22]

Henry's unease about the future of his ranching business in Culbertson was exacerbated when profits at the Diamond Ranch began to dip in 1906. Jim Spurgeon recalled that while Frank Arnette was a great boss, he just did not have a head for business: "Frank never made any money and finally Henry had to sell the ranch. Frank was, well he was a good operator, but . . . he never made any money. [He was] a little extravagant."[23] Jim remembered walking in Culbertson with his father one afternoon when they bumped into Henry on the street, likely when Henry was in town in the fall of 1906 to assist with the roundup and shipment of cattle. Henry complained to Jim's father that Frank was not doing well. Jim quoted Henry as saying: "You know Frank's never made any money for himself or me either." Jim's father had to side with Henry, because he knew Frank well enough to know he was a "top operator" but he never made any money. Henry knew that in poker, as in life, you show greatness by the hands you fold, not the hands you play, so Henry quit while he was ahead.

Henry dissolved his partnership in the Diamond Ranch in 1906, unloading the last shipment of steers in 1908.[24] But Henry had not left Frank in a pickle. In December 1907, the two men traveled to their hometown of Geneseo, Illinois, to attend Henry's sister and Frank's mother, Margaret Arnette's, golden wedding anniversary celebration. Like Henry, Margaret had no head start in life, but she and her husband, George, worked hard to develop a farming business in Geneseo. Over the years, they invested in real estate in Henry County, Illinois, and throughout Minnesota, becoming some of the most extensive landowners in Illinois. At the wedding anniversary celebration, Margaret and George gave $30,000 (approximately $1 million today) to each of their six children and their orphaned niece, Inez Hudnell. It was time for Frank to now paddle his own canoe.[25]

In selling his range cattle operation in Culbertson, Henry again proved to be ahead of the curve. In 1909, Congress enacted the Enlarged Homestead Act, which offered a 320-acre (half-section) of land free to settlers in the West. In 1912, Congress supplemented the law with the Three-Year Homestead Act, which reduced the waiting period for ownership from five to three years and permitted a homesteader to be absent from his homestead for five months of each year. The westward-looking home seeker, not realizing that even 320 acres was usually far too little land on the semi-arid plains, responded eagerly. Eventually, nearly thirty-two million acres of Montana land passed from public to private hands under the various homestead acts. The ready availability of free or inexpensive land and the new methods of dry farming made the Montana homestead boom possible. But what really launched it was the great promotional campaign that began in 1908. There were many powerful promoters including chambers of commerce, bankers' groups, eastern newspapers, as well as real estate brokers. And there were the railroads, which had a vital stake in building up the region they served and had immense advertising resources.[26]

James J. Hill, who controlled three of the five regional railroads in Montana, had an obvious financial interest in promoting immigration. But he pursued motives other than financial gain. Hill believed in rural virtues and saw the family farm as the backbone of American society. He envisioned the fertile plains of Montana as the granary of the world, neatly divided into family farms and populated by thousands. In his massive settlement campaign, he saw the fulfillment of a great national purpose. "Population without the prairie," he once observed, "is a mob, and the prairie without population is a desert."[27] And a population producing grain and demanding consumer goods is a railroad magnate's gold mine.

As Henry predicted, under the stimulus of the advertising barrage, homesteaders swept into east-central Montana after the turn of the twentieth century. In 1908 to 1909, the railroads started moving farming families into northern and eastern Montana. New boomtowns such as Plentywood, Scobey, Rudyard, Ryegate, Baker, and Hardin sprang up. By 1910, agriculture had surpassed mining to become Montana's major source of income. The state's population climbed from 234,329 in 1900 to 376,053 in 1910.[28]

A new decade dawned for Henry as he concentrated his business operations closer to home in 1907. He had turned sixty years old on February 1 and had now spent forty-three years in Montana building a business, a home, a family, and, according to local newspapers in 1908, a fortune. An interesting article ran in several newspapers throughout the state that year under different titles such as "Rich Men of Helena and How They Got It" and "Monied Men of Montana."[29] The piece delved into a question of endless fascination for the everyday citizens of the state—just how did Helena's rich men make their money? The piece offers insight into Henry's status in society and how others viewed him and other successful men.

The article highlights the prosperity that abounded in Montana in the early 1900s. It states that Helena had three millionaires (they would be worth thirty times that today) and scores of others whose wealth ranged from a quarter of a million to a million dollars. The papers identify the three millionaires as Henry's friends and business associates W.G. Conrad, T.C. Power, and Thomas Cruse. Like Henry, the three men had arrived in the early days of Montana Territory, and the adjectives used to describe them—"plenty of initiative," "shrewd," "energetic," "sound judgement," "far-sighted," "careful"—were just as applicable to Henry. The entire list of wealthy men in the article reads like the invitation list to one of the Siebens' parties: John T. Murphy, Ben D. Phillips, Louis Stadler, Louis Kaufman, D.A.G. Floweree, and A.K. Prescott. Other old-time friends listed included Henry's attorney friend T.J. Walsh, brewers Fred and Charles Kessler, Colonel Broadwater's nephew T.A. Marlow, real estate magnate Richard Lockey, merchant R.C. Wallace, and mining and lumber empresario Anton M. Holter.

Henry is prominently highlighted in the article. The journalists guessed he was worth somewhere in the region of $250,000 ($8.5 million dollars today). They wrote that the open range largely helped in Sieben's success but noted he was a "shrewd, systematic and careful man of business." He is described as a liberal man who kept a strict methodical account of his financial affairs. Henry likely agreed that "the rich men of any time are those who not only gained wealth but kept it." The theme of failure also crops up several times in the article. Henry knew better than most that failure was an important part of the path to success. Furthermore, he always understood that one learned the most from failures when they had the "ability to drop an unsuccessful undertaking and go on to something else that has been very valuable."[30]

The year 1907 marked a fresh chapter for Henry's business enterprises. He began focusing his business interests on raising sheep and producing wool at the Mitchell Place. Although he was no longer working with Frank Arnette as a partner at the Diamond ranch in eastern Montana, he did not fully divest of his interest in cattle. Instead, Henry took the helm of the Northern Montana Roundup Association and served as president for the year. In May, he made another strategic move to showcase his continued interest in cattle. Henry formed a business partnership with his neighbor, T.C. Power, and Helena rancher Perry P. Kline, to incorporate the Big Hole Ranch Company. The partners started with a capital of $50,000, and their intention was to acquire and operate ranch property in the Big Hole Basin.

This marked Henry's first foray into conducting cattle business in southwestern Montana. Perry P. Kline began his career in Montana as a butcher in Dillon and then worked as a livestock agent for the Great Northern Railway. Henry and T.C. Power likely became acquainted with Kline in his capacity working for the railroad. Perry Kline's headquarters were in Helena, but he was accustomed to traveling the state as a livestock agent. Kline took on the role of manager of the Big Hole Ranch Company, spending his summers on the ranch and traveling statewide and spending winters in Butte. Henry got to work immediately and traveled with Kline to Dillon after the official incorporation of their company in May 1907. The partners were searching for young steers to stock the ranch. The following month they purchased 480 acres of titled land and a school section under fence and lease by the state from Len Pendleton of Dillon. By 1908, they had 400 head of beef steers and numerous horses at the ranch. In 1909, Henry traveled to Red Rock, a railroad stop just to the southeast of the Big Hole, to help unload 488 steers for the ranch. In 1910, he sold 599 wethers from the Mitchell Place to Perry Kline at $4.39 per head, taking home $2,611.56 ($85,000 today). Henry also sold 119 cows and 255 steers to a man he noted as "Frazier" for $6,691 ($220,000 today's value).[31]

It appears the Big Hole Ranch Company partnership was a success. Henry traveled frequently to the ranch and assisted with operations. The partners had at least 2,000 head of steers, horses, and sheep. While Perry Kline continued to unload trainloads of steers from Red Rock in 1912, it appears Henry's direct involvement in the ranch slowed down between 1911 and 1915. His ledgers and pocketbooks do not suggest he took any trips to the area during that time. However, in 1916, Henry bought 4,000 head of cattle that were likely kept at the Big Hole Ranch. To manage his diverse stock business interests at the time, Henry decided to set up a business corporation in his own name.[32]

So, Henry established the Sieben Sheep and Cattle Co. (likely a precursor to what would become the Sieben Live Stock Co.). Henry's

Henry Sieben, once again in business attire, loading cattle at the Adel Ranch near Cascade, 1926.
Courtesy of the Hibbard family private collection.

cattle account ledger documents Sieben Co. activities for just the last six months of 1907 and the first two months of 1908, but it highlights that Henry infused the company with his own cash as well as profits from sheep sales and rent on school land. His pocketbook for 1908 indicates he traveled to the Big Hole Ranch to look after horses belonging to the Sieben Sheep and Cattle Co. This suggests that while Henry shared land and responsibilities with Thomas A. Grimes at the Mitchell Place and with Power and Kline at the Big Hole Ranch, he kept his other business affairs separate. This business structure enabled Henry to maintain financial independence within his partnerships, something that would become increasingly important as his daughters became more interested in the business and he continued to expand his operations.[33]

Henry's next major purchase was a ranch he knew well. The idea to establish a ranch in the Chestnut Valley region had been percolating in the back of his mind since his return visit there with Leonard in honor of their younger brother, Jake's, death in 1905. In 1907, just two years after that nostalgic trip, Henry jumped on an opportunity to purchase

Henry Sieben with daughter Margaret along Pole Creek at the Adel Ranch. Courtesy of the Hibbard family private collection.

the Cannon Brothers Ranch at Adel, located northeast of Cascade. For the first time, Henry purchased a ranch solely in his own name, without family members or business associates joining him in the venture. He finally owned the "hole in the wall."

Montana newspapers reported on the remarkable purchase. Henry paid Charles and Henry Cannon $87,500 ($2.9 million in today's value) for the Adel Ranch. Henry's recent sale of his shares in the Diamond Ranch to Frank Arnette undoubtedly supplied much of this cash investment. The purchase included 16,000 acres of land and 1,735 head of cattle. Like Henry, the Cannon brothers were wealthy and influential self-made men who resided in Helena. They arrived in Montana Territory with Charles Cannon eking out a successful living as a baker in Helena's mining camp while his brother, Henry Cannon, worked in the cattle business. Together, they purchased land west of Helena that figured largely in the making of their fortunes. Henry Cannon invested profitably in cattle and both brothers were known as cautious and frugal businessmen.[34] Having made such a substantial gamble on the Adel Ranch, it was not surprising that Henry got to work straightaway in ensuring its prosperity. Henry brought in 2,200 head of sheep from Chinook plus 712 head of cattle and forty-five bucks from the Sieben & Grimes ranch. A fellow rancher in the Wolf Creek area, Don Brown, painted a vivid picture of Henry as a man of action, never accepting complacency: "He walked active. He has action you know. There's something about him . . . Henry Sieben moved quick when he was going."[35]

From the years 1907 to 1912, Henry actively participated in the establishment of the Adel Ranch as one of the largest and most successful sheep and cattle ranches in Montana. Fortunately, a post office had been established at Adel in 1896, which enabled Henry's crew to stay in relatively constant communication with their boss and surrounding communities. The post office was housed in the home of Jimmy and Bessie Birch. Bessie was the only postmaster at Adel and Jimmy held the contract to deliver mail via wagon from Cascade to Adel twice a week.[36]

Nature, it seems, conspired with Henry as he built his new stock operation at the Adel Ranch and expanded his holdings at the Mitchell Place from 1909 to 1916. It was a time of ample rainfall, averaging sixteen inches of precipitation a year. Furthermore, the rains came at the right time, during the late spring and early summer. In 1909, total wheat production in Montana reached nearly eleven million bushels.

Newcomers naively assumed this was the normal, predictable climate in Montana. However, forty years of experience on the range had taught Henry better. He understood the fortunate weather conditions would not last.[37]

The first order of business for Henry was to put an efficient and trustworthy crew together to run the Adel Ranch. Henry was known as one of the best livestock operators and ranch managers in the state and somebody who had the knack for hiring good men who stayed with him. Henry's pocketbooks for 1907 to 1911 indicate he made numerous trips to the Adel Ranch during that time, sometimes going every three to four weeks when the weather allowed. Those records indicate that within just a couple of weeks of purchasing the Adel Ranch, Henry had hired a steady and regular crew of workers. Some of the regular crew included Herbert Gilmore, Henry Iverson, William Pritchard, and Jack Schumacher. These men built stables and corrals, threshed hay, sheared sheep, shoed horses, herded cattle, and worked as blacksmiths and cooks.

Henry Sieben (third from the right) poses with the Adel Ranch crew, ca. 1912. Courtesy of the Hibbard family private collection.

One of the men included on Henry's regular labor roster was Alberta's younger brother, Merrill Gordon. Henry made Merrill the first foreman of the Adel Ranch. Merrill had by now spent nearly a decade in Montana, proving himself to Henry as a hardy and industrious person, first at the Diamond Ranch and then putting in fence lines for Henry at the Mitchell Place. A neighboring rancher in Cascade, Frank Sterling, recalled the reasons why Merrill and Henry's successive foremen thrived at the Adel Ranch: "Because he had foremen that stayed at Adel ranch . . . he [the foreman] had full control of everything. He could run the place without Mr. Sieben and [the foreman] listened to . . . and thought a lot of Mr. Sieben."[38]

As Henry assembled his crew, he also stocked and equipped the ranch, making the purchases locally from Cascade Mercantile Co. as well as from Holter Hardware and the T.C. Power Co. in Helena. Supplies ranged from items such as salt for preserving meat, to newspapers, to even a tea kettle. Henry also bought materials necessary for the teams to efficiently carry out their tasks. Henry spent thousands of dollars providing lumber and other materials for the crews to construct and repair buildings, batteries to operate tools, blacksmithing tools, and cow-whips. In addition to everyday materials, Henry also invested in either improving existing farm and ranch equipment or purchasing new ones. Henry paid $650 ($20,000 today's value) for a grain separator, $300 ($10,000 today's value) for six wagons, $140 ($5,000 today's value) for two sulky plows, $70 ($2,300 today's value) for two Fresno scrapers, $60 ($2,000 today's value) for a mowing machine, $45 ($1,500) for a grinder, and $30 ($1,000) for four walking plows.

In the midst of hiring crews and supplying the Adel Ranch, Henry significantly increased his livestock holdings from 1907 to 1911. In 1907, Henry stocked forty-two horses at the Adel Ranch that included nineteen work horses, eight saddle horses, four unbroken mares, and eleven colts. His horses alone were worth $2,860 (approximately $100,000 today). By 1910, the herd increased to forty-eight horses at the ranch, ranging in value from $50 ($1,600 today's value) to a stallion worth $650 ($20,000 today's value). Henry entered one of his prized stallions into the "aged stallion" category of the Montana Livestock Fair held in Bozeman in 1913 and won third place. Cattle became an important component of the Adel Ranch. In July 1907, Henry recorded 594 cows, 346 yearlings, and 262 steers at Adel. By 1908, Henry had 1,253 cattle of a wide variety. This consisted of 100 branded calves, 129 heifers, 257 cows and calves, 286 yearlings, 149 two-year-old steers, 120 three-year-old steers, and 212 dry cows. His only tally number for cattle in 1910 is a total cattle count of 607 and a single bull.

While horses and cattle formed a portion of the Adel Ranch's livestock numbers, they paled in comparison with the thousands of sheep there. In November 1907, Henry stocked 2,920 ewes and forty-five bucks. By January 1908, that number increased to 5,163 ewes and lambs and fifty-one bucks. The Adel Ranch sheep numbers had increased to a total of 8,813 by end of year 1910. This number included a wide range of wethers, lambs, two-year-old ewes, and one-year-old ewes. Henry purchased several different breeds of bucks so he could produce a variety of wool types. In 1910, his preferred buck was a Cotswold sheep—a long wool breed that historically grazed in the Cotswold hills of England known for its long, lustrous fleece and mild-flavored meat. Henry also owned Rambouillets, a popular sheep breed in Montana known for their quality wool as well as their meat. Besides these two popular sheep breeds, Henry recorded owning five "scrub" sheep—likely "Florida Cracker" sheep. This hardy breed could withstand heat and cold, high wind, poor forage, and drought. Henry's Cotswolds were worth $28.75 ($950 today's value) a head while the scrubs were just $4 ($130 today's value) a head. At the end of 1911, Henry owned 9,883 sheep at the Adel Ranch.

Shipping sheep or wool from the Adel Ranch was quite an arduous endeavor that required cooperation from neighbors to load at the railroad loading facilities at Craig or Cascade. Both were arduous twenty-mile journeys over the mountains. Frank Sterling, the rancher near Craig, recalled that Henry ran an average of 10,000 sheep at the ranch, and his crew usually brought down 4,000 sheep in the fall to ship. Henry's crew trailed the sheep in two bands of 2,000 sheep each. Sterling kept one band in his corrals and the other band stayed in corrals at Craig. The sheep and crew rested overnight before the crew loaded and shipped the sheep the next day. Henry also paid Frank Sterling to provide summer pasture for some his sheep. Frank routinely pastured two bands of Henry's sheep for a few months in the spring and then took them back to the Adel Ranch to be sheared in June. Once sheared, Frank trailed them back to Craig and kept them until October when he would return them to the Adel Ranch.

Frank Sterling remembered Henry as a very good neighbor, which was invaluable in those days as they "could always figure out some way if one or the other of us were in trouble with stock . . . and they would help us. We'd help them and they would help us."[39] And those times certainly arose. One winter, Henry shipped sheep to Washington to winter, and when they were shipped back in the spring, the snow in Craig made the journey back to the Adel Ranch impossible. Sterling invited Henry to bring the sheep to his ranch where he corralled two bands and kept watch over them for three weeks until the snow cleared.

Red Wolrich, a former crew member at the ranch, recalled the hard work it took to ship wool. He remembered it took a team of three or four wagons and four horses an entire day to bring wool to Cascade.

The crew stored the wool in a stock house, loaded up 4,000 pounds of salt for the ranch, and then made a two-day trek back to the Adel Ranch. Again, they loaded more wool and returned to Cascade. Once back in town, they piled the two loads of wool as high as they could into boxcars for shipping.[40] If Henry's records are any indication, the crew made numerous trips back and forth to load wool every season.

Henry shipped vast amounts of wool to market in 1910, 1911, and 1912. In 1910 he shipped 60,000 pounds of wool worth $9,398.02 ($307,000 today's value), and in 1911 he shipped 58,000 pounds. Henry recorded in his pocketbook for 1912 that he sheared 9,074 sheep and produced 126,085 pounds of wool. His shipping exposed him to a new opportunity. Henry purchased shares in a National Wool Waterhouse and Storage Company in Chicago in 1910. The company was organized to provide warehouses where sheep men could store their clips (large piles of wool sheared from many sheep) instead of sending them on consignment to the eastern buyers. By purchasing shares in the company, Henry received profits on his investment as well as reduced costs of storing and handling wool. The Mitchell Place and Adel Ranch were now firmly established among the largest sheep and wool producing outfits in the state.[41]

Henry Sieben, loading sheep at Adel Ranch, August 1926. Courtesy of the Hibbard family private collection.

With growing operations at both ranches and mounting success, Henry decided to incorporate the Sieben Live Stock Company in October 1909. He dissolved the Sieben Sheep and Cattle Co. in the process. The new company had an authorized capital of $50,000 and included just three initial people—Henry as president, Alberta as secretary, and Merrill K. Gordon as foreman.

At the time, Alberta continued to be the heart and soul of Helena society, and her work ethic illustrated her industriousness, aptitude, and care for the causes and people she loved. Alberta had spent the last two decades showcasing her diverse skillset in Helena by hosting weekly social events that ranged in scale from card parties in her home to organizing balls in honor of charities. She was also a leader in many important organizations. She served as president of the Ladies' Auxiliary of the Montana Children's Home Society, an organization dear to Henry and one he was proud she led and expanded in her tenure as president.

Alberta was also contributing in Henry's business circles. In 1908, Alberta chaired the committee that entertained the wives and daughters of sheep men in town for the annual Woolgrowers Association meeting. In 1911, Alberta sought to share information on preventing the spread of tuberculosis, a disease that was circulating widely in towns across the nation, particularly in towns where people lived and worked close together with inadequate sewers and polluted water. Montana had recently passed a law making it illegal to dump raw sewage into rivers people used for drinking water. The law was one of the first clean water acts passed in the country. Alberta and Henry felt passionately that Helena should have access to clean water, and so Alberta helped bring a speaker from the National Association for the Prevention and Study of Tuberculosis to Helena to discuss the importance of recent legislation and providing proper sanitation. An exhibition of real-life photos and objects were on display, and all Helena schoolchildren attended the exhibition.

Alberta's philanthropic endeavors dovetailed with Henry's interest in improving Helena's amenities by attracting professionals to Helena. Henry's endeavors in this matter included contributing to the building of the finest hotel in town (the Placer Hotel); providing $200 ($6,500 today's value) to the fundraising efforts in 1912 to build a permanent campus for the Montana Wesleyan University near the capitol building on the eastside of Helena; and donating $500 ($14,500 today's value) in 1916 to the construction of the Marlow Theater. Alberta's organizational skills and her varied experience benefited the Sieben Live Stock Company. Henry tried to instill a love of the Adel Ranch and Mitchell Place in Alberta and his daughters. He could only dream that those efforts would ensure the ranches remain in his family even today.[42]

After purchasing the Adel Ranch in 1907, the entire Sieben family spent at least two or three weeks there every summer. Margaret recalled they could not stay longer because the cook was too busy with the hay crew and Henry did not want to add to her demands. The family traveled to the ranch via train and stagecoach. It wasn't long before Margaret and Berneice began to view the Adel Ranch and the Mitchell Place as second homes. Margaret recalled the family taking the Great Northern train from Helena to Cascade. There was a conductor selling candies and peanuts on the train who pointed out all the places of interest along the journey. Margaret recalled that when they traveled through the Chestnut Valley, the conductor, knowing Henry was on the train, pointed to a little cabin on the Missouri River and called it out as "Sieben's Bottom." Margaret and Berneice were tickled by the information. When the Siebens arrived at Cascade, they stayed overnight at the Cascade Hotel. Margaret was not fond of the accommodation, recalling: "That was terrible because there were many more bed bugs than there were people staying in the hotel."[43] The next morning, the hotel provided breakfast and a picnic lunch for their stagecoach journey to the Adel Ranch. The stagecoach was a wagon and Margaret and Berneice sat on blankets on the back for the ride. On one rainy trip, Margaret and Berneice had to get out of the wagon and remove the thick mud from the spokes of the coach's wheels.

When the family arrived at the Adel Ranch, they stayed in the old home. There was no electricity or running water in the house. Instead, they had a pump in the kitchen and filled bowls and pitchers as needed.

There was no bathroom, just a privy behind the home. Heat was secured from wood stoves. Margaret and Berneice spent their days riding all over the ranch with their father. Margaret recalled that she had "nothing but happy memories of all of that. It wasn't hard work, we all just pitched in and that was just the way it was . . . we just loved every bit of it."[44] As Montana's road infrastructure improved in the early 1900s, the Sieben family soon traveled to the ranches in a machine Henry could never have dreamed possible he would own—an automobile.

It is not known precisely when the first automobile appeared in Montana, but by 1913, there were over 6,000 vehicles registered to Montanans. As early as August 1910, *The Great Falls Leader* reported that Henry and his family had visited Great Falls for a few hours, arriving by automobile. Henry was likely among the first Montana residents to own and operate an automobile. Henry always had an eye to the future, and given his love of tools, technology, and societal improvements it is not surprising that in 1913 he purchased the latest model Stevens-Duryea from the Silver-Bow Automobile Company. The new car was a seven-passenger model CC. Automobile travel was confined to cities and towns in those early days. Long distance trips like Henry's to Great Falls in 1910 were rare, an endeavor for only the most adventurous. The most serious obstacle to drivers at the time was the lack of good roads, something Henry soon learned on a fateful trip on August 1, 1911.[45]

On that day, Henry and Alberta were riding in an automobile on a public road near Prickly Pear Schoolhouse on Canyon Creek Road, just a few miles from the mining town of Marysville. Henry and a teenager, C.J. Keyes, who was employed as a chauffeur, were in the front seat while Alberta likely enjoyed the ride in the back. Henry decided he wanted to drive for a while, so he and C.J. exchanged seats. William Shean was driving a horse-drawn wagon in the opposite direction, and at a narrow point in the road, Henry came upon the man suddenly. He was driving at twenty-five miles per hour, and the car startled Shean's horses so badly they threw Shean from the wagon to the ground. The horses backed up on William Shean and trampled him. He died six days later. Henry and Alberta were devastated by the incident.

In one of the last photographs taken of Henry and Alberta together (Henry at the wheel, Alberta second from right), they are enjoying an automobile outing with friends, spring 1911. Courtesy of the Hibbard and Baucus family private collection.

In November 1912, William Shean's teenage daughters, Mabel and Edna, filed a suit against Henry and Fred E. Kessler (who was administrator for the Sieben estate) for $15,000 ($500,000 today's value). They argued their father lost his life through the negligence and carelessness of the drivers. Their attorney posited that Henry and C.J. did not sound the horn or use ordinary care in the operation or speed of the machine. Henry settled the case, but the event deeply troubled him, and from that point onwards he always used a chauffeur to drive for him.[46]

In the winter of 1911, Alberta was in ill health. Her doctor believed it was rheumatism of the throat. It got increasingly worse over the following months to the point where she could hardly swallow. Henry decided to take the family to Los Angeles where Alberta could visit specialist doctors. The whole family hoped the climate would improve Alberta's condition. The family left on December 28, 1911. Henry's pocketbooks reveal that most of January and February were spent consulting different doctors but to no avail.

Alberta's health continued to deteriorate, and she was admitted to Pottinger Sanitarium. Specialists at the facility diagnosed Alberta as having contracted anthrax. Margaret recalled that while at the ranches, Alberta had a habit of pulling up hay as she walked and eating the white ends. The doctors believed she likely picked up anthrax from infected cattle. Henry returned to Montana on March 10 for business, leaving Margaret and Berneice to visit their mother daily. A group of local ladies took the girls under their wing in Henry's absence. When he returned later that spring, Henry knew the outlook was poor. Toward the end, Alberta could scarcely swallow or talk to her family. At the age of forty-eight, Alberta died on the morning of May 31, 1912.[47]

Henry sent an urgent telegram to Alberta's sister, Florence, in Helena, and the local newspapers soon reported her unexpected death. The funeral was held at the Sieben family home with several hundred friends attending to pay their respects. Alberta's remains were taken to the nearby Forestvale cemetery for internment. Pallbearers included Henry's longtime friends A.K. Prescott, J.H. Longmaid, N.J. Gould, and Frank K. Turner. Margaret remembered snippets from the day. She recalled the difficulty the men had in getting the casket down the steps of their home to the waiting car. She remembered how difficult it was for her and Berneice to see their mother on display in the parlor of their home.[48] Henry left no record of his feelings on this devastating blow to his family. The only entry he made in his pocketbooks about Alberta's death reads "Mamma passed away 5:30 A.M."[49]

Life went on for the Henry Sieben family, however. Berneice continued attending a finishing school at Mount Vernon in Washington D.C. and Henry ensured that Alberta's wish for Margaret to attend Dana Hall in Massachusetts was fulfilled. Margaret left in fall of 1912, just months after her mother's death. Henry threw himself into work, allowing himself scarcely any time alone to dwell on the loss of his wife. First, he immersed himself in financial roles that occupied his time while he was in Helena. Henry had been appointed director of the Conrad Trust & Savings Bank in 1910 and reveled in his role as a bank director. In fact, he enjoyed the work and company of like-minded businessmen so much he accepted the position of director at the American National Bank in 1912. His fellow directors included good friends T.C. Power, Louis Heitman, A.C. Johnson, and N.J. Gould. When the weather allowed, Henry frequently traveled back and forth to his ranches at the Mitchell Place and the Adel Ranch. He focused on expanding his sheep holdings and wool production at both of those properties.[50] ❖

Chapter 8

1915–1937

"HE KNEW WHEN HE HAD THE BEST HAND AND HE PLAYED IT HARD"

During and immediately after World War I was a complicated time for the Sieben family and for Montana. A severe drought, war, and Prohibition combined to produce a serious economic depression in Montana and the Northern Plains. The agricultural boom turned to bust, the flood of immigration reversed itself, and many Montanans faced hard times. At a personal level, life was also changing rapidly in front of Henry's eyes. As he approached seventy years old, Henry was now a widower, lived alone, and his dear friends were passing away. On top of that, Berneice and Margaret were establishing their own families. In his typical pragmatic and progressive manner, Henry met these changes head on. Amid the swirling tides around him, he remained the steady, industrious, and intentional anchor at the middle of it all, guiding himself and others through the challenges.

Shortly after Alberta's death in 1912, Henry had begun to reckon with the fact that Berneice and Margaret would soon leave his home to start their own lives. Furthermore, Henry's social circles had gotten increasingly smaller. He still regularly met with friends and business associates at the American National Bank and Montana Club, but he was never at ease socializing with family friends alone. Henry was lonely and longed for a partner with whom he could share his life and family. As luck would have it, a local woman by the name of Jessie Dean Green offered Henry another shot at finding happiness in the last chapter of

Henry Sieben portrait (artist unknown), ca. 1930. Courtesy of the Hibbard family private collection.

his life. Jessie was born in 1864 in Minnesota, the year Henry had traveled to Montana. She moved with her parents to Deep Creek Valley near Townsend in the early 1880s and married railroad contractor William Henry Green in 1884. The couple moved to Helena where they had three daughters, Gertrude Carroll (who died in infancy), Verna Ellsworth, and Dorothy Dean. William died unexpectedly in 1894, leaving his family in financial peril. Jessie trained herself in secretarial skills and took a position as assistant manager of the A.M. Holter Hardware Company, which is where she likely met Henry. Not only was Henry a friend of Anton Holter, he was also a regular customer at the hardware store in the early 1900s. Jessie was known for her competence in business dealings as well as her kind and charming demeanor—traits Henry undoubtedly appreciated. Henry wed Jessie in an intimate family gathering at St. Peter's Episcopal Church on July 14, 1915. The couple celebrated their marriage by traveling to California and Seattle in fall 1915.

Henry was practical and direct with Jessie about the financial aspect of their union. He had worked for decades to build his business enterprises and was forthright about the fact he would ensure those enterprises remained in his daughters' hands. Henry's goal was to avoid misunderstandings or ambiguity after his death. Henry's betrothed agreed, and two days before their wedding, Henry and Jessie signed a prenuptial agreement. The terms agreed to by both parties included if Henry passed before Jessie and they had remained married before his death, she, or upon her death her heirs, would receive $15,000 (roughly half a million dollars today). After this lump sum payment, Jessie would receive $3,000 (nearly $100,000 today) per year for the remainder of her lifetime.

Berneice and Margaret were happy for their father and supportive of his marriage to Jessie. In fact, the Siebens had known the Green family for quite some time. Jessie's daughter Dorothy, known as "Dolly," was a friend of Berneice's and even joined the Sieben family on a trip to Yellowstone in 1909. Margaret recalled Jessie was very different from Alberta, describing Jessie as a smart "businesswoman" who had raised her children alone and singlehandedly made enough money to provide them with a wonderful education. Margaret believed Jessie had her eye on Henry for quite some time and that she got what she wanted. Berneice and Margaret were very fond of Jessie, but they could never call her mother. Instead, they settled on *"Madre."*

It did not take long for Jessie to integrate into Henry's social circle. She also carved out a philanthropic role for herself. By 1916, just a year after marrying Henry, Jessie had taken up the cause close to Henry's

Three years after Alberta's death, Henry married Jessie Green. Pictured here from left to right: Margaret Sieben, General Gregory, Jessie Green Sieben, Verna Green, Henry Sieben, Berneice Sieben, and A. T. Hibbard. Courtesy of the Hibbard family private collection.

heart—supporting the Montana Children's Home. Jessie worked with Alberta's friends and family, including Alberta's sister, Florence, to organize fundraiser balls for the Children's Home. Jessie joined the YWCA finance committee and brought back conviviality and parties to the Sieben home. Henry and Jessie hosted dinners with friends, and Jessie threw bridge parties. Jessie's company and support grounded Henry at a time when he needed it most. Jessie's daughter Dolly Green also lived with the Siebens for a number of years and was an accomplished violinist.[1]

Time took some of Henry's closest friends in the stock industry. The deaths one after another highlighted the fact that time marched on regardless of how young Henry still felt. In the three years prior to his marriage to Jessie, Henry was honorary pallbearer for numerous close friends, including his longtime associate D.A.G. Floweree, miner John Longmaid, and rancher Jesse I. Phelps. Phelps's tragic death by suicide in 1915 had particularly rattled Henry and his daughters. Jesse Phelps's wife had passed away the previous year, and local newspapers reported that Phelps, unable to get over her death, shot and killed himself at his home at 433 Lawrence Street. Henry and Jesse Phelps had been longtime friends and business associates and lived just four blocks from one another.[2]

Henry's daughters also soon married. The first celebration centered on Berneice's nuptials to Fred Sheriff in June 1915. Once Fred completed his degree in mechanical engineering at the University of Wisconsin in 1912, he returned to Helena and got a job working with the Banking Corporation. He was now ready to propose to Berneice, and the couple were engaged in June 1915. Berneice and Fred married at the Sieben home in Helena, just six weeks before Henry and Jessie's marriage. Alberta's sister, Florence, and her sister-in-law, Sarah Kessler, along with Fred's mother and sister helped Margaret organize the big day for Berneice.

But Berneice probably needed little help from others. She had learned well from her mother and exquisitely decorated the family home for her wedding. According to the *Independent Record*[3], every available space was adorned with vines and flowers such as pink and white honeysuckles as well as white lilacs. The bridal party, with Margaret as maid of honor and her cousins, Louise and Helen Kessler, as flower girls, descended the staircase of the home to Mendelssohn's wedding march. Last to come down the stairs was Henry who proudly held his daughter's arm as they made their way to the drawing room where the pastor of the Unitarian church waited to officiate the ceremony. Berneice wore an elegant gown of white satin with tulle sleeves and a tulle pointed tunic with sprays of orange blossoms. After the ceremony and wedding dinner concluded, the younger generation of guests danced in the ballroom on the third floor. Berneice and Fred enjoyed a short wedding trip to Hamilton, Montana, before returning to Helena to begin their lives together.

Since his arrival in the territory in 1864, Henry's goal had been to establish long-term financial security for himself and his family. When he purchased the lot for the Sieben home at 520 Harrison Avenue in

Berneice Sieben around the time of her marriage to Fred Sheriff in 1915. Courtesy of the Hibbard and Baucus family private collection.

1898, he also bought the available property around it to ensure his family could also live in the area. As a wedding gift to his daughter, Henry gave Berneice Lots 1 and 2 in block "O" of the Mauldin Addition of Helena—essentially two homes at 700 and 704 Power Avenue. In the official deed, Henry wrote the gift was in consideration "of the love and affection which [Henry] has and bears unto [Berneice]," and to ensure Berneice's "better maintenance, support, protection, and livelihood." Henry had grown up with so little and was always determined to provide more for his children. Berneice and Fred moved into their home at 704 Power Street.[4]

Just a couple of years later, A.T. Hibbard proposed to Henry's younger daughter, Margaret. Margaret declared that her decision to marry A.T. was the "best thing I ever did."[5] During the early 1900s, Wednesdays were considered the "wedding" day, and so on Wednesday, August 1, 1917, Margaret and A.T. married at St. Peter's Episcopal Church in Helena. As with Berneice's wedding two years earlier, Henry hosted a beautiful celebration in honor of his daughter's nuptials. Margaret's bridal party consisted of her cousins, Louise and Helen, as well as close friends. Berneice did not take part in the bridal party, as she had just given birth to a daughter, Jean, a few weeks earlier. In the early 1900s, women usually did not resume social activity for at least a month

Margaret Sieben on the day of her marriage to A.T. Hibbard in 1917. Courtesy of the Hibbard family private collection.

after giving birth. Berneice did, however, attend the wedding reception at the Sieben home, and Fred Sheriff was A.T.'s best man. Henry had the honor of giving Margaret away. Margaret wore a gown of silver cloth and had a long tulle veil with a dainty spray of orange blossoms. Her bridal party were dressed in pink charmeuse. For the reception, the Sieben home was beautifully decorated with roses and gladiolas, and the lawn was lit with Japanese lanterns while Madame Ericke-Zimmerman's orchestra played throughout the evening. After a short honeymoon to Glacier National Park, Margaret and A.T. returned to Helena where they rented temporarily at 814 Gilbert Street before moving into their home at 626 North Benton. Just as he had with Berneice after she married, Henry also helped Margaret purchase her first home. All members of the Sieben family had found partners with whom they would navigate a new and complex chapter of their family's and Montana's story.[6]

Since the early 1900s, Henry and Alberta, alongside many thoughtful Montanans, had taken up the cause of reform to combat rising social problems. Progressives, including many women particularly in homestead communities, viewed saloons and alcohol as social evils, and they wanted to remove them through Prohibition. The campaign had gained strength during the Progressive period of the early 1900s, and when Montanans voted on the referendum in November 1916, they overwhelmingly approved the prohibition of alcoholic beverages. Montana went "dry" at the end of 1918, and in 1920 Prohibition became national law through the Eighteenth Amendment to the United States Constitution.

Henry's family had remained very close with Alberta's sister, Florence, her husband, Fred Kessler, and her brother-in-law, Charles Kessler. They witnessed firsthand the devastating impact Prohibition had on the Kessler Brewery, one of the state's first and longest-running brewing operations. After Prohibition went into effect in January 1919, the U.S. Collector of Internal Revenue certified the destruction of 588 gallons of Kessler beer and the brewery closed.

Despite Prohibition, one of Henry's most important social outlets had always been, and was still, the Montana Club. It was here that he

Henry Sieben was known to enjoy a game of cards and to gamble with his friends, as seen here at a game of poker in Helena, ca. 1932. Courtesy of the Montana Historical Society Library & Archives, PAc 2006-15.03.

met with his old-time friends and business peers to play the card game "solo" (which originated in Germany) as well as poker.

Conrad Kohrs was the leader of the card playing group at the Montana Club that called themselves the "Juvenile Club." Even though the group was made up of some of Helena's most distinguished businessmen, it is clear they did not take themselves too seriously. This is particularly evident in a witty article that appeared in the *Montana-Record Herald* a few years earlier in May 1915. The piece shared that T.C. Power had been admitted "on probation" to the Juvenile Club in 1914, and on his seventy-sixth birthday in 1915, the group admitted him to full membership. They also gifted him seventy-six carnations and joked he was the youngest man among the old-timers. The men continued to gather throughout Prohibition. Margaret remembered that her father and his friends never played for money; instead, the loser bought the drinks for the group. Henry may have told his daughter that story, but his pocketbooks throughout the years of Prohibition tell another.

They indicate the men played for money (but never too much for frugal Henry). Henry frequently noted his losses and takings and was particularly pleased with himself in summer of 1927 when he recorded that he rarely lost and took home $81.60 (nearly $1,500 today) in winnings.

The Juvenile Club looked forward to meeting with the well-known and liked bartender Julian Anderson, who had presided over the bar in the elegant reading room and the Rathskeller, the club's speakeasy-style basement watering hole since the club's opening in 1893. Anderson had an impeccable reputation for crafting superb cocktails and, in 1919, he even published his drinks recipes in a small, twenty-page volume titled *Julian's Recipes. Julian's Recipes* was just the second book of cocktails to be published by an African American and was a point of pride for the club, enhancing its status and that of Helena as a cosmopolitan city. Unfortunately for Anderson, this was just as Prohibition came into effect. But even though prohibitionists concluded they had securely won, it failed across the country, and nowhere more spectacularly than in Montana, even among the well-to-do members of the Montana Club.[7]

Once Prohibition took effect, Julian Anderson's job title was abruptly modified to "elevator operator," but the only thing Anderson apparently transported between floors was members' illicit stores of booze from their hidden basement lockers. In November 1920, Henry recorded in his pocketbook a $10 ($150 today's value) donation for Julian at the Montana Club. Without public bar service, Julian was not earning tips, and the collection was likely an effort on the part of club members to ensure Julian could continue working at the business and was still being adequately compensated. Throughout the 1920s, Henry recorded cash entries to his friend Louis Heitman in his pocketbooks for beer and the Juvenile Club kept a stash of liquor underneath Jackson Street. The group sometimes met at one another's homes for card games where they raffled one of the bottles.

"Whiskey roads" that stretched across the United States-Canada border became commonplace in Montana throughout the 1920s.

Prohibition failed in the hard-drinking state of Montana. Alcohol flowed openly in working-class towns such as Butte and Havre and in government towns such as Helena. When Prohibition ended in 1933, most Montanans, including Henry, were relieved. But Prohibition was not the only drastic change to occur in Montana in the second decade of the twentieth century. When war erupted in Europe during the summer of 1914, Montana quickly felt the impact.

The onset of World War I created a sudden and substantial demand for Montana's metals, lumber, and wheat from the United States' allies. Montana's mines, sawmills, and farms all increased production to meet the demand, and nearly 40,000 Montana men including thousands of Native Americans went to war. This accounted for ten percent of Montana's population, a greater percentage than any other state. Henry's son-in-law A.T. Hibbard enlisted in the U.S. Army in 1917 to serve as second lieutenant in the Quartermaster Corps, and Henry's chauffeur, James Trenary, was selected to enlist in the hospital corps of the U.S. Navy. While most Montanans supported the war, believing it would lead to lasting peace, many people openly opposed the nation's involvement in the effort.

In Montana, as elsewhere, German-Americans and suspected opponents of war were pestered. Will Campbell, editor of the *Helena Independent,* wrote fiery editorials condemning anyone who did not support the war and accused foreigners of being spies. On September 9, 1917, he wrote, "Are the Germans about to bomb the capital of Montana?" and offered $100 ($2,500 today's value) to anyone who could spot German aircraft circling over Helena. County committees of the Montana Council of Defense began patrolling for spies in their communities and encouraged people to report non-conformists and anyone who seemed suspicious or unpatriotic. People quickly took advantage and figured out they could turn in neighbors for any reason.

Germans in Montana were victims of various and serious attacks. The Council drew up rules for all Montanans to follow during wartime. They banned dancing, parades, and public assemblies. They even prohibited speaking the German language in schools, churches, or at private gatherings. The thousands of German-speaking immigrants who populated rural Montana were not allowed to speak their own language—even in church—for two years.[8]

The anti-German sentiment of the era rattled Henry. He left Germany when he was five years old and showed little interest in cultivating his native language or culture in his life in Montana. In contrast to some of his German immigrant friends such as Conrad Kohrs, who traveled to Germany for extended stays with his family in the late 1800s, there is no evidence to suggest Henry ever returned to his homeland, joined a German fraternity, read a German newspaper, or encouraged Berneice or Margaret to engage with their heritage.[9] Therefore, it is unlikely Henry was the direct subject of anti-German sentiments, but he certainly felt ethnic tension during the war years. In fact, Henry left no pocketbook from 1918. It may have been misplaced over the years (pocketbooks from the years 1898–1900 and 1930–44 are also missing) or he intentionally did not keep a pocketbook during that fraught year. Another possibility is he destroyed it.

Until World War I, Helena had a thriving German ethnic community. As early as 1878, a local German immigrant, Miss Molitor, offered German language lessons to children at the schoolhouse. And in 1893, a German language school opened on 668 North Rodney. German language newspapers were also popular, with the *Montana Freie Presse* circulating in the 1880s and the *Staats-Zeitung* in the early 1900s, particularly among the town's southside German-speaking district. A local branch of the Sons of Hermann lodge held picnics, festivals, and balls. But in the face of World War I–era suppression and violence, German language newspapers ceased publication, and the Sons of Hermann lodges and other German-American organizations disbanded statewide.[10]

Shortly after Margaret and A.T.'s marriage in summer 1917, A.T. enlisted in the U.S. Army and was stationed on the East Coast throughout the war. Margaret stopped renting their home on 814 Gilbert Street and moved back home to 520 Harrison Avenue. In fall 1918, Margaret received word from A.T. that he was to be deployed overseas imminently and wanted to see her. Henry and Jessie encouraged her to go, and so

Margaret packed up some of her belongings and traveled to Florida, stopping for a time to visit a friend in Louisville. The army made her wait quite a time in Louisville before she could visit her husband. Not only was a war engulfing the country, an international debacle of different sorts had also struck: influenza.

As the troops began to return in 1918, they brought the Spanish Flu with them. The virus, now confirmed as H1N1, was particularly deadly to those between the ages of twenty and forty. Hospitals were full to overflowing, funeral homes ran out of caskets, and children, suddenly orphaned, were roaming the streets. In the United States, more than 675,000 people died, and the Spanish Flu took the lives of 100 million people worldwide. A.T.'s brother, Harrell, died due to complications of the flu that year. The army was understandably reluctant to allow soldiers' wives to visit. Eventually, Margaret was given permission to go to Florida. She traveled by train and described the horrific images engrained in her memory of coffins piled up like cord wood in the station. Apart from A.T.'s brother, Harrell, Margaret was relieved that the rest of her family made it through the epidemic unscathed.[11]

The ending of World War I resulted in an international decline of farm prices, and drought replaced the ample rainfall of the previous decade. This combination of events produced a major depression in Montana and the Northern Plains. Henry knew it signaled the end of the homestead boom and the beginning of a new chapter in Montana's history—one of drought, wind, and poverty that would change the course of the state's development. But Henry's experience of the Hard Winter of 1886 to 1887 had prepared him for scenarios like this.

Henry understood that cycles of drought were a natural part of the Great Plains climate. Before and during the beginning of the homestead boom in 1909, Henry had been quietly and systematically growing his property portfolio and investing in an increasingly profitable sheep market. Now, ten years later, he was one of the state's largest sheep ranchers. Henry accomplished his goals with a penny-wise mindset and approach, never buying into the hysteria and excitement that encouraged farmers to go into debt to expand their farms.

Henry still had the energy of a man half his age. His daughters were married, and he wanted more than ever to divest his interests in the ranches and begin the process of transitioning ownership to the next generation, but Henry knew better than to act on feelings. His practicality kicked in, and as he took in events that were occurring locally, nationally, and internationally, he knew that now was not the time to hand over the business reins to the Sheriffs and Hibbards. Henry needed to lead operations and the ranch teams through the tumult for one final and monumental push. Along the way, he planned to gradually involve his daughters and sons-in-law and ensure the generational interest, stability, and success he had always dreamed of for his family and legacy. With Jessie's support, Henry dug in his heels for one last hurrah.[12]

When the drought cycle began in 1917, it mostly affected counties north of the Missouri River. It spread to the eastern two-thirds of the state in 1918, and by the following year, it affected the normally well-watered valleys of the western mountains. The drought had a devastating effect on crop production. Farmers accustomed to yields of twenty-five bushels of wheat to the acre averaged just 2.4 bushels per acre in 1919. Furthermore, forest fires swept across western Montana and high winds in 1920 whipped away topsoil. As if the natural devastation was not enough, economic instability following World War I brought additional headaches to Montanans. By 1920, Europe was once more supplying its own food needs, and grain and crop prices dropped dramatically in the United States Between August and October 1920, the price of a bushel of wheat dropped from $2.40 to $1.25 (approximately $40 to $20 today). Montana's mining and lumber towns also suffered. There was no more need for wartime raw materials, so companies shut down and unemployment numbers rose significantly. Montanans suffered and the government offered little assistance. The Wilson administration extended seed loans to local farmers from 1918 to 1920, but this aid barely scratched the surface of the overwhelming need. Many homesteaders had spent the last decade caught up in the excitement and seemingly endless good times, borrowing money that banks were only too pleased to supply. In summer 1919, 3,000 residents of

Hill County faced the oncoming winter without sufficient means of support.

From 1919 to 1925, Montana had the highest rate of bankruptcy in the nation, and roughly two million acres passed out of production and 11,000 farms, about twenty percent of the state's population, were vacated. Half of Montana farmers lost their land, and the average acre value of farmland fell by fifty percent. Banks also folded across the state. Between 1920 and 1926, more than half of the state's banks failed, taking thousands of family savings accounts down with them. An estimated 60,000 people left Montana during the 1920s, many moving on to Washington, Oregon, or California. As they departed, some homesteaders held up darkly humorous signs such as "Goodbye Old Dry!"

The postwar recession affected the entire country, but the national economy generally recovered by 1922. However, in Montana where agriculture is king, the recession lasted until the return of sufficient rainfall in the mid-1920s. Montana was the only state to lose population during the roaring twenties.[13] When discussing the fallout of the post-1919 era in Montana, Brian Hilger, a neighboring rancher, declared that Henry "was the only rancher in the state probably that didn't go broke in 1919." While Henry was not the "only" one, his frugality, ingenuity, and management skills ensured he was not one of the thousands of Montana ranchers and farmers who went bankrupt. Instead, Henry's strong financial standing enabled him to swoop in and buy up small ranches and homesteads from desperate owners at bargain prices. Henry gathered information from his ranch crews about farmers or ranchers who needed a quick sale. Additionally, as a director of the American National Bank and president of the Central Investment Company, he had invaluable insight on homesteaders and farmers who were defaulting. In fact, many of the ownership transfers of homestead lands within the Sieben & Grimes Ranch and possibly the Adel Ranch, were handled by Sieben's sons-in-law at the Montana Livestock Loan Company.[14]

One particularly insightful example of Henry's approach to land acquisition during these years was his purchase of Nicholas Hilger Jr.'s ranch in 1920. Hilger's father, Nicholas Hilger Sr., was a contemporary of Henry Sieben's. He arrived with his family to the territory in 1867, and they made their home in Helena where Nicholas Sr. served as a probate judge. In 1873, Hilger bought acreage, later known as the Hilger Ranch, at the Gates of the Mountains on the Missouri River. The Hilgers began raising cattle on the ranch and were soon also offering guided boat tours through the Gates of the Mountains. He launched the steamboat service "The Rose of Helena" on June 2, 1886. The business took off and his son Joe operated it. Over the years, the judge expanded his properties and in 1904 dispersed his property to three surviving sons, Nicholas Jr., David, and Joe.

Joe and his wife, Carrie, managed to hold onto and expand their ranch properties in the post–World War I era. David and Nicholas were not so fortunate. David had moved to Lewistown in Fergus County where he became a successful sheep producer and investor in real estate and banking. Despite his vast holdings, the drought of 1919 left him bankrupt. Nicholas Jr. inherited the home ranch at the Gates of the Mountains where he worked with Sieben and Grimes. The two ranches occasionally had troubles, but Nicholas Jr.'s son, Brian Hilger, recalled they got along "one way or another without too much problem." But two floods, one caused by the bursting of the Hauser Dam in 1908 and the other by the building of the Holter Dam from 1909 to 1918, flooded Nicholas Jr.'s hay ground forcing him to buy hay shipped from Minnesota at $60 ($1,200 today's value) per ton. Brian Hilger remembered his father borrowed money to buy a ranch across the divide, and as part of the purchase he got the hay to winter his cattle. Nicholas Jr. got most of his cattle through the winter storms of 1918 to 1919 expecting to sell in the spring. But beef prices went down and when spring came there was no market. Brian Hilger recalled that if his father had sold the cattle in fall 1918, he would have been all right. Instead, Nicholas Jr. tried to save the cattle, couldn't pay back the money he borrowed, and, like so many other ranchers and farmers at the time, lost everything. Henry Sieben bought Nicholas Jr.'s land on a tax deed from the company that loaned Nicholas the money. Fortunately, Brian and his siblings hung on to some parcels of land in the area and bought other homestead properties. Eventually, their land became mixed up with the Sieben & Grimes Ranch in a checkerboard pattern. As a result, cattle drifted onto Sieben land and Sieben sheep did the same on Hilger property. Finally, the two families got together and traded land in the early 1930s. This deal enabled them to square up the land and use it clearly and equitably, smoothing out neighborly relations thereafter.[15]

The Hilger story is just one example of many where Henry seized an opportunity to expand his holdings. But once frugal, always frugal. Brian Hilger described Henry as sometimes being "too conservative" in his approach to purchasing homestead land. According to Hilger, Henry often missed out on opportunities to expand the Sieben & Grimes Ranch as he did not want to pay homesteaders the price they sought. In one story, Hilger recalled that Henry Sieben had 320 acres of land in one section and then a homesteader by the name of Walker came in and took up a section that surrounded those 320 acres. The situation prevented Henry from accessing his land. When Walker asked Henry if he wanted to purchase his property, which included water rights, Henry told him he would pay $0.50 ($10 today's value) an acre. Walker was not happy with the offer and so he brought the same proposition to neighboring rancher, John Syness, who paid Walker $0.60 ($12 today's value) an acre. In another story, a female homesteader wanted to sell her land in the area for $3 an acre but Henry refused to pay more than $2 ($60 and $40 in today's value, respectively) an acre. Brian Hilger ended up purchasing that land. Hilger summed it up by stating, "[He] was a little too saving sometimes."[16]

With his many successes, Henry inevitably attracted the envy of others, particularly of those who were suffering during periods of great financial calamity. One livestock operator, Brian O'Connell, said "I would like to be like him . . . I would say they [people] might envy a man like that."[17] Merrill Gordon's daughter, Peggy Gordon Lestz, further expanded on this opinion stating that anyone who is successful has people who "want to gossip" and feel they "should be equally rich."[18] Henry's methods of acquiring and holding onto land did result in some ill feelings and complicated business transactions. For example, in 1900, two years after Henry and Thomas Grimes purchased the Mitchell Place from Martin A. Mitchell, they were forced to bring Mitchell to court as there were rumblings his children were claiming interest in the property. The District Court issued a decree stating that upon investigation of the case, it was discovered a clerk erroneously omitted Martin A. Mitchell's name from letters of administration and that descriptions of some portions of the land were incorrect. These mistakes were corrected. The judge declared Sieben and Grimes the rightful owners of all the Mitchell Place property Martin A. Mitchell sold to them in 1898 and stated that Martin A. Mitchell and his children were barred from claiming or asserting any interest in the premises.

A similar situation transpired after Henry's business partner, Thomas Grimes, died in 1921. After battling a long illness, Thomas Grimes died in November 1921 at the age of sixty-nine. He left behind a wife, a daughter, Edith, and two sons, Lee and Walter. Peggy Gordon Lestz recalled that after Henry bought out Thomas Grimes' share of their operation at the Mitchell Place, Lee Grimes's always held a grudge, believing he and his family should have gotten more than they received. Lestz claimed Lee was misguided about the amount of money the family should have made on the sale of their portion of the ranch. Minutes from the Sieben & Grimes Livestock Company (incorporated in 1915) indicate that while Thomas Grimes was alive, his wife, Eva B. Grimes, served on the board of directors along with Henry, Thomas Grimes, and Margaret Hibbard. Upon Thomas Grimes's death in 1921, Eva's children were also included on the board of directors. However, due to ill feelings between the two families, all members of the Grimes family had left the board by January 1923. The Sieben & Grimes Livestock Company was now solely run by the Siebens, Hibbards, and Sheriffs.

Henry's records, legal documents, and the testaments of others he worked with indicate he was a careful and efficient businessman who conducted his business affairs with professionalism. In Henry's mind, business was business, and he knew better than to pay heed to the noise of others. Furthermore, for every negative opinion, there were ten positive opinions that highlighted Henry's integrity and the respect with which he treated others. Business associate Brian O'Connell stated: "I admired him very much . . . he was a gentleman . . . just one of a kind." Rancher Royal Smith echoed those sentiments, stating Henry "was a great man." Instead of grandiose gestures of generosity, Henry quietly went about helping ranchers in need in his own inimitable style and with considerable impact.[19]

During those postwar recession years, Henry met most weekday mornings with his friends and business associates Louis Kaufman and Louis Stadler in the lobby of the Harvey Hotel on 10 North Main Street in Helena. The three old-time friends chatted about business and local news while sipping coffee in large rocking chairs in front of the glass front window that looked across at the Placer Hotel. Brian O'Connell described he would "get a kick out of listening to them,"[20] and rancher Don Brown, whose father had known Henry well in the early days of Montana, stated he always enjoyed talking with Henry and that "everybody always had a lot of respect for all three of them. They had done well, they came in . . . real early from Germany and they were always interesting too."[21] Henry's intentional visibility at the hotel most mornings and then at the American National Bank in the afternoons meant that people knew where to find him to ask advice and favors.

Rancher Royal Smith recalled a time during the drought years of the 1920s when he was in financial dire straits, and like many others in his situation the banks refused to lend to him. Instead, Royal Smith sought out Henry downtown, told him he needed $1,500 (approximately $20,000 today) and that he had stock as collateral. Henry looked him straight in the eye, put his hand in his pocket, and gave Smith the money there and then. Both men signed a note as a contract. Henry did this for many Montanans in similar situations. In the process, Henry became known as the "hip-pocket banker." Of course, Henry only gambled on good bets. Smith described him as a "good judge of people . . . he'd look a man straight in the eye and he'd know if he wanted anything to do with him or not."[22] Over the years, Smith often approached Henry at the bank or the hotel and asked for a

$100 ($1,500 today's value). Henry would just pull the money out of his pocket and give it to Smith.

In a similar situation a few years later, local rancher Don Brown let Henry know that he was in financial trouble but wanted to keep his cattle. He assured Henry he had plenty of feed and hay, and Henry let him know he would think about it. A little while went by and Don Brown, worried sick about his future, visited Henry at the American National Bank. Henry was chatting with A.T. Hibbard and Fred Sheriff at the time but welcomed Don Brown inside. Brown once again made his case for financial assistance. Henry responded by just quietly nodding yes at him and gave him the money. Don Brown described how he "had a warm spot in [his] heart for him after, always after that."[23] Henry knew better than anyone how just a little assistance and belief in someone during hard times could make all the difference. He had learned that lesson after the Hard Winter of 1886 to 1887 when the kindness and confidence of others had made all the difference to him. Henry's "hip-pocket banking" was his small but impactful way of contributing to the survival and success of those in dire straits like he had been all those years before.

Some of Henry's hip-pocket banking experiences also resulted in him acquiring some of the best crew he ever worked with. A Swedish man by the name of Pete Nelson had his own small sheep operation and, like Royal Smith, Don Brown, and many before and after him, Pete went to Henry for help during the lean years after World War I. Henry looked Pete over and agreed to lend him the money, but Pete couldn't pay Henry back and instead returned looking for more money. Henry said no. Instead, he told Pete he wanted him as a foreman at the Adel Ranch. Henry showed Pete his checkbook and told him to buy and sell as he pleased and not bother him. Royal Smith recalled that Henry told Pete, "You've got the ability, you've got the head, and you've got the money behind you."[24] Henry's instinct that Pete would steer the Adel Ranch through the postwar recession and beyond proved more than accurate.

Bill Shanklin, a former ranch hand who worked for Pete Nelson, described him as "one of the best foremen I ever worked for."[25]

Shanklin also recalled "he was the most efficient manager I ever knew" and remembered that no matter what Pete Nelson was doing on the ranch, if a storm or something else came up that meant he and the crew had to switch gears, Pete would have the entire team doing something else within fifteen minutes. During downtime at the ranch, Pete Nelson played Henry's favorite card game, solo, at the bunkhouse. If the ranch crew didn't want to play, their other option was to split wood for the fires instead. Not surprisingly, Bill Shanklin and many others opted for solo and spent many hours playing cards with Nelson. He had a gruff demeanor and a reputation for hollering instructions loudly and colorfully at his ranch crew, but Pete's hard exterior apparently hid his big heart. If any of the ranch herders went broke in the off-season in Helena, they sent word to Pete, who sent them money or told them to come back out to the ranch where he found something for them to do.

In addition to leading Henry's crew through the turbulent economic period of the 1920s and 1930s, it appears Pete Nelson may have also aided Henry in expanding the Adel Ranch. Royal Smith suggested Pete Nelson was responsible for Henry acquiring an adjacent 6,000-acre ranch, The Wooden Shoe, in 1920. The ranch was so named for the Belgians who brought their wooden shoes with them across the ocean and wore them at the ranch. The Wooden Shoe was a cattle and hay ranch owned by the Belgo-Montana Livestock Company. This momentous purchase greatly expanded Henry Sieben's footprint in the area, enlarging the ranch all the way south to Stickney Creek near Craig.

With the departure of so many homesteaders in the 1920s, it was difficult for Pete Nelson to hire and retain ranch crew for the expanding operation at the Adel Ranch. Henry and Pete enticed workers by offering them a steady job, good wages, and the opportunity to (temporarily) take up homesteads on land surrounding the Adel Ranch. Pete Nelson selected the crew who filed for the homestead, built a cabin on the land, and then gave them three horses to plow twenty acres and sow oats. Once the ranch hand had proved up, the crew member may have sold the land and water rights to Henry Sieben. While Pete Nelson excelled in his role as foreman of the Adel Ranch, it required a bit more of Henry's time to solidify that position at the Mitchell Place, known by the early 1920s as the Sieben Ranch.[26]

Shortly after Fred Sheriff married Berneice in 1917, Henry thought it would be a good idea to provide Fred with some hands-on experience of managing the Sieben Ranch, so Berneice, Fred, and their infant daughter, Jean, moved into a small house on the ranch. It had wood heat and a wood stove but no electricity. Fred tried his hardest to oversee operations and make a success of his time as ranch foreman, but he just could not adapt to the lifestyle. Year-round ranch living and managing a crew was not for him. Henry understood this almost immediately, and never one to dither, he hired a foreman by the name of Henry Fisher to replace Fred. The Sheriffs moved back into Helena after one year on the Sieben Ranch. When Henry Fisher retired, Henry Sieben hired Axel Holmstrom as ranch foreman. Brian Hilger described him as a "good, tough, ornery guy."[27] Hilger mentioned that from time to time, his family had issues with Axel Holmstrom, but he was a good ranch manager who made Henry Sieben a lot more money.

Berneice's husband, Fred Sheriff (on tractor), takes instruction from Henry's business partner, Thomas Grimes, on the Sieben Ranch (formerly known as the Mitchell Ranch), ca. 1920. Courtesy of the Hibbard family private collection.

By 1922, Henry was satisfied that he had accomplished, as best he could, his goals of steering the Sieben and Adel Ranches through the war period, the postwar depression, and the drought. He had expanded the ranch acreages and hired capable foremen who were at the helm of both operations. Henry was satisfied he could confidently pass on the reins of ranch management to his daughters and sons-in-law. Like Henry, the Sheriffs and Hibbards both made Helena their home and were eager to manage the ranches from that location. It was no small task. According to Brian Hilger, the Sieben Ranch ran approximately 12,000-15,000 sheep in the 1920s and 1930s. The Adel Ranch in the 1920s ran 9,000-10,000 sheep. A.T. and Fred accompanied Henry on business meetings to learn about operating the ranches as corporations that employed hundreds of workers. Henry had included Berneice and Margaret on the board of the Sieben Ranch Company since 1915 and, from 1923 onwards, his daughters were primary shareholders (285 shares each) and vice-presidents of the company. Henry included A.T. as treasurer and Fred as secretary, both men holding ten shares each. Henry served as president and also held ten shares, but the title was honorary in nature. As primary shareholders, Henry expected his daughters and their husbands to lead operations. Henry had other preoccupations.[28]

Henry's pocketbooks during the 1920s and 1930s indicate his days were filled with meetings at the American National Bank and with his peers at the Harvey Hotel and the Montana Club. He was also actively involved in the Montana Stockgrowers Association, the Montana Woolgrowers Association, and the Montana Children's Home Society. From 1922 onwards, he no longer recorded business transactions in his pocketbooks. His personal matters and interests took precedence.

In 1920, Henry was ready to invest in something new. The recent development of oil fields in eastern Montana yielded impressive profits. Production near Mosby was amounting to 10,000 barrels a day, two pipelines into Winnett were equaling 7,000 barrels, and at least seventy-five rigs drilled in various fields in Fergus and adjacent counties. Never one to shy away from a calculated risk, Henry organized and invested in a new company, the Texas-Montana Oil & Gas Company. Henry was president of the company and four other prominent businessmen served as board directors. The company had various holdings in Texas, including in the salt domes of Texas's Gulf Coast region, which consisted of 710 leased and owned acres as well as an interest in a 10,000-acre lease on which drilling occurred. In Montana, the company owned leases in the Cat Creek, Porcupine, Big Wall, Fish Creek, and Roundup districts, comprising 1,600 acres.

To top it off, Henry added still another dimension to his life with his first airplane flight in June 1922. A. W. Stephenson, a pioneer Montana pilot, flew Henry to the shearing pens on the Sieben Ranch. In the words of the *Montana-Record Herald* journalist, "The air trip completed the cycle from ox to airplane." In an interview he gave after the flight, Henry reported he had traveled those hills in every conceivable manner, "by foot, by ox team, horseback, wagon, automobile and . . . airplane." He enjoyed every minute of the flight, sharing that "the air certainly gives you a great view and the sensation is very enjoyable. I wouldn't have missed it." Pilot Stephenson was impressed by how naturally Henry took to the air,

Having traveled thousands of miles on foot, by horse, wagon, train, and automobile during his lifetime, Henry Sieben enthusiastically embraced air travel at age seventy-five. Here, he poses with his grandchildren, Jean Sheriff and Hank Hibbard, before his first flight in 1922. Courtesy of the Hibbard family private collection.

Henry Sieben in aviator gear, 1922. Courtesy of the Hibbard family private collection.

stating, "I never had one take the air more as matter of course than did Mr. Sieben . . . he was so thoroughly interested and lacked the timidity which characterizes so many who are taking their first ride."[29]

Henry intended to usher in a modern period of stewardship under the Hibbard and Sheriff families, one that would survive longer and more successfully than he could ever have imagined.[30]

Henry had been planning the business transition for years. His goal in purchasing the Sieben and Adel Ranches, and expanding both at a similar rate, was that he could eventually leave a ranch of equal size, value, and profitability in the hands of each daughter. Henry gave the Sieben Ranch, managed by the Sieben Ranch Company, to Berneice and Fred Sheriff. He gave the Adel Ranch, managed by the Sieben Live Stock Company, to Margaret and A.T. Hibbard. But before each family took over, Henry wanted them all to serve as directors and shareholders of both corporations so they could learn about the working of each ranch and support one another. Henry had ensured that Berneice and Margaret's connection with the ranches ran deep, so it is not surprising that they were more than up to the task. From 1922 onwards, the five directors and shareholders attended annual meetings of the Sieben Ranch and Live Stock Company. They held the Sieben Ranch annual company meeting on February 1, Henry's birthday. As a minority shareholder, Henry's wish was to attend the meetings and advise only if needed and/or requested.

From 1922 to 1928, land purchases, taxes, interest on money borrowed from majority shareholders (Margaret and Berneice) to pay for land, rising labor costs, and late-season snowstorms in 1927 all combined to provide relentless headaches for the Sheriffs and Hibbards. The rain cycle returned during the middle and late 1920s, and with it came quality grass for sheep and cattle. At the same time, the great nationwide boom of 1922 to 1929 began to improve the state's dormant economy, as local industries responded to rising nationwide demands for metals, lumber, and oil. Wool was also in high demand, and in 1926 the Sieben Ranch Company ran in excess of 200,000 pounds. The bad times seemed to be over and the Sheriffs and Hibbards were optimistic that the first few years of their tenure were just growing pains.

Henry, however, was worried. He knew the brief period of prosperity keeping the ranch operations afloat during the late 1920s could vanish at any time. Although racked with inner turmoil, Henry remained tactful, swallowed his desire to take charge, and, as always, listened more than he spoke. At the annual company meetings, Henry occasionally offered his family "the benefit of some of his ideas and conclusions regarding the policy of the company"[31] in particular, cautioning them against making further land purchases when they weren't turning profits. Perhaps to instill in the next generation the lessons he had learned over his years in the stock industry, in December 1926, Henry invited Margaret and A.T. to join him on a trip to Chicago to attend the International Livestock Exposition.

On the return journey, the family stopped at Geneseo, Illinois, to visit Henry's older brother, Leonard Sieben, and his family. The reunion inspired the two brothers, now aged eighty-two and seventy-nine, respectively, to reminisce and share tales of their adventures and trials. Leonard and Henry regaled A.T. and Margaret with stories about their wagon journey from Illinois to Montana, freighting in Montana Territory, driving cattle from Utah to the Chestnut Valley, and introducing sheep to the area in the 1870s. Like Henry, Leonard was a respected businessman in his local town, and the Sieben brothers' reunion sparked the interest of local newspapers. The *Moline Daily Dispatch* reported on Leonard and Henry's reunion, titling the article "Covered Wagon Pioneers Hold Reunion in Geneseo."[32]

Margaret and A.T. were amazed to see in person the parallels between the two brothers' lives. Since his return to Illinois in 1879, Leonard and his wife Sarah had successfully built a farming operation in Henry County, Illinois. Like Henry, Leonard moved his young family to the small town of Geneseo to raise his five children and provide them with the best education he could offer them. Leonard became involved in civic affairs in the community and was elected to the office of assessor in 1884. Like Henry, Leonard was still active in business. Leonard owned and rented 331 acres of arable land in Henry County and also owned 20.5 acres of timber land and 40 acres of improved land, which was his old homestead. The *Henry County Record* would later describe Leonard as follows:

> [Leonard] affords a good illustration of what a life devoted to worthy effort may bring forth with nothing to aid him but a determination to make good use of his time in taking advantage of the opportunities afforded in a free land . . . he has made his way to a position, not only of comfort and ease, but to one of confidence and trust in the gift of his fellow citizens.[33]

Perhaps emboldened by the stories of the plucky brothers' early day adventures, on Henry's eightieth birthday on February 1, 1927, A.T. Hibbard proposed that he, Margaret, Fred, and Berneice could from

This is the only surviving photograph of Henry (at left) with his brother Leonard Sieben reunited in Geneseo, Illinois, 1926. Courtesy of the Hibbard family private collection.

that point forward be solely responsible for conducting the ranch operations on their own. Although racked with uncertainty, Henry knew there was never a perfect time to take over a large operation. The next generation needed to take the reins, so at the 1927 directors' meeting, Henry stated it had been his desire for some time to entirely relieve himself of any responsibility in connection with the company. While the proposition was warmly received by all involved, it never came to fruition. A new ordeal of drought and depression began in Montana during 1929 and1930, and Henry's counsel was sorely needed.

This time, the droughts would last longer than before, intermittently for nearly a decade. And this time, a terrible nationwide and worldwide depression greatly complicated Montana's problems. The drought began intermittently in 1929, intensified in 1930, and reached disastrous proportions in 1931. The mid- to late 1930s brought more serious drought and dust-laden winds. Along with the drought came a substantial drop in food prices, as the global depression led to declining food purchases and mounting crop surpluses. An amount of wheat worth $100 ($1,500 today's value) in 1920 brought only $19.23 ($450 today's value) in 1932. Furthermore, meat and wool prices collapsed. Beef cattle that sold for $9.10 ($160 today's value) per hundredweight in 1929 sold for only $3.34 ($80 today's value) in 1934. Sheep brought $8.14 ($150 today's value) per hundredweight in 1929 but only $3.12 ($70 today's value) in 1934. Once again, poverty and hunger engulfed rural Montana. After touring the eastern half of Montana in 1931, Governor John Erickson buried his head in his hands and lamented he would gladly embrace any solution somebody could find. The Great Depression had arrived.

Although Montana did not lie in the heart of the Dust Bowl of the "dirty thirties," it experienced the ravages of drought, dust, and depopulation. Like ten years previously, many farmers left the land and joined the general exodus of poverty-stricken people toward the West Coast. To a greater extent than in the depression of 1918 to 1922, Montana's industries and cities suffered along with the farmers and ranchers. When the Great Depression hit, it flattened the competitive copper industry. Copper prices steadily fell throughout the early 1930s, and it spelled disaster for Montana's mining towns. In Butte and in the smelting and refining towns of Anaconda, Great Falls, and East Helena, machinery ground to a halt and thousands of workers lost their jobs. Tens of thousands of Montanans were in desperate need of relief by the early 1930s, but the federal and state government offered little help and from 1929 to 1932, Montana and the nation sank deeper into depression. Ranching operations at Sieben and Adel were equally hit.[34]

In 1929, business finances plummeted, and Henry decided to stay on as president of the board of directors. The company's accountant provided the directors with consistently disheartening news about company finances. From 1928 to 1936, things went from bad to worse. At the February 1, 1933, annual meeting, perhaps overwhelmingly discouraged himself or frustrated at his advisory status and inability to lead the business, Henry suggested someone else take over his role as president of the company. But his family refused. They needed him to stay abreast of events, even just to participate as a sounding board for their worries and questions. Henry obliged.

The family was reenergized. Henry knew that the best lessons were learned in hard times, and he was proud his daughters and sons-in-law had overcome the many and diverse challenges that had presented themselves over the previous decade. The hard-won experience also bolstered the next generation's confidence. Margaret's and Berneice's knowledge of the land and crews had proven invaluable. A.T.'s wide breadth of financial expertise helped the group navigate the ups, downs, and bureaucracy. A.T. had become a banking expert, serving as president of the Union Bank from 1933 until 1955. A.T. was also president of the Montana Bankers Association and a member of the American Bankers Association. With a degree in mechanical engineering, Fred Sheriff brought technical expertise to the ranches. Fred was also president of the Montana Livestock Marketing Association and, inspired by Henry's flight in 1922, he took up flying himself, becoming the first Commissioner of Aeronautics of Montana. Henry was thrilled when Fred joined Amelia Earhart and Northwest Airlines company executives in planning a route from Minneapolis to Seattle in 1928. Together, the Sheriffs and Hibbards made a formidable team, capable of bringing Henry's enterprises into the modern era.[35]

Amid the strain of running such large enterprises in the 1920s and 1930s, the Sheriffs and Hibbards reveled in the time spent with their children at the Sieben and Adel Ranches during the summers. They divided most of their time between both ranches, taking turns staying at the cabin at the Sieben Ranch and often jointly staying at the Adel Ranch. They experienced many fun times together, creating traditions for their families. Bill Shanklin recalled that Margaret

and Hank spent most of their summers at Adel with A.T. coming and going depending on work demands at the Union Bank in Helena.

Margaret and Berneice threw great Fourth of July parties at Adel in the 1920s. They played all types of games in front of the ranch house such as "pompom pull away," which involved pulling on a rope to see who could win. Another game had two people sitting on the ground with their feet together. They each took hold of one end of a broom and pulled to see which person could pull the other off the ground. When one person managed to pull the other up, Berneice and Margaret slipped a pie tin full of water under the

Above two photos: Margaret and Berneice remained close throughout their lives and their children grew up together, as seen here: Jean Sheriff and Hank Hibbard with a mule and a horse at the Adel Ranch, ca. 1929. Courtesy of the Hibbard family private collection.

person in the air and they'd have a fun wet landing. The families and the ranch crew members all enjoyed ice cream and cake, and when it got dark, A.T. and Fred climbed the hill to the left of the house and set off fireworks. Margaret remembered, "It was just beautiful . . . I remember those 4th of Julys . . . they were just wonderful times."[36]

Henry Sieben enjoyed being a grandfather, as shown here with Margaret's daughter, Jean Sheriff, ca. 1918. Courtesy of the Hibbard family private collection.

Henry often accompanied his daughters and grandchildren to the ranches throughout the 1920s and 1930s. Even though A.T. and Fred were the ranch bosses at the time, everyone on the crew knew Henry was the owner. Bill Shanklin recalled that when he was working at Adel, Henry "always had something up and going . . . you could tell he never loafed . . . he'd always be doing something."[37] Henry indulged his favorite pastimes of fishing and hunting at the ranches during the 1920s and 1930s. He was an excellent shot and often asked ranch crew members to join him to hunt grouse or other game. By then Henry didn't mount or dismount as easily as he had in his youth, so he trained a little mare named Cobra to stand while he shot from her back.

Henry also continued to indulge his newfound interest in flying. In July 1931, he took a momentous flight in the company of his wife, Jessie, and fellow pioneers, including rancher David Hilger, from Helena to Salt Lake City. The pioneers boarded the National Parks Airways passenger and mail plane and retraced the route that had taken them weeks to make trudging behind ox teams in the 1860s. This air trip took them just four hours. The group was scheduled to attend the "Covered Wagon Days" celebration in Salt Lake City. As the reporter for the *Helena Daily Independent* noted:

> It would be interesting could one follow their thoughts as they contrast the mode of travel they are now employing with the painfully slow, torturous progress over the same trail between Corinne, Utah, and Helena . . . how many incidents of the past will come crowding to their minds.[38]

Many honors came to Henry through the years. In 1892 Henry was named a charter member of the International Livestock Exposition of Chicago. One not-so-welcome accolade arrived in 1926 when the speaker at the Montana Stockgrowers dinner mixed up his notes and Henry was treated to hearing his own eulogy. The speaker paid tribute to the late, great Henry Sieben while Henry sat quietly in the crowd. Once the speaker concluded, Henry rose to deny the allegation, sharing that the eulogy was fine, just premature. In 1932, the Montana Woolgrowers Association elected Henry as Honorary Lifetime President, and shortly afterwards the organization commissioned a portrait of Henry by Robert W. Grafton. They presented the portrait to the Saddle and Sirloin Club, a club consisting of some of the nation's most influential figures in the livestock industry in the Chicago Stockyards. Henry's portrait hung alongside Conrad Kohrs' portrait at the club until a fire engulfed the building in 1934 and destroyed the contents.[39]

During the last few years of his life, Henry also gave quite extensive and insightful personal interviews to local newspapers. The first article in January 1930 was spurred by a meeting of the Montana Woolgrowers Association in Helena where members hailed Henry as "the dean of Montana woolgrowers." This prompted the *Montana-Record Herald* to sit down with Henry and record his story. In December 1934, Montana Senator W. R. Church wrote a thorough synopsis of Henry's life for *The Mountaineer.* Both texts provide invaluable details on Henry's life spanning from his childhood in Illinois to his airplane flight in Montana in 1922. On November 26, 1937, Henry passed away at home with his family.[40]

Margaret remembered *Madre's* kindness during the time of Henry's passing. Jessie left Margaret alone with her father for two or three hours on the night he died. The pair had a conversation Margaret never forgot. Henry's legs and feet were cold, and he knew he was going to die. In his typical direct and practical fashion, Henry shared there was nothing wrong with him, his body was just worn out. After his vast, fortunate life that spanned nine decades and was full of adventure and love, he didn't mind dying. He just felt badly that "I won't know what's going to happen to tomorrow." But as his friend Don Brown declared, "He'll live on. Those people live on."[41] ◈

Epilogue

1937–2024

THE SIEBEN LEGACY

Henry Sieben at the Sieben Ranch. Courtesy of the Hibbard family private collection.

The intertwined tale of Henry Sieben and the Montana story continues long after the stockman's death. Four generations have succeeded Henry, each embodying his legacy in unique ways. They have met and overcome challenges, some similar, some different to what Henry encountered. Through innovation, adaptability, and business smarts, the Sieben and Adel Ranches are thriving in the twenty-first century. In each era, it's clear the family has drawn inspiration from Henry's remarkable tale to ensure they steward the land for generations to come.

The original goal of leaving the land in a better place at the end of each generation's watch continues.

Only a handful of short tributes to Henry existed when Berneice and Margaret gathered biographical information on their father and successfully nominated him to the "Hall of Great Westerners" in 1961. Just two years later in 1963, the interstate exit to the Sieben Ranch was officially named "Sieben." Henry's epic story has receded from the public memory. He did not contribute to subscription biographies of the "who's who" of Montana, and he left no memoirs. Instead, and perhaps more fittingly, the stories of Henry's life have been preserved in the two ranches he placed in stewardship of his daughters. The Sieben and Adel Ranches are successfully operated today by the fifth generation of Henry Sieben's descendants. That is perhaps the most fitting tribute of all.

THE SECOND GENERATION, 1922–1946

Henry's daughters, Berneice and Margaret, were devastated by his death in 1937, but they followed their father's advice and became successful business and ranch women. Henry's funeral service was held at St. Peter's Episcopal Cathedral in Helena. It was a simple occasion, just as Henry would have wanted. He was buried at the nearby Forestvale Cemetery among friends and associates he had known since he first arrived in Montana. Many of his friends and colleagues from his seventy years in Montana are buried nearby: Colonel Charles Broadwater, James Fergus, Daniel Floweree, Nicholas Kessler, Harry W. Child, Chief Justice Theodore Brantley, and Louis Stadler.

Shortly after Henry's death, his daughters and their husbands made decisive and practical decisions regarding the ranches they now possessed. Berneice became president of the Sieben Ranch Company and vice-president of the Sieben Live Stock Company. Margaret was president of the Sieben Live Stock Company and vice-president of the Sieben Ranch Company. Berneice and Fred Sheriff oversaw the Sieben Ranch with Fred in charge of daily operations. Margaret and A.T. Hibbard managed the Adel Ranch with A.T. in charge of business operations.

This arrangement enabled each couple to focus on one ranching operation, but it also allowed them to continue working together.[1]

The combined business acumen of the two families enabled them to successfully operate the Sieben and Adel Ranches from 1939 to 1946. During the war years, the families experienced poor markets for wool, intermittent drought, high operating costs, and new demand for summer range. Minutes of shareholder meetings from the period demonstrate a thoughtful, comprehensive, and cautious approach to navigating the economic and global difficulties—traits they had learned from Henry Sieben. It was no easy task for either family to ensure the survival of the ranches, but they were resilient and tenacious, just as Henry Sieben had been.[2]

One of the primary difficulties this generation faced was finding and retaining employees during World War II. Ranch operations at the time still primarily required manpower and needed a large and experienced crew. For example, at the Adel Ranch the crew oversaw approximately 11,000 sheep, fifty to seventy-five cattle, numerous saddle and draft horses as well as many pigs. Crew member Bill Shanklin remembered there was just one tractor and no mowing machine on the tractor. They used it for some plowing, but the crew did the mowing, raking, and stacking of hay with horses. In order to ship sheep to market from the Adel Ranch in the fall, six to eight crew members trailed two bands of 5,000 sheep to Craig, a job that took three days. Furthermore, the ranch had a sawmill where the men cut their own lumber. A sawmill man came in to saw the lumber and a lot of it was sold locally. These tasks required strong and experienced workers. But according to Bill Shanklin, able-bodied men were going to Portland or Seattle for work, and any crew the Hibbards or Sheriffs could find during the war years were usually temporary, leaving soon after lambing or shearing in the spring to pursue other opportunities.

During the war, the responsibility of managing the Adel Ranch fell on Margaret's shoulders. Family lore passed down through the generations shares that during the war, Margaret resorted to visiting bars in Cascade and Great Falls, pulling young men from their stools, offering them a good wage and meals at the Adel Ranch. And those who took her offer were rarely sorry. Some of the sheepherders were Romanian with little English, but that didn't faze Margaret. She talked to everyone, always interested in learning about her employees. Crew members later remarked that they would "have gone to hell for her." A pocketbook diary she kept in 1943 highlights Margaret's thoughtful and personable nature. It was in this book that she noted each of the crew member's birthdays so she would not forget to acknowledge them.[3]

Margaret also contributed to the war effort by assuming the role of knitting chairman of the Red Cross. Spurred on by reports of five million refugees in France, Montana women from Augusta, Marysville, Wolf Creek, and East Helena gathered in Helena to knit clothing for the displaced people in Europe. While Margaret and A.T. kept the ranch and Union Bank afloat during the war, their only son, Hank, graduated with a degree in Agriculture from Montana State College in 1941 and returned to Adel to assume the role of general manager.

Henry was very proud of how his family managed their ranches. Pictured here are three generations (right to left): Henry, grandson Hank Hibbard, ranch manager Pete Nelson, and son-in-law A.T. Hibbard. Courtesy of the Hibbard family private collection.

Just as Henry Sieben had trained them to do, Berneice, Margaret, and their husbands steered the ranches through the war and set about ensuring his land and legacy would be passed on to the next generation. By the time Germany surrendered on September 2, 1945, Henry's two daughters agreed that it was time to divide the holdings. In July 1946, Margaret resigned from her position as vice-president of the Sieben Ranch Company and donated her shares back to the company. Berneice did the same for the Sieben Live Stock Company. Since then, Berneice's descendants have operated the Sieben Ranch Company near Helena while Margaret's descendants undertook sole operation of the Sieben Live Stock Company at Adel near Cascade.

The Sieben and Adel Ranches have remained in the hands of Henry's daughters and their descendants. In 1946, the Sheriffs brought their daughter, Jean, on as vice-president of the Sieben Ranch Company and her cousin, Hank, became a director of the Sieben Live Stock Company operation. Henry's legacy and the process by which future generations would continue to steward the land was firmly in place.[4]

THE THIRD GENERATION, 1946–1976

During the 1920s and 1930s, Jean and Hank spent their childhood and teens in the company of their grandfather, Henry Sieben, on the Sieben and Adel Ranches. The experience instilled in them from an early age the importance of stewarding the land for a purpose greater than their own needs. When Henry passed away, Jean was twenty and Hank was eighteen.

Just as Henry had done a generation before with Fred and Berneice, the Sheriffs mentored Jean's husband, John J. Baucus, in the operations of the Sieben ranch near Helena. John was elected as treasurer and assistant secretary of the Sieben Ranch Company and began working for his father-in-law, Fred Sheriff. John J. had grown up in the sheep industry in Great Falls and took easily to ranch work at Sieben. Fred instilled in John J. the value of education and being involved in the development of the stock industry. The ranch soon became a gathering spot for Baucus family and friends, which delighted Berneice and transported her back to her childhood with Margaret and her friends playing on the ranch in the early 1900s. Berneice Sieben died unexpectedly in 1964, and her husband, Fred, passed away in 1972. They died assured in the knowledge that the Sieben Ranch would continue to stay in the family, safely in the hands of Jean and John J. who were in the process of raising the fourth generation to understand the ranch's legacy and the hard work it took to steward and nurture the land.[5]

After the war, Hank called upon a childhood friend, Jane Goodsill, in New York. The two soon married and, after Hank received his MBA from the Harvard Business School, the couple returned to Montana. Having grown up steeped in the ranch's history and having worked on the land most of his life, Hank was ready to take over operations. Like his grandfather, Henry Sieben, he possessed an independent and entrepreneurial spirit. While the ranch transition process differed greatly from that which occurred when Henry Sieben passed on the ranch to Margaret and A.T., Hank's parents entrusted him to lead the business into the future. They had invested in his formal education and practical training on the Adel Ranch and were content that they had stewarded the ranch as best they could, providing Hank with the opportunity to build on their tenure.

Like Henry Sieben fifty years earlier, Hank understood the importance of participating in conversations about agricultural developments and challenges, and he became a well-regarded promoter of the livestock industry. Hank served as president of the Montana Woolgrowers Association, vice-president of the National Woolgrowers Association, and president of the American Sheep Producers Council. He even joined a delegation of American stockmen on a visit to Australia and New Zealand to discuss quotas and cooperation to protect their industry.[6]

Hank also had an interest in civic affairs. While Henry Sieben's unsuccessful forays into local politics led him to later remark that politics "stink to high heaven,"[7] Hank was determined to succeed. He served as a member of the Montana House of Representatives in 1961 and 1963 and in the Montana Senate from 1965 to 1972. Hank's father, A.T., was immensely proud of Hank's work not only on the ranch but in his endeavors to develop Helena and Montana society. In 1972, Hank ran for the U.S. Senate, leaving his eldest sons, Chase and Scott, to manage the Adel Ranch.[8]

During his Senate campaign, Hank cited the need for jobs, welfare reform, and veteran help. In his campaign flyer, Hank quoted Henry David Thoreau, but the words could just as easily have been applied to Henry Sieben: "Be not simply good—be good for something." Hank narrowly lost the senate race, by just one vote per precinct, to incumbent Lee Metcalf in 1972.

In 1976, while flying over the ranch in his Piper Super Cub looking for a missing bull, Hank hit a powerline and he and a young ranch hand, Wayne Pursley, of Great Falls were killed instantly. The ranch's attorney and accountant recommended that Chase, Scott, and Whit sell the ranch. The brothers refused. Chase later remarked, "The ranch was our family history, identity and heritage, and an important piece of this region's landscape and history. To sell the ranch would be akin to losing an arm or a leg, or more accurately a big chunk of our soul, not to mention that of the community around us."[9] Chase returned to Adel to take over management and day-to-day operations of the ranch and Scott assisted him, while Whit returned later in 1984.

A similar transition began about this time on the Sieben Ranch. Jean and John J. Baucus's son, John F., had graduated with a degree in Agricultural Production from Montana State University in 1971 and had been in management training since then. By the late 1970s, Jean and John J. were satisfied that John F. had the education and experience to steward the land into its fourth generation.[10]

As the new generation began to take the reins of the Sieben and Adel Ranches in the 1970s, Margaret Hibbard and Jean Baucus, the last two remaining members of the family who knew Henry Sieben, took on the roles of preservers and cultivators of Henry's story. They instilled in the current stewards the importance of bettering the local community. Margaret continued the charitable work of her parents, Henry and Alberta. She continued the family's longtime support of the causes closest to Henry's heart—the Montana Children's Home (now Shodair

Children's Hospital), the Red Cross, and the YWCA. Margaret inherited her father, Henry Sieben's, resilient and no-nonsense approach to life, traits apparent in an interview she gave to the *Independent Record* a year after her son Hank's death in 1976. In the piece, Margaret declared she was "one of those funny old people who can change with the times." Despite the challenges and tragedies she endured, Margaret was grateful for the good fortune of sharing her life with her son and her husband and having a happy marriage. She remarked, "I just think I've been a very very fortunate person" and that she had "that thing in me . . . I won't give up." Margaret and Jean's passion, perseverance, family values, respect for the past, love of the land and animals, and can-do attitude for the future remain core tenets of the Sieben and Adel Ranches today.[11]

THE FOURTH GENERATION, 1976–2010s

By the end of the 1970s, the fourth generation were stewards of the Sieben and Adel Ranches, guiding them through the end of the twentieth century and into the twenty-first century. Much had changed socially, economically, and politically since Henry Sieben had handed the ranches down to Berneice and Margaret in the 1920s. The mainstays of the Montana economy, agriculture and metal mining, had sharply declined since the 1920s. New growth in lumber, tourism, and government employment filled the gap.[12] When Chase Hibbard and John F. Baucus took over the reins of their respective ranches, the economy was good and so was the weather. But as Henry Sieben had learned, neither stayed that way for long, and the 1980s brought a return to hard times. Severe drought hit the state and commodity prices plummeted because of rising global productivity and crop surpluses. Agriculture was still Montana's number one industry, but its share of the state's economic base declined. Mechanization and concentration of the production of two major commodities—wheat and beef—robbed the industry of both population and social influence. Farm and ranch workers who once sacked wheat, baled hay, or dug sugar beets now sought employment in Montana's growing lumber, petroleum, tourism, and government sectors.[13]

To confront these challenges, the fourth generation implemented Henry Sieben's timeless strategy of adaptation and innovation. As John F. Baucus put it, "Hopefully you innovate enough and stay open to different ideas."[14] On the Sieben Ranch, John and his wife, Nina, encountered many of the same problems that challenged Henry. One of these was a significant predator problem. Wolves, grizzlies, mountain lions, and coyotes threatened the ranch's sheep, and because of the mountainous terrain, the Baucus family couldn't fence in the livestock. Instead, they brought in llamas and guard dogs to protect the sheep, and while it didn't eliminate the predator problem, it greatly reduced it. Just as Henry dealt with poisonous plants and weeds, the Baucuses also encountered issues surrounding weed control and pine tree encroachment in the 1990s. John F. tried spraying chemicals, which was expensive. Nina was taking care of a dozen or so dairy goats at the time and noted they required rough forage for feed, so they tried using goats to eradicate knapweed and pine tree encroachment. It was slow, but effective. By the early 2000s, they had approximately 1,200 goats. At the time, many agricultural research projects were underway and grant money was available. The Baucuses took advantage of this and partnered with Montana State University to document the long-term benefits of using goats to help with weed control and pine tree encroachment. They also turned bugs loose to reduce the number of leafy spurge and knapweed. John F. and Nina, inspired by teachings passed down from previous generations, knew that they had to think ahead and stay curious to survive. Their innovative approaches were not overnight tools, but over a few years they began to show promise and reduce operating costs.

Revenue from wool production dropped significantly in the 2000s, which meant sheep ranchers needed to get creative with revenue streams. During John J.'s tenure in the 1950s and 1960s, approximately forty percent of income on the ranch came from wool. When John F. and Nina ran operations, that number dropped to around five to ten percent. Much of the innovations in sheep shearing came from Australia, and the technology was often expensive. John F. Baucus and Chase Hibbard approached the challenge by investing in a hydraulic wool press that enabled them and neighboring ranchers to share the expensive equipment.[15] Meat took on a more important role as ranch income, and this was challenging due to the instability in the lamb and mutton market since the 1980s. John F. joined a lamb co-op in North Dakota, and they began to sell goats to California and Oregon meat markets.

Close attention to matters of succession has remained an important value for Henry's descendants. After his father's death in 1993, John F. became the sole operator of the Sieben Ranch. This freed Max to pursue his political career as a Democrat in the U.S. Senate. He served from 1978 until 2014 and then as ambassador to the People's Republic of China from 2014 to 2017. John F. and Max's sister, Karen, moved to California where she married Nick Kallay and raised their three children. Since 2000, John F. and Nina have worked with their son John H. and his wife, Cathy, in the transition of taking over management duties. By 2015, John and Cathy Baucus had assumed management. Thanks to methodical, long-term planning, the fifth generation is now thriving at the helm of the Sieben Ranch.[16]

Chase Hibbard took over the management of the Adel Ranch in 1976 after his father's death. He learned the importance of listening to the land for management cues and taking risks to innovate and adapt to changing environmental circumstances throughout his tenure as steward of the land. The land at Adel holds water better than at Sieben where much of the ground is shaly and steep. This results in better grass production at Adel. However, one of Chase's first realizations when he began to operate the ranch was that he could develop traditional grazing practices to improve sustainability at Adel. Stories passed down from his grandparents, Margaret and A.T., and his father, Hank, about Henry Sieben's long-range planning to meet the challenges of overgrazing motivated Chase to begin exploring more sustainable grazing techniques. Like Henry, Chase understood he needed to innovate. He worked with rest-rotation grazing expert, Gus Hormay, to develop a three-pasture rest-rotation grazing system, enabling Chase to lead the Adel Ranch through the periods of drought in the 1980s and again in the early 2000s when the land suffered severe drought. Chase also implemented other innovative and often risky approaches to improve the land and stock. He altered livestock numbers, changed the calving season, and adopted environmentally friendly strategies, such as pulling cattle away from riparian areas to improve water quality and quantity. Chase also incorporated his brothers, Scott and Whitney's, respective expertise in business management and low-stress livestock handling to adapt to the ever-changing business climate.[17]

Chase also followed in his father's political footsteps and served in the Montana House of Representatives from 1993 to 2000. He carries on the legacy of collaboration rather than conflict from previous generations, which led him to help found the "Devil's Kitchen Management Team" in 1989. The group, which continues today, is composed of representatives from wildlife agencies, state and federal forest managers, sportsmen, and neighboring landowners. The group gathers three times per year around the "kitchen table" to listen to each other's ideas and needs for preserving and controlling wildlife and habitat. They set goals for the area, focusing primarily on game management. Through a controlled expansion of the game herd, they have produced a greater quantity of larger bulls and have taken a lot of the onerous hunter management away from private landowners by using the Department of Fish, Wildlife and Parks block management program to manage hunters. This allowed Chase and other ranchers to do some limited outfitting by taking in some outside hunters. In addition to helping manage wildlife, the scheme helped diversify ranch income. Commensurate with the family's values, in 2008, Chase, Scott, and Whit led a process to put a conservation easement on a vast acreage at the core of the Adel Ranch. These bold moves helped ensure the Adel Ranch's prosperity and perpetuity, and encouraged Scott's son, Cooper Hibbard, to begin transitioning into the role of ranch manager in the 2010s.[18]

THE FIFTH GENERATION, CURRENT OPERATORS

On the Sieben Ranch today, John H. Baucus and his wife, Cathy, run operations. A mixture of sheep and cattle still dot the shaly terrain where signs of the area's history are everywhere. From Malcolm Clarke's grave and original cabins to Thomas Grimes's home to the stone milkhouse, the ranch still proudly holds and shares its rich history. Its stewards regularly host gatherings at the ranch to share its rich history with the community. John H. has endeavored to stay ahead of issues such as economic recessions, the changing nature of labor, and compliance with federal and state regulations by investing in mechanization and looking into everything from the sale of timber and landscape rock to putting up cell towers, solar panels, and using government programs for income protection. He also explored developing a wind farm and drilling for fossil fuels—neither of which worked out. Like Henry Sieben, John H. has always enjoyed working with cattle, but for now he sees the value of sheep—their economic value for the Sieben Ranch and their part in the land's and his family's history. John H. is an expert in heavy machine work, which has helped with the technology that is used on the ranch today.[19]

At the Adel Ranch, Cooper Hibbard and his wife, Ashley, oversee operations. Chase Hibbard remains chairman of the board of directors, assisting Cooper as needed. Cooper's brother, Tyrrell, manages and operates the Blossburg unit for Sieben Live Stock Company. They face many of the same obstacles that previous generations have endured and overcome, including fluctuations in labor quantity, quality, and affordability, along with rising expenses. Other new challenges have presented themselves. These include more restrictive government regulations including permitting for certain ranch activities, decreased precipitation, and more severe wildfire seasons, as well as a larger, more spread-out generation of Hibbards with varying degrees of involvement in ranch activities.

FINAL WORD

Henry Sieben grew up with Montana. He traveled into the territory in 1864 with John Bozeman. Starting out as a nearly penniless German immigrant of seventeen, he created a successful enterprise based around family, land, sheep, and cattle. From Henry and his brother Leonard's stewardship of the Chestnut Valley Ranch over 150 years ago, the simple values of family and hard work have been the threads that kept his two ranches intact. A strong sense of family, an appreciation for history, and courage in the face of adversity are Henry's lasting legacy. The Adel and Sieben Ranches have continued to expand and thrive through multiple generations and pivotal moments in local, national, and global history. Since Henry's original purchase of the Sieben Ranch, its size has increased eighty times over. The Adel Ranch is now ten times larger than when Henry purchased it in 1907. Henry's descendants have preserved and built upon the land to a scale and scope that very few others have

A freshly shorn sheep looks out of the shearing shed at the Sieben Live Stock (Adel) Ranch in 1995. Courtesy of J.M. Cooper, photographer.

achieved. With the fifth generation of his family now at the helm, we see Henry's stamp on his family and on Montana. The current generation is inspired by Henry Sieben's remarkable tale, creating an annual "ranch camp" to engage and educate the sixth generation and preserve the sense of stewardship for the land. The story of Henry Sieben, a thoughtful businessman, a brilliant strategist, and a committed rule breaker and trailblazer who shaped Montana's history, is as relevant to Montana today as it was in his own time.[20] ◈

Appendix I

HENRY SIEBEN FAMILY TREE

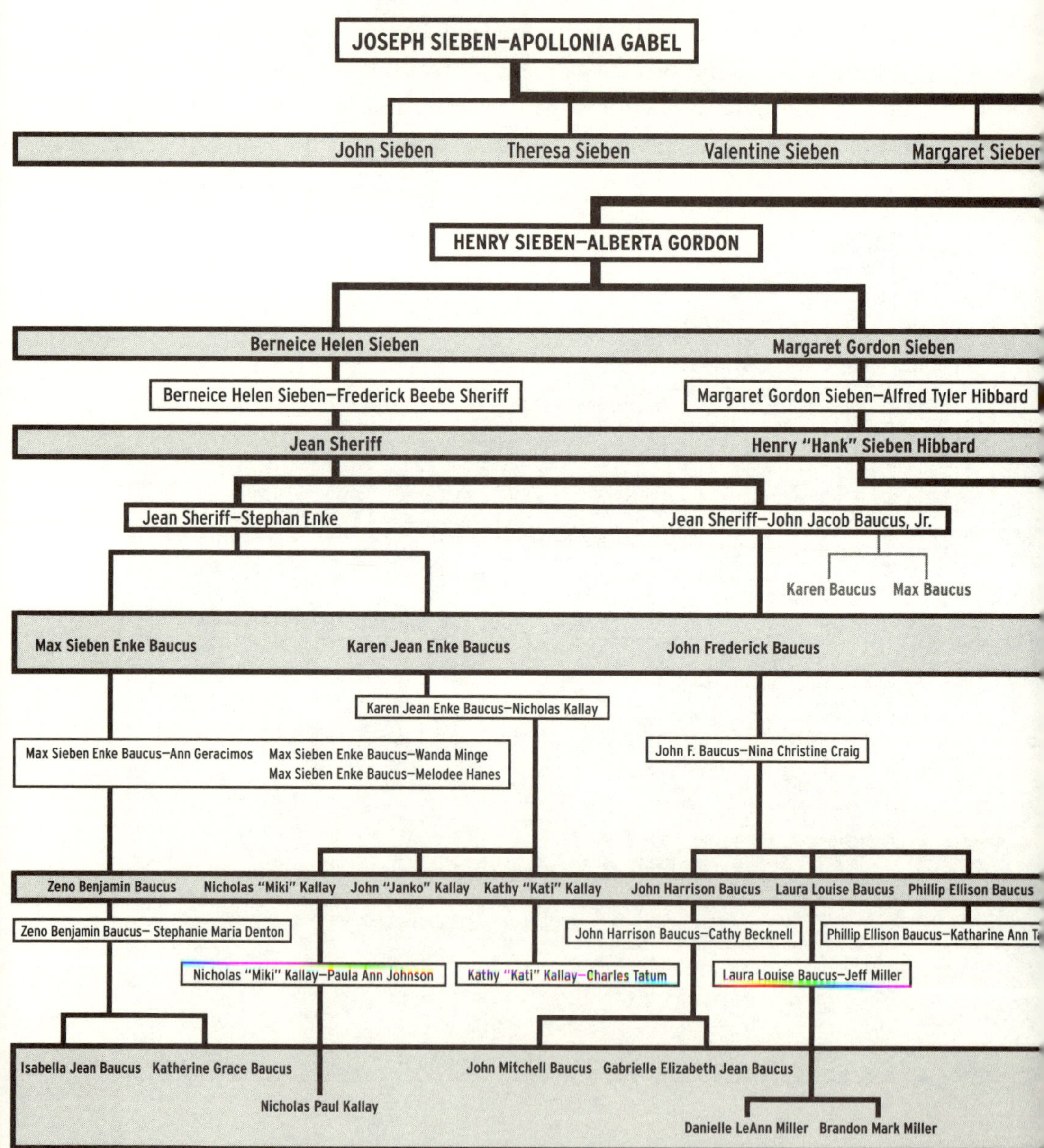

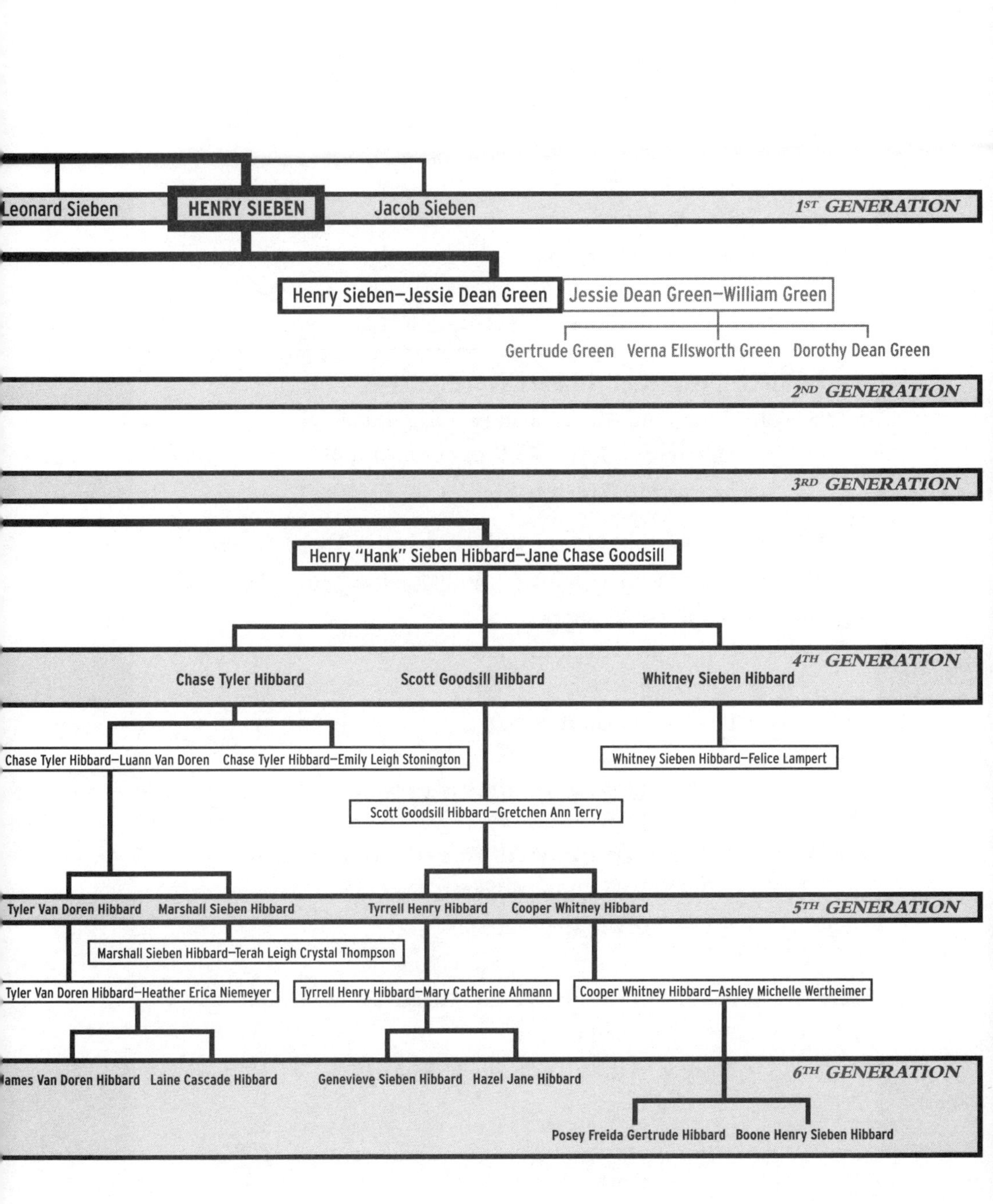
Leonard Sieben
HENRY SIEBEN
Jacob Sieben
1ST GENERATION
Henry Sieben–Jessie Dean Green
Jessie Dean Green–William Green
Gertrude Green
Verna Ellsworth Green
Dorothy Dean Green
2ND GENERATION
3RD GENERATION
Henry "Hank" Sieben Hibbard–Jane Chase Goodsill
4TH GENERATION
Chase Tyler Hibbard
Scott Goodsill Hibbard
Whitney Sieben Hibbard
Chase Tyler Hibbard–Luann Van Doren
Chase Tyler Hibbard–Emily Leigh Stonington
Whitney Sieben Hibbard–Felice Lampert
Scott Goodsill Hibbard–Gretchen Ann Terry
Tyler Van Doren Hibbard
Marshall Sieben Hibbard
Tyrrell Henry Hibbard
Cooper Whitney Hibbard
5TH GENERATION
Marshall Sieben Hibbard–Terah Leigh Crystal Thompson
Tyler Van Doren Hibbard–Heather Erica Niemeyer
Tyrrell Henry Hibbard–Mary Catherine Ahmann
Cooper Whitney Hibbard–Ashley Michelle Wertheimer
James Van Doren Hibbard
Laine Cascade Hibbard
Genevieve Sieben Hibbard
Hazel Jane Hibbard
6TH GENERATION
Posey Freida Gertrude Hibbard
Boone Henry Sieben Hibbard

Joseph Sieben (1810–1859) **married Apollonia Gabel** (1808–1853) in 1835. They had seven children:

- John (1836–1909)
- Theresa (1838–1925)
- Valentine (1840-1886)
- Margaret (1841–1915)
- Leonard (1844–1933)
- **Henry** (1848–1937)
- Jacob (1850–1904)

FIRST GENERATION

Henry Sieben married Alberta Gordon (1864–1912) in 1886. Henry and Alberta had two daughters:

- **Berneice Helen Sieben** (1890–1964)
- **Margaret Gordon Sieben** (1895–1986)

After Alberta's death, **Henry married Jessie Dean Green** (1864–1943). Jessie had married William Green in 1884. They had three daughters:

- Gertrude (1885–86)
- Verna Ellsworth (b. 1880)
- Dorothy Dean (b. 1890)

SECOND GENERATION

Berneice Helen Sieben married Frederick Beebe Sheriff (1890–1972). They had one daughter:

- **Jean Sheriff** (1917–2011)

Margaret Gordon Sieben married Alfred Tyler Hibbard (1890–1968). They had one son:

- **Henry "Hank" Sieben Hibbard** (1919-1976)

THIRD GENERATION

Jean Sheriff married Stephan Enke (1916–1974) in 1940.
They had two children:

- **Max Sieben Enke Baucus** (1941–)
- **Karen Jean Enke Baucus** (1943–)

Jean and Stephan divorced. **Jean got remarried to John Jacob Baucus, Jr.** (1915–1993) in 1947. John J. Baucus adopted Karen and Max. Jean and John J. Baucus had one child:

- **John Frederick Baucus** (1949–)

Henry "Hank" Sieben Hibbard married Jane Chase Goodsill (1922–2011). They had three sons:

- **Chase Tyler Hibbard** (1948–)
- **Scott Goodsill Hibbard** (1951–)
- **Whitney Sieben Hibbard** (1951–)

FOURTH GENERATION

Max Sieben Enke Baucus married Ann Geracimos (1936–) in 1975. They have one son:

- **Zeno Benjamin Baucus** (1976–)

Max and Ann divorced in 1982. **Max got remarried to Wanda Minge** in 1983. Max and Wanda divorced in 2009. **Max got remarried to Melodee Hanes** (1956–) in 2011.

Karen Jean Enke Baucus married Nicholas Kallay (1934–) in 1967. They have three children:

- **Nicholas "Miki" Kallay** (1970–)
- **John "Janko" Kallay** (1973–)
- **Kathy "Kati" Kallay** (1974–)

Karen and Nicholas divorced in 2002.

John F. Baucus married Nina Christine Craig (1948–).

They have three children:

- **John Harrison Baucus** (1973–)
- **Laura Louise Baucus** (1974–)
- **Phillip Ellison Baucus** (1977–2006)

Chase Tyler Hibbard married Luann Van Doren in 1975.

They have two sons:

- **Tyler Van Doren Hibbard** (1978–)
- **Marshall Sieben Hibbard** (1981–)

Chase and Luann divorced in 2000. **Chase remarried Emily Leigh Stonington** (1947–2019) in 2004.

Scott Goodsill Hibbard married Gretchen Ann Terry (1953–) in 1977. They have two sons:

- **Tyrrell Henry Hibbard** (1981–)
- **Cooper Whitney Hibbard** (1984–)

Whitney Sieben Hibbard married Felice Lampert (1957–) in 2013. No children.

FIFTH AND SIXTH GENERATIONS

Zeno Benjamin Baucus married Stephanie Maria Denton (1977–) in 2008. They have two daughters:

- **Isabella Jean** (2015–)
- **Katherine Grace** (2018–)

Nicholas "Miki" Kallay married Paula Ann Johnson (1965–) in 2001. They have one son:

- Nicholas Paul Kallay (2003–)

John "Janko" Kallay: unmarried

Kathy "Kati" Kallay married Charles Tatum in 2003.

John Harrison Baucus married Cathy Becknell (1967–) in 1998. They have two children:

- **John Mitchell Baucus** (2000–)
- **Gabrielle Elizabeth Jean Baucus** (2002–)

Laura Louise Baucus married Jeff Miller (1974–) in 1997. They have two children:

- **Danielle LeAnn Miller** (2005–)
- **Brandon Mark Miller** (2008–)

Phillip Ellison Baucus married Katharine Ann Taylor (1977–). Phillip was in killed in action in Iraq in 2006.

Tyler Van Doren Hibbard married Heather Erica Niemeyer (1980–) in 2008. They have two children:

- **James Van Doren Hibbard** (2013–)
- **Laine Cascade Hibbard** (2016–)

Marshall Sieben Hibbard married Terah Leigh Crystal Thompson (1980–) in 2009.

Tyrrell Henry Hibbard married Mary Catherine Ahmann (1981–) in 2010. They have two daughters:

- **Genevieve Sieben Hibbard** (2011–)
- **Hazel Jane Hibbard** (2013–)

Cooper Whitney Hibbard married Ashley Michelle Wertheimer (1986–) in 2018. They have two children:

- **Posey Freida Gertrude Hibbard** (2021–)
- **Boone Henry Sieben Hibbard** (2024–) ❖

Appendix II

SIEBEN BRANDS

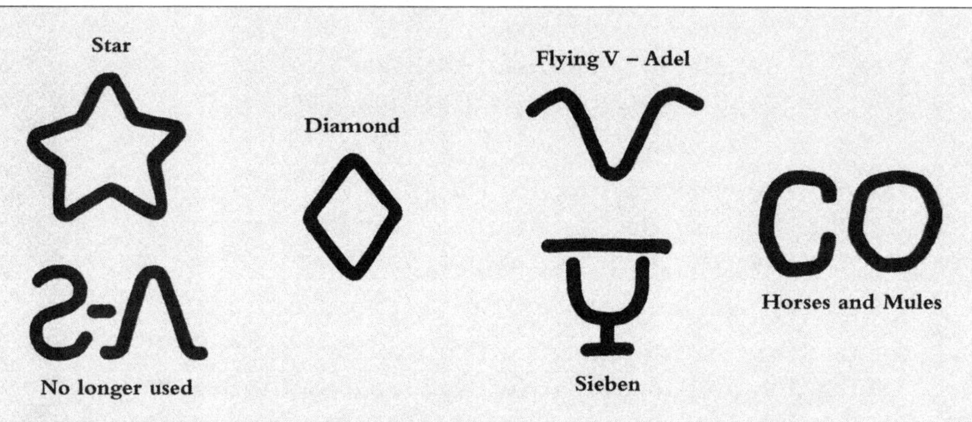

Henry Sieben recorded his first cattle brand, the Diamond Brand, in 1874. Source: Jean Baucus, *Henry Sieben, 1846-1937: Legacy of Livestock and Land.* Self-Published, 1995 (reprinted here with permission of the family).

- Henry Sieben's first registerd brand in Montana was the Diamond Brand.
- The Sieben Ranch Company (Baucus family) today mainly uses the Bar Wineglass.
- The Sieben Live Stock Company (Hibbard family) today uses the Flying V and the Diamond. ❖

Appendix III

—OTHER CHARACTERS—

Teddy Blue Abbott.......... Cowboy poet who worked for Granville Stuart, 1880s.

Nolan Armstrong........... Foreman of the Diamond Ranch, Culbertson.

Louis Arnett..................... Henry and Leonard Sieben's companion on journey west.

Frank Arnette................... Henry Sieben's nephew. Son of Margaret Sieben.

Charles H. Austin........... Chestnut Valley rancher.

E.C. Babcock.................. Proprietor of gentlemen's furnishings business and friend of Henry Sieben's.

Minnie Babcock............. Friend of Alberta Gordon Sieben and wife of E.C. Babcock.

Harvey Barbour............... Horse owner and friend of Henry Sieben's in Helena.

John Bielenberg.............. Conrad Kohrs' son-in law.

Henry N. Blake................ Attorney and Chief Justice of the Montana Territorial Supreme Court.

John M. Boardman.......... Manager of Pioneer Cattle Company, Conrad Kohrs's son-in-law.

John Bozeman................ Pioneer who established the Bozeman Trail into southwestern Montana Territory in the 1860s.

Theodore M. Brantley.... Longest serving Chief Justice of the Montana Supreme Court (1899–1922), friend of Henry Sieben's.

Charles H. Bray............... Superintendent of Kessler Brickworks. Ran against Henry Sieben for the Republican seat in Montana's 1899 legislature.

Horace Brewster.............Henry Sieben's foreman on his ranch at Flatwillow, 1880s.

Paul O. Brewster.............Partner with Henry in the Diamond Ranch, Culbertson.

Jim Bridger...................... Pioneer who established the Bridger Trail into southwestern Montana Territory in the 1860s.

Charles A. Broadwater.... Freighting, railroad and banking magnate. Leonard Sieben worked for Broadwater's Diamond R. Freighting Company in the 1860s.

Julie Broadwater............. Friend of Alberta Gordon Sieben and wife of Charles A. Broadwater.

H. P. Brooks..................... Rancher on the Fort Maginnis range with Henry Sieben, 1880s.

Don Brown...................... Helena area rancher.

John Brown...................... Prospector who mined with Henry Sieben at Madison Gulch, 1865.

Martha Jane Canary........ American frontierswoman and storyteller known as "Calamity Jane." Canary and Henry Sieben likely crossed paths in Virginia City, 1864, and in Castle in the 1880s.

Charles Cannon.............. Businessman and owner of Cannon Ranch (now known as the Adel Ranch).

Henry Cannon................. Businessman and owner of Cannon Ranch (now known as the Adel Ranch).

Robert Chesnut............... Namesake of the Chestnut Valley and first settler in the area.

William Chessman.......... Helena area businessman.

Adelaide Child................ Friend of Alberta Gordon Sieben and wife of Harry W. Child.

Harry W. Child................. Businessman who founded Yellowstone Park Company and friend of Henry Sieben's.

William Andrews Clark.. Miner, banker and politician.

Thomas Clary.................. Wagon master with the Diamond R Freight Company.

Robert "Bob" Coburn.... Henry Sieben's partner in Flatwillow Ranch, 1880s.

Walt Coburn.................... Bob Coburn's son.

Timothy E. Collins.......... Great Falls businessman and attorney; partner with Henry Sieben in White Sulphur Springs Association.

Joseph Conrad................ Fort Benton area rancher and business associate of Henry Sieben's.

W.G. Conrad.................... Banker and business partner of Henry Sieben's.

Margaret Cruse................ Friend of Alberta Gordon Sieben and wife of Thomas Cruse.

Thomas Cruse................. Helena area miner, rancher and businessman.

Marcus Daly..................... Butte mine owner and businessman.

A.J. Davis.......................... Businessman and owner of DHS Ranch, 1880s.

Nelson J. Dovenspeck..... Rancher in Meagher County.

Sidney Edgerton............. First Territorial Governor of Montana, 1864–1866.

James Fergus.................... Miner, rancher and politician. Ranched with Henry Sieben on the Fort Maginnis range. Purchased Malcolm Clarke's ranch in the 1870s.

Henry Fisher.................... Foreman at Sieben Ranch.

A.J. Fisk............................ Helena newspaper owner.

Dan Floweree.................. Rancher who operated one of the largest ranches in the state—the Floweree Horse and Sheep Company.

Bartholomew Gehring.... Rancher in Prickly Pear Valley, Helena.

Nate Gibson..................... Operator of the *Mayflower* ferry boat at Chestnut Valley.

Paris Gibson..................... U.S. Senator, sheep rancher, businessman, founder of Great Falls.

Joe Goey........................... Rancher who first employed Henry Sieben when he reached Virginia City, 1864.

Edward I. Goodkind....... Helena area wholesaler.

Thomas Gorham............ Manager of Steele's mercantile at The Ferry, Chestnut Valley.

Jeff Gowen........................ Rancher who first employed Henry Sieben when he reached Virginia City, 1864. Also freighted with Henry.

N.J. Gould........................ Banker and friend of Henry Sieben's.

Richard Grant.................Former fur-trader who, along with his sons, brought cattle from the Oregon Trail into southwestern Montana for grazing, 1850.

Theodore Grimaud.........Sheepherder who killed Sieben ranch herder, Jesse Liefer.

Thomas A Grimes...........Sheep rancher and business partner in Sieben & Grimes operation, 1898–1921.

H.H. Guthrie.................. Helena area businessman, friend of Henry Sieben's.

Charles S. Haire..............Celebrated architect who designed Henry Sieben's home at 520 Harrison Avenue.

Rufus J. Hardy................ Chestnut Valley rancher.

Samuel Hauser.................Territorial Governor and Helena area banker and businessman.

Cornelius Hedges...........Attorney and Montana superintendent of schools (1872–1878 and 1883–1885). Helped found Yellowstone National Park, 1872.

Edna Hedges....................Friend of Alberta Gordon Sieben and wife of miner and attorney Cornelius Hedges.

Louis Heller.................... Henry and Leonard Sieben's companion on journey west in 1864.

Holly J. Herrin............... Rancher adjacent to the Sieben ranch, Prickly Pear Valley, Helena.

Aaron Hershfield............. Helena area banker and partner with Henry Sieben in White Sulphur Springs Association.

Susanna Hilger................ Rancher adjacent to the Sieben Ranch, Prickly Pear Valley, Helena.

James J. Hill......................CEO of the Great Northern Railway, 1870s–1900s.

S.S. Hobson......................Rancher in the Judith Basin area.

Alvin Hodson..................Operator of the *Mayflower* ferry boat at Chestnut Valley.

Axel Holmstrom.............Foreman at Sieben Ranch.

Anton M. Holter.............Helena area businessman and politician, friend of Henry Sieben's.

Mary Holter.................... Friend of Alberta Gordon Sieben and wife of Anton M. Holter.

Allen Hurlbut..................Gold prospector who led a train over the Bozeman Trail in 1864.

Louis Kaufman................ Partner with Louis Stadler in the OH Ranch near Utica and a Helena butcher shop. Good friend of Henry Sieben's.

Percy Kennett.................. Rancher and friend of Henry Sieben's.

Nickolas Kessler...............Brewer, brickmaker, and businessman.

C.J. Keyes..........................Henry Sieben's chauffeur.

Mary Kleinschmidt..........Friend of Alberta Gordon Sieben and wife of Theodore Kleinschmidt.

Theodore Kleinschmidt..Helena area banker and friend of Henry Sieben's.

Perry P. Kline.................. Rancher and Henry Sieben's business partner in Big Hole Ranch Company.

Conrad Kohrs.................. Owned some of the largest ranches in Montana including the DHS Ranch and Pioneer Cattle Company. Good friend of Henry Sieben.

John Lepley...................... Fort Benton area rancher, friend of Henry Sieben's in White Sulphur Springs.

Jesse Liefer........................ Sheepherder at Sieben Ranch.

Henry Liston.................... Rancher, friend of Henry Sieben's.

John H. Longmaid........... Marysville mining businessman, friend of Henry's.

Philip Lovell..................... Rancher, 1860s.

J.L.B. Mayer..................... Rancher, ran against Henry Sieben for the Republican seat in Montana's 1899 legislature.

Frank B. McCann............ Culbertson rancher who acquired the Diamond Ranch in the 1940s.

Len McFarland................ Sheep rancher on the Fort Maginnis range.

M.E. Milner...................... Rancher who owned the Square Butte enterprise, worked closely with Henry in the Northern Montana Roundup Association.

John H. Ming.................. Helena area rancher and theater owner.

Jeanette Morrow............. Friend of Henry's in White Sulphur Springs.

John T. Murphy................ Rancher and businessman, friend of Henry Sieben's.

Pat Nacey......................... Employee of the Diamond Ranch.

Pete Nelson....................... Foreman of Adel Ranch.

Eva Nolan.......................... Original settler in the Chestnut Valley.

Brian O'Connell.............. Rancher adjacent to the Sieben Ranch, Prickly Pear Valley, Helena.

William C. Orr................ Partner in the Poindexter and Orr Livestock Company.

Dr. William Parberry...... Owner of White Sulphur Hot Springs, 1870–83, partner with Henry Sieben in White Sulphur Springs Association.

Henry Parchen................. Drugstore owner and friend of Henry Sieben's in Helena.

J.L. Perkins........................ Chestnut Valley rancher.

Jesse I. Phelps................... Rancher and friend of Henry Sieben's.

Benjamin D. Phillips....... Rancher, friend of Henry Sieben's.

W.T. Pigott........................ Great Falls attorney.

Henry Plummer.............. Sheriff of Bannack and outlaw. Hung just before Henry arrived in Montana.

George Powell.................. Immigrant who hunted with Henry Sieben and an Irishman named Collins near Crow Creek, 1865.

Mary Power....................... Friend of Alberta Gordon Sieben and wife of Thomas C. Power

Thomas C. Power............ U.S. Senator, rancher and businessman. Partnered with Henry Sieben in the Big Hole Ranching Company, 1907.

A.K. Prescott.................... Sheep rancher, friend of Henry Sieben's.

Theodore Roosevelt........ U.S. President (1901–09), rancher and businessman. Member of Montana Stockgrowers Association, 1880s.

Charles Marion Russell... Celebrated Montana artist who sketched *Waiting for a Chinook* for Louis Stadler and Louis Kaufman, 1887.

Wilbur F. Sanders............ Attorney and U.S. Senator from Montana.

Henry Schrammeck........ Ranch manager for the Sieben brothers in the Chestnut Valley, 1870s.

A.J. Seligman.................. Helena area businessman, friend of Henry Sieben's.

Bill Shanklin................... Ranch hand at Adel Ranch.

William Shean................ Killed when car Henry Sieben was driving struck his wagon, 1911.

John T. Smith.................. Diarist who left a record of the journey into Montana with John Bozeman, 1864.

Royal Smith..................... Helena area rancher.

Jim Spurgeon.................. Ranch manager for Conrad Kohrs.

Louis Stadler................... Partner with Louis Kaufman in the OH Ranch near Utica and a Helena butcher shop. Friend of Henry Sieben's.

George Steele.................. Founder of "The Ferry" community in the Chestnut Valley and proprietor of Steele's mercantile.

Frank Sterling................. Cascade area rancher.

Nelson Story................... Pioneer rancher and businessman who drove the first Texas longhorns into Montana, 1865

F.E. Stranahan.................. Helena area attorney, ran against Henry Sieben for the Republican seat in Montana's 1899 legislature.

Granville Stuart............... Rancher and manager of DHS Ranch, Fort Maginnis range. Left his memoirs.

John Survant.................... Rancher in the Malta area.

Charles W. Swett............. Chestnut Valley rancher.

William Swett.................. Chestnut Valley rancher.

Anna E. Thoroughman... Original settler in the Chestnut Valley.

Lily Tool........................... Friend of Alberta Gordon Sieben and wife of E.C. Babcock.

Joseph K. Toole................ Politician and Governor of Montana (1889–1893, 1901–1908), friend of Henry Sieben's.

James Trenary.................. Henry Sieben's chauffeur.

Frank K. Turner............... Helena area grocer and friend of Henry Sieben's.

Abram H. Voorhees......... Diarist who kept a record of the journey into Montana with Captain Hurlbut, 1864.

R.C. Wallace.......................Helena area grocer, ran against Henry Sieben for the Republican seat in Montana's 1899 legislature.

Charles Watson................Marysville businessman. Ran against Henry Sieben for the Republican seat in Montana's 1899 legislature.

William Wheeler............. Helena area businessman, friend of Henry Sieben's.

Pierre Wibaux.................. French stockman who ranched in the Beaver Valley, Montana.

Red Wolrich..................... Crew member at Adel Ranch.

Henry Zimmerman........ Operator of the *Mayflower* ferry boat at Chestnut Valley. ◈

ENDNOTES

INTRODUCTION

[1] John Russell, *Treasure State Tycoon: Nelson Story and the Making of Montana* (Helena: Montana Historical Society Press, 2019) and Bill Vaughn, *The Last Heir: The Triumphs and Tragedies of Two Montana Families* (Lincoln: Bison Books, 2022).

[2] Dick Pace, "Henry Sieben: Pioneer Montana Stockman," 1979.

[3] Whitney Hibbard interview with Peggy Gordwon Lestz, January 15, 1982. Oral Histories about the Life of Henry Sieben, Montana History Portal, Oral Histories about the Life of Henry Sieben, *https://www.mtmemory.org/nodes/view/106564*

PROLOGUE

[1] Kiner, *History of Henry County, Illinois,* 559-61.

[2] A.T. Hibbard written notes from conversation with Henry Sieben, Hibbard family private collection; Whitney Hibbard interview with Ruth Sieben Hagelin, November 28, 1982. Oral Histories about the Life of Henry Sieben, Montana History Portal, Oral Histories about the Life of Henry Sieben, *https://www.mtmemory.org/nodes/view/106564*

[3] Bob Sieben private collection; Baucus, *Henry Sieben,* 8; Pace, "Henry Sieben," 4; Office of the Illinois Secretary of State, *https://www.ilsos.gov/departments/archives/teaching_packages/early_chicago/doc23.html;* Wilkerson and Richmond, *Germans in Illinois,* 1-62; "Geneseoans will Celebrate Golden Wedding Anniversary," *The Dispatch,* April 7, 1928; Burns, *The Civil War,* 1990.

CHAPTER 1

[1] "Henry Sieben, Oldest of Montana Stockmen," *The Mountaineer,* 17 December 1934; "Henry Sieben, Gold Days Pioneer," *The Montana Record-Herald,* 24 January 1930; "Geneseoans will Celebrate Golden Wedding Anniversary," *The Dispatch,* 7 April 1928.

[2] "Henry Sieben, Gold Days Pioneer," *The Montana Record-Herald,* 24 January 1930; Doyle, *Journeys to the Land of Gold,* Vol. 1, 39-42.

[3] Egan, *1864,* 162-73.

[4] Egan, *1864,* 74-78.

[5] Doyle, *Journeys to the Land of Gold,* Vol. 1, 143; Johnson, *Some Went West.*

[6] Johnson, *The Bloody Bozeman,* 56-58.

[7] Doyle, *Journeys to the Land of Gold,* Vol. 1, 162-63; Enzler, *Jim Bridger,* 247-51.

[8] Doyle, *Journeys to the Land of Gold,* Vol. 1, 142-49.

[9] Doyle, *Journeys to the Land of Gold,* Vol. 1, 204.

[10] "Henry Sieben, Gold Days Pioneer," *The Montana Record-Herald,* 24 January 1930.

[11] Doyle, *Journeys to the Land of Gold,* Vol. 1, 142-49; 158-66; 201-5; Johnson, *The Bloody Bozeman,* 57-65.

[12] "Henry Sieben, Gold Days Pioneer," *The Montana Record-Herald,* 24 January 1930.

[13] Egan, *1864,* 12-13. Johnson, "Great Falls is a White Man's City," 45; Johnson, *The Middle Kingdom,* 16-17; U.S. Census 1870, https://www.ancestrycdn.com/support/us/2016/11/montana.pdf

[14] "Henry Sieben, Gold Days Pioneer," *The Montana Record-Herald,* 24 January 1930; Malone, *Montana,* 78-81.

[15] "Gold in Alder Gulch," *https://www.hmdb.org/m.asp?m=117023,* accessed November 3, 2024.

[16] Sibell Wolle, *Montana Pay Dirt,* 20-46; Baumler, *Girl from the Gulches.*

[17] Stuart, *Forty Years,* 23.

[18] Stuart, *Forty Years,* 263-66; "Covered Wagon Pioneers," *The Dispatch,* 4 December 1926.

[19] "Letter List," *The Montana Post,* 9 December 1865, 11 August 1866.

[20] "Henry Sieben, Oldest of Montana Stockmen," *The Mountaineer,* 17 December 1934; Stuart, *Forty Years,* 16.

[21] Egan, *1864,* 215.

[22] Stuart, *Forty Years,* 28-31; Holmes, *Montana,* 107-8; Johnson, "Flour Famine," 18-27.

[23] For more on the Mullan and Montana roads, see: Axline, *Taming Big Sky Country,* 14-17.

[24] Axline, *Taming Big Sky Country,* 9, 13-14.

[25] Axline, *Taming Big Sky Country,* 13-14; 17-21.

[26] "Henry Sieben, Oldest of Montana Stockmen," *The Mountaineer,* 17 December 1934.

[27] "Henry Sieben, Gold Days Pioneer," *The Montana Record-Herald,* 24 January 1930

[28] Egan, *1864,* 141-44.

[29] "Henry Sieben, Oldest of Montana Stockmen," *The Mountaineer,* 17 December 1934.

[30] Axline, *Taming Big Sky Country,* 20-21.

[31] Egan, *1864,* 35-37.

[32] Henry Sieben, Oldest of Montana Stockmen," *The Mountaineer,* 17 December 1934.

[33] Henry Sieben, Oldest of Montana Stockmen," *The Mountaineer,* 17 December 1934.

[34] Stuart, *Forty Years,* 31; Egan, 1864, 134-36.

[35] "Henry Sieben, Oldest of Montana Stockmen," *The Mountaineer,* 17 December 1934.

[36] Malone, *Montana,* 145-6; Russell, *Treasure State Tycoon.*

[37] "Henry Sieben, Oldest of Montana Stockmen," *The Mountaineer,* 17 December,1934.

CHAPTER 2

[1] "Pioneer's Funeral Largely Attended," *The Great Falls Tribune,* 10 April 1913; Rowe, *Mountains and Meadows,* 251-52; "Henry Sieben, Gold Days Pioneer," *The Montana-Record Herald,* 23 January 1930; Henry Sieben, Oldest of Montana Stockmen," *The Mountaineer,* 17 December 1934.

[2] Malone, *Montana,* 148-50.

[3] "Henry Sieben, Gold Days Pioneer," *The Montana-Record Herald,* 23 January 1930; Henry Sieben, Oldest of Montana Stockmen," *The Mountaineer,* 17 December 1934.

[4] Kinsey Howard, *Montana: High Wide and Handsome;* Malone, *Montana,* 119-23; Holmes, *Montana,* 124-44; Henderson, "The Piikuni and the U.S. Army's Piegan Expedition," 48-70. For more on Métis history, see Candi Zion, *In Between People: The Métis of Central Montana* (2021) and *Walkin Down the Middle: The Hi-Line Metis* (2022).

[5] Malone, *Montana,* 148; Kohrs, *Conrad Kohrs: An Autobiography,* 58.

[6] "Henry Sieben, Gold Days Pioneer," *The Montana-Record Herald,* 23 January 1930; Henry Sieben, Oldest of Montana Stockmen," *The Mountaineer,* 17 December 1934; Robert F. Clary Jr., *https://www.legacy.com/us/obituaries/greatfallstribune/name/robert-clary-obituary?id=21917466,* accessed 15 December 2022; Kohrs, *Conrad Kohrs: An Autobiography,* 55.

[7] Kohrs, *Conrad Kohrs: An Autobiography,* 63.

[8] Hibbard family collection, conversation notes between Henry and his daughter Margaret; "Henry Sieben, Gold Days Pioneer," *The Montana-Record Herald,* 23 January 1930; MC 64 (4:4-1), "Jake Sieben," Recollections from Anna E. Bickett Thoroughman, Montana Historical Society Pioneers' Reminiscences; "Chestnut," *The Old Town Promoter,* 7 August 1944; Eva Nolan Reminiscences, pp. 1-4; Rowe, *Mountains and Meadows,* 4; Malone, *Montana,* 151-52.

[9] "Henry Sieben, Gold Days Pioneer," *The Montana-Record Herald,* 23 January 1930; John F. Baucus, personal communication, October 2022.

[10] "Meagher County News," *Helena Weekly Herald,* 8 June 1876; "Local News," *Rocky Mountain Husbandman,* 8 June 1876; "Loss of Sheep by Drowning," *Helena Weekly Herald,* 1 February 1877; "Stock Growing in Montana," *Helena Weekly Herald,* 20 November 1879.

[11] "Sun River Items," *The Benton Record,* 5 February 1876; "Personal," *The Montana Record-Herald,* 23 December 1875.

[12] "Brevities," *Helena Weekly Herald,* 9 March 1876.

[13] Malone, *Montana,* 158-59.

[14] "Passenger List," *Helena Weekly Herald,* 4 May 1876; "Jacob Sieben," Recollections from Anna E. Bickett Thoroughman, Montana Historical Society Pioneers' Reminiscences; Rowe, *Mountains and Meadows,* 16-21.

[15] "Jacob Sieben," Recollections from Anna E. Bickett Thoroughman, Montana Historical Society Pioneers' Reminiscences.

[16] "Jacob Sieben," Recollections from Anna E. Bickett Thoroughman, Montana Historical Society Pioneers' Reminiscences; "Territorial News," *The Benton Record,* 19 January 1877.

[17] Rowe, *Mountains and Meadows,* 19-22; Eva Nolan James Writings 1950, Montana Historical Society, pp. 1-3.

[18] Rowe, *Mountains and Meadows,* 26.

[19] Eva Nolan James Writings 1950, Montana Historical Society, p. 2.

[20] Rowe, *Mountains and Meadows,* 26.

[21] "Henry Sieben, Oldest of Montana Stockmen," *The Mountaineer,* 17 December 1934.

[22] Hotel Arrivals," *Helena Weekly Herald,* 19 November 1874; "Brevities," *Helena Weekly Herald,* 25 January 1877; "Personal," *Helena Weekly Herald,* 15 March 1877; *Rocky Mountain Husbandman,* 11 June 1877.

[23] "The Bachelors of Sun River," *The Benton Record,* 26 February 1876.

[24] "Special Correspondence," *Rocky Mountain Husbandman,* 15 June 1876.

[25] "Steamer Arrivals-Manifests and Passenger Lists," *The Benton Record,* 31 May 1878 "Local News," *Helena Weekly Herald,* 17 January 1878; "Local News," *Rocky Mountain Husbandman,* 21 February 1878; "Brevities," *Rocky Mountain Husbandman,* 5 June 1879; "Henry Sieben, Gold Days Pioneer," *The Montana-Record Herald,* 23 January 1930.

[26] Letter from Henry Sieben to Ike Greenhood, 1879; and letter from Jake Sieben to Messrs Greenhood Bohm & Co., 1879. Montana Historical Society Library and Archives, MC 130.

[27] "Henry Sieben, Oldest of Montana Stockmen," *The Mountaineer,* 17 December 1934; "Local News," *Rocky Mountain Husbandman,* 29 May 1879.

[28] Axline, *Taming Big Sky Country,* 30-31; "Annual Report of the Receipts and Expenditures of the County of Meagher, M.T." *Rocky Mountain Husbandman,* 13 March 1879; "Road District No. 8 Fund," *Rocky Mountain Husbandman,* 20 March 1879.

[29] *The Biographical Record of Henry County, Illinois,* pp. 286-87; Hibbard family collection, conversation notes between Henry and his daughter Margaret.

[30] "More Sheep," *Helena Weekly Herald,* 25 September 1879; "Henry Sieben, Oldest of Montana Stockmen," *The Mountaineer,* 17 December 1934.

[31] Henry Sieben, Oldest of Montana Stockmen," *The Mountaineer,* 17 December 1934.

CHAPTER 3

[1] "Northern Montana," *Helena Weekly Herald,* 1 January 1880.

[2] "A Good Winter for Stock," *Helena Weekly Herald,* 12 February 1880.

[3] "Rambles of Our Traveling Man," *Rocky Mountain Husbandman,* 5 August 1880.

[4] "Rambles of Our Traveling Man," *Rocky Mountain Husbandman,* 5 August 1880.

[5] "Chestnut Valley," *Rocky Mountain Husbandman,* 20 July 1882.

[6] Kiner, *History of Henry County, Illinois,* 559-61; *Roosevelt County's Treasured Years,* 264-65; *History of Montana,* 921-22.

[7] Author in communication with Chase Hibbard, John F. Baucus, Brent Roeder (Sheep and Wool Extension Specialist, Montana State University), August 8, 2023 [e-mail].

[8] "Brevities," *Helena Weekly Herald,* 25 March 1880; "Fatal Disease Among Sheep," *Rocky Mountain Husbandman,* 13 May 1880.

[9] "Lady Attacked by an Enraged Cow," *Helena Weekly Herald,* 24 February 1881.

[10] Malone, *Montana,* 154.

[11] "Rambles of Our Traveling Man," *Rocky Mountain Husbandman,* 5 August 1880.

[12] Coburn, *Pioneer Cattleman in Montana,* 8; "Local News," *Rocky Mountain Husbandman,* 14 July 1881.

[13] "Montana Matters," *The River Press,* 20 July, 1881; "Which Refer to the Cattle and Sheep on a Thousand Hills in Montana," *The River Press,* 1 March 1882.

[14] "An Important Sale," *The River Press,* 1 March 1882; Dale, *Ties, Rails, and Telegraph Wires.*

[15] Henry Sieben, Oldest of Montana Stockmen," *the Mountaineer,* 17 December 1934.

[16] "Local News," *The Benton Weekly Record,* 30 March 1882.

[17] "Henry Sieben, Oldest of Montana Stockmen," *the Mountaineer,* 17 December 1934; "Chestnut Valley," *Rocky Mountain Husbandman,* 20 July 1882; "From Friday's Daily," *The Benton Weekly Record,* 22 September 1882; Coburn, *Pioneer Cattleman in Montana,* 8; Malone, *Montana,* 163-64.

[18] Malone, *Montana,* 146-56.

[19] "Notice to Stock Growers," *Rocky Mountain Husbandman,* May 1883-4.

[20] "White Sulphur Hot Springs Sold," *Helena Weekly Herald,* 4 January 1883; "Stocked for $80,000," *Rocky Mountain Husbandman,* 4 January 1883; "White Sulphur Springs," *The River Press,* 17 January 1883.

[21] Merchants National Bank Collection, Box 31, folder 7 & 10, Montana Historical Society.

[22] Whitney Hibbard in conversation with Pearl Leede Rhein, 1980s. Pearl's mother was Jeanette Morrow and her uncle was Robert Coburn, Henry's one-time business partner; "Personalities," *The River Press,* 4 July 1883; "Local News," *Rocky Mountain Husbandman,* 4 October 1883.

[23] 14 November 1882, Granville Stuart to Samuel Hauser, MC 37, Box 20, folder 21, Montana Historical Society.

[24] "Henry Sieben, Oldest of Montana Stockmen," *The Mountaineer,* 17 December 1934.

[25] 13 August 1881; 7 Aug 1882; 31 Dec 1883, Granville Stuart to Samuel Hauser, MC 37, Box 20, folder 21, Montana Historical Society; *The Stockgrowers Journal,* 1 August 1885; Burns, *The American Buffalo,* 2023.

[26] 10 Nov 1885; 16 Jan 1886, Granville Stuart to Samuel Hauser, MC 37, Box 20, folder 21, Montana Historical Society. 23 September 1885, Henry Sieben to Mr Hershfield, MC 115 Box 8, Folder 20, Montana Historical Society.

[27] "A Big Enterprise," *Helena Weekly Herald,* 3 December 1885.

[28] Malone, *Montana,* 160.

[29] Author in communication with Chase Hibbard, June 2023.

[30] Stuart, *Forty Years on the Frontier,* 175-80; Malone, *Montana,* 160-63; Mueller, *The Central Montana Vigilante Raids,* 27-29; Montana Stockgrowers Association Records, 1885-1912, Vol. 3, MC 45, Montana Historical Society.

[31] The 1885 Legislature created two new functions of government: a territorial veterinary surgeon who could quarantine cattle and the Board of Stock Commissioners. This board would conduct brand inspection at marketing points and supervise the range industry in general.

[32] "Stock Notes," *The River Press,* 28 April 1886; 8 September 1886; "Stock Market," *The River Press,* 8 September 1886; *Stockgrowers Journal,* 27 March 1886.

[33] "Local Notes," *The River Press,* 22 December 1886; "Married," *Helena Weekly Herald,* 23 December 1886; "Personal," *Helena Weekly Herald,* 23 December 1886.

CHAPTER 4

[1] Aarstad et al, *Montana Place Names,* 86; Kohrs, *An Autobiography,* 76; Stuart, *Forty Years,* 184-87.

[2] Whitney Hibbard interview with Jim Spurgeon, September 20, 1981. Oral Histories about the Life of Henry Sieben, Montana History Portal, Oral Histories about the Life of Henry Sieben, *https://www.mtmemory.org/nodes/view/106564*

[3] "City and County." *The Billings Gazette,* 11 November 1887.

[4] Horace Brewster Reminiscences, 1922-1926, SC 468, Montana Historical Society.

[5] Stuart, *Forty Years,* 180-84.

[6] Stuart, *Forty Years,* 180-84.

[7] Pace, "Henry Sieben" 8-9; Whitney Hibbard in conversation with Margaret Hibbard, September 20, 1981. Oral Histories about the Life of Henry Sieben, Montana History Portal, Oral Histories about the Life of Henry Sieben, *https://www.mtmemory.org/nodes/view/106564*

[8] Malone, *Montana,* 155.

[9] Malone, *Montana,* 156.

[10] Malone, *Montana,* 156-57.

[11] Malone, *Montana,* 155-59.

[12] Stuart, *Forty Years,* 228-30; "Local Notes," *The Glendive Independent,* 7 March 1885.

[13] Stuart, *Forty Years,* 230.

[14] "Henry Sieben, Oldest of Montana Stockmen," *The Mountaineer,* 17 December 1934; "Stock Notes," *The River Press,* 8 September 1886; "City and County," *The Billings Gazette,* 31 August 1886.

[15] Stuart, *Pioneering in Montana I,* 234.

[16] Whitney Hibbard interview with Margaret Hibbard, September 20, 1981.

[17] Malone, *Montana,* 165; "Stadler and Kaufman Homes," *Independent Record,* 19 December 2016; "Waiting on a Chinook (Last of 5,000)," *https://cmrussell.org/product/waiting-on-a-chinook-last-of-the-5000,* accessed November 4, 2024.

[18] Stuart, *Forty Years,* 230-39; *History of Montana,* 921-22.

[19] Kohrs, *An Autobiography,* 82-85.

[20] Malone, *Montana,* 165-66; "Henry Sieben, Oldest of Montana Stockmen," *The Mountaineer,* 17 December 1934.

[21] Kohrs, *An Autobiography,* 86.

[22] Kohrs, *An Autobiography,* 82-5; Stuart, *Forty Years,* 230-39.

[23] Whitney Hibbard interview with Brian O'Connell, January 2, 1982. Oral Histories about the Life of Henry Sieben, Montana History Portal,

Oral Histories about the Life of Henry Sieben, *https://www.mtmemory.org/nodes/view/106564*

[24] "Local News," *The River Press,* 25 February 1891.

[25] Stuart, *Forty Years,* 228.

[26] Holmes, *Montana Stories of the Land,* 152, 170–75.

[27] Kohrs, *An Autobiography,* 86–94; "Reservation Notes," *The River Press,* 10 October 1888; "Cattle Shipments," *The River Press,* 24 October 1888; "Personal," *Helena Weekly Herald,* 12 December 1889; Malone, *Montana,* 167.

[28] Whitney Hibbard interview with Margaret Hibbard, 20 September 1981; Coburn, *Pioneer Cattlemen,* 201.

[29] "Record your Patents," *Great Falls Tribune,* 28 January 1891.

[30] Aarstad et al, *Montana Place Names;* 41; "The Mining History," *https://www.mininghistoryassociation.org/ButteHistory.htm,* accessed 20 November, 2023; "Castle Town, Montana," *https://www.legendsofamerica.com/castle-town-montana,* accessed 20 November, 2023; Etulain, *The Life and Legends of Calamity Jane.*

[31] Meagher County Clerk and Recorder, 9 August 1890; 25 August 1890; 27 January 1891; 10 February 1891; "Mining Notes," *The Montana Mining Review,* 25 February 1891; "Around the Courts," *Great Falls Tribune,* 17 October 1891; "Court House," *Great Falls Tribune,* 10 December 1891; "District Court Proceedings, *Rocky Mountain Husbandman,* 11 May 1893.

[32] "Application for Patent," *Helena Evening Herald,* 1 November 1897; Whitney Hibbard interview with Margaret Hibbard, September 20, 1981; Whitney Hibbard interview with Brian O'Connell, January 2, 1982.

[33] Whitney Hibbard interview with Margaret Hibbard, September 20, 1981; "Barbour and Bickett," *Helena Semi Weekly Herald,* 7 June 1894.

[34] Whitney Hibbard interview with Margaret Hibbard, September 20, 1981.

[35] Whitney Hibbard interview with Margaret Hibbard, September 20, 1981; *The Independent Record,* 11 December 1892; "Blue Ribbon Day," *Helena Semi-Weekly Herald,* 6 September 1894.

[36] Whitney Hibbard interview with Margaret Hibbard, September 20, 1981.

[37] "History of Butte," Butte Silver Bow County; *https://co.silverbow.mt.us/DocumentCenter/View/15538/History-of-Buttedocx;* "Population of Montana 1890-1920," *www.census.gov;* Kohrs, *An Autobiography,* 95.

[38] "Democratic Primaries," *The Independent Record,* 27 March 1889; "Republican Co. Convention," *Great Falls Leader,* 5 September 1889.

[39] Emmons, *The Butte Irish,* 99-103; Malone, *Montana,* 211-12; Kohrs, *An Autobiography,* 93-94.

[40] Kohrs, *An Autobiography,* 93–94; Malone, *Montana,* 210–14; author in conversation with Professor David Emmons, December 2023.

[41] Author in conversation with Professor Amy McKinney, January 22, 2024.

[42] "Covering Cattle Kate," Tom Rea, November 15, 2014, *www.wyohistory.org;* "The Johnson County War," John W. Davis, November 8, 2014, *www.wyohistory.org.*

[43] "Local Notes," *The River Press,* 10 August 1898.

CHAPTER 5

[1] Kohrs, *An Autobiography,* 92-94; Holmes, *Montana,* 198.

[2] Whitney Hibbard interview with Margaret Hibbard, September 20, 1981.

[3] Whitney Hibbard interview with Jim Spurgeon, September 20, 1981. Oral Histories about the Life of Henry Sieben, Montana History Portal, Oral Histories about the Life of Henry Sieben, *https://www.mtmemory.org/nodes/view/106564;* "Personal and General," *The Independent Record,* 7 May 1883.

[4] "Havre Items," *The Chinook Opinion,* 3 October 1895.

[5] "A Fine Programme," *The Daily Helena Herald,* 25 May 1894.

[6] "Personal Points," *The Cheyenne Daily Leader,* 16 July 1889; "Annual Meeting," *The Cheyenne Daily Leader,* 26 November 1891; "Personals," *The Chinook Opinion,* 21 April 1892; *The Chinook Opinion,* 13 August 1891 and 8 October 1891.

[7] Whitney Hibbard interview with Jim Spurgeon, September 20, 1981.

[8] "Natawista," *Dictionary of Canadian Biography,* accessed December 4, 2024, *https://www.biographi.ca/en/bio/natawista_12E.html;* Malone, *Montana,* 56-59.

[9] Aarstad et al, *Montana Place Names,* 60-61; *100 Years in Culbertson,* 43.

[10] Whitney Hibbard interview with Frank B. McCann, September 17, 1981. Oral Histories about the Life of Henry Sieben, Montana History Portal, Oral Histories about the Life of Henry Sieben, *https://www.mtmemory.org/nodes/view/106564*

[11] Whitney Hibbard interview with Frank B. McCann, September 17, 1981; Baucus, *Henry Sieben,* 14-15; Malone, *Montana,* 163-64; Holmes, *Montana,* 153-54; Kinsey Howard, *Montana,* 104-05; author in conversation with Professor David Emmons, January 16, 2024 [e-mail].

[12] Author in conversation with Whitney Hibbard, January 18, 2024.

[13] Whitney Hibbard interview with Margaret Hibbard, September 20, 1981.

[14] "Henry Sieben," *The Mountaineer,* 17 December 1934.

[15] "Henry Sieben," *The Mountaineer,* 17 December 1934. Pace, "Henry Sieben," 9; Whitney Hibbard in conversation with Frank B. McCann, September 17, 1981; *100 Years in Culbertson,* 43.

[16] Whitney Hibbard interview with Frank B. McCann, September 17, 1981; Kohrs, *An Autobiography,* 96-97; "Of Local Interest," *The Silver State Post,* 17 July 1895; *100 Years in Culberson,* 46; Baucus, *Henry Sieben,* 10.

[17] Whitney Hibbard interview with Margaret Hibbard, September 20, 1981.

[18] "A Round-Up Association," *The Chinook Opinion,* 25 April 1895; To Help One Another," *The River Press,* 31 July 1895.

[19] "To Help One Another," *The River Press,* 31 July 1895.

[20] "The Cattlemen Deliberate," *Great Falls Tribune,* 10 December 1895; "Meeting of the Northern Montana Roundup," *Rocky Mountain Husbandman,* 19 December 1895.

[21] Montana Club Constitution Book 1, 1890, 367 M76m Montana Club, Montana Historical Society.

[22]Whitney Hibbard interview with Margaret Hibbard, September 20, 1981; "Sixth Avenue Apartments," National Register of Historic Places marker, Montana Historical Society; Montana National Register Sign Program, "Chessman Flats," Historic Montana, accessed December 1, 2023, *https://historicmt.org/items/show/2698.*

[23]Whitney Hibbard interview with Margaret Hibbard, September 20, 1981.

[24]"Spray of the Falls," *Great Falls Tribune,* 23 February 1895.

[25]"Spray of the Falls," *Great Falls Tribune,* 29 November 1894; "Spray of the Falls," *Great Falls Tribune,* 6 February 1896.

[26]"Stockgrowers Meet," *The Rocky Mountain Husbandman,* 30 April 1896.

[27]"The Stockmen," *The Chinook Opinion,* 30 April 1896.

[28]"The Stockmen," *The Chinook Opinion,* 30 April 1896.

[29]Malone, *Montana,* 211-18; Holmes, *Montana,* 197-99

[30]"Stock Notes and News," *The Rocky Mountain Husbandman,* 14 May 1896; "Locals," *The Montana Citizen,* 27 June 1896; "City and State," *Daily River Press,* 30 July 1896; "Town, County and State," *The Chinook Opinion,* 6 August 1896; *Helena Evening Herald,* 8 August 1896.

[31]"North Montana Round-Up Association," *Helena Evening Herald,* 30 November 1896; "O'Brien Appeal Dismissed," *Great Falls Tribune,* 4 December 1896.

[32]Whitney Hibbard interview with Margaret Hibbard, September 20, 1981.

[33]"The Farmers' Institute," *The Chinook Opinion,* 25 February 1897; *The Montana Citizen,* 27 February 1897; "Personals," *Helena Evening Herald,* 18 May 1897.

[34]"Official Proceedings of the Choteau County Board of Equalization for 1897," *Daily River Press,* 28 July 1897; "City and State," *The River Press,* 4 August 1897; "New County Offices," *Great Falls Tribune,* 4 July 1894; Stock Commissioners," *The River Press,* 3 Feb 1897.

[35]"Stock Notes and News," *The Chicago Drovers' Journal,* 11 November 1897; Sheep and Wool," *Rocky Mountain Husbandman,* 15 April 1897; "Chief Wool State," *The Livingston Post,* 6 May 1897; "To Fatten Sheep," *Helena Evening Herald,* 16 August 1897.

[36]"City and State," *Daily River Press,* 30 July 1896.

[37]Whitney Hibbard interview with Margaret Hibbard, September 20, 1981.

[38]Whitney Hibbard in conversation with Jim Spurgeon, September 20, 1981; *Roosevelt County's Treasured Years,* 264-65; *History of Montana,* 921-22

[39]*The Harrison Sun,* 15 September 1905.

CHAPTER 6

[1] The ledger contains detailed accounting, not in Henry's script, for each of his properties. In fact, Henry did not record any of the accounting entries in his surviving ledgers. It appears he hired an accountant to record his business transactions. This is not unusual given Henry's limited writing skills. However,

he did record his day-to-day transactions in thirty surviving pocketbooks dating from 1897 to 1937. "Property ledger," Hibbard family private collection; Henry Sieben Pocketbooks 1897-1937, Hibbard family private collection.

2 Whitney Hibbard interview with Margaret Hibbard, September 20, 1981.

3 "Spray of the Falls," *Great Falls Tribune,* 19 July 1898.

4 "1898 Sieben Residence Day Book," Hibbard family private collection.

5 Whitney Hibbard interview with Margaret Hibbard, September 20, 1981.

6 "Link and Haire, Architects," *https://archiveswest.orbiscascade.org/ark:/80444/xv73544;* "Helena's Historic West Side," *https://mhs.mt.gov/Shpo/docs/WestSideHelenaArchitectureWalkingTour.pdf.*

7 Whitney Hibbard interview with Ruth Sieben Hagelin, November 28, 1982. Oral Histories about the Life of Henry Sieben, Montana History Portal, Oral Histories about the Life of Henry Sieben, *https://www.mtmemory.org/nodes/view/106564*

8 "Henry Sieben Home," *https://historicmt.org/items/show/745?tour=42&index=70;* Whitney Hibbard in conversation with Margaret Hibbard, September 20, 1981; Baucus, *Henry Sieben,* 39.

9 "Open House," *Helena Evening Herald,* 2 January 1899; *The Great Falls Leader,* 7 January 1899.

10 Malone, *Montana,* 218; the Seventeenth Amendment to the Constitution, which provided for popular election of senators, was not adopted until 1913. "Landmark Legislation," *https://www.senate.gov/about/origins-foundations/senate-and-constitution/seventeenth-amendment.htm,* accessed November 3, 2024.

11 Malone, *Montana,* 254-57.

12 "It's Harmony Personified," *Helena Evening Herald,* 23 September 1898.

13 "Legislative Nominees," *Helena Evening Herald,* 8 October 1898.

14 "Legislative Nominees," *Helena Evening Herald,* 8 October 1898.

15 "Certificate of Nominations," *Montana German Press and Montana Staats Zeitung,* 8 November, 1898; "Boodle Wins," *Helena Semi Weekly Herald,* 10 November 1898.

16 Malone, *Montana,* 219.

17 Malone, *Montana,* 221-23; Swibold, *Copper Chorus;* "The Election Case of William A. Clark of Montana (1900)," *https://www.senate.gov/about/origins-foundations/electing-appointing-senators/contested-senate-elections/089William_Clark.htm,* accessed November 3, 2024.

18 Malone, *Montana,* 254-55.

19 Petrik, *No Step Backward,* Appendix 2, Tables 1 and 2; Paladin and Baucus, *Helena: An Illustrated History.*

20 "Will Visit the River," *The Independent Record,* 23 June 1898; "Larger Damages," *The Helena Semi-Weekly Herald,* 30 June 1898.

21 "City Council," *The Montana Record Herald,* 28 August 1898; "Helena, Montana," *http://www.waterworkshistory.us/MT/Helena.,* accessed February 8, 2024.

22 "For Larger Site," *Helena Evening Herald,* 20 June, 1899; "Federal Building," *https://historicmt.org/items/show/2218,* accessed February 6, 2024.

[23] Malone, *Montana,* 255.

[24] "Are Ready to Resume," *The Montana Record Herald,* 12 October 1900; "Improvement of the City," *The Montana-Record Herald,* 11 January 1902; "Society," *The Montana Record-Herald,* 11 April 1903.

[25] "A Service of Interest," *Helena Evening Herald,* 1 May 1899.

[26] "Seventh Anniversary," *Helena Evening Herald,* 16 November 1898.

[27] "Cash for New Church," *The Montana-Record Herald,* 14 March 1901; Whitney Hibbard interview with Margaret Hibbard, September 20, 1981.

[28] "Seventh Anniversary," *Helena Evening Herald,* 16 November 1898; "Monday's Musical," *Helena Evening Herald,* March 9 1899; "A Service of Interest," *Helena Evening Herald,* 1 May 1899.

[29] Many Cattle for Chicago Markets," *Great Falls Tribune,* 24 September 1899; "The State Lawmakers," *The Anaconda Standard,* 2 February 1899; "To Protect Montana Stockmen," *Midland Empire News,* 15 August 1899; Whitney Hibbard interview with F.B. McCann, September 17, 1981; "Cattle and House Account Ledger, 1895–1928," Hibbard family private collection; "Henry Sieben Pocketbooks 1897–1906," Hibbard family private collection.

[30] Whitney Hibbard interview with Margaret Hibbard, September 20, 1981.

[31] Whitney Hibbard interview with F.B. McCann, September 17, 1981.

[32] Whitney Hibbard interview with Peggy Gordon Lestz, January 15, 1982.

[33] Rowe, *Mountains and Meadows,* 168-69.

[34] Whitney Hibbard in conversation with Jim Spurgeon, September 20, 1981.

[35] "Fatal Shooting Affray," *The Anaconda Standard,* 24 January 1900.

[36] "Eder was Set Free," *The Helena Independent,* 27 February 1900.

[37] Whitney Hibbard interview with Margaret Hibbard, September 20, 1981.

[38] Whitney Hibbard interview with Ruth Sieben Hagelin, November 28, 1982.

[39] First National Bank," *The Kalispell Journal,* 21 May 1903; "Kalispell Banks Elect Officers," *The Western News,* 21 January 1904; "Bankers' Dividend," *The Kalispell Bee,* 13 January 1905; Whitney Hibbard interview with Margaret Hibbard, September 20, 1981.

[40] "The Chinook Meeting," *The Choteau Acantha,* 27 April 1899; "Gray Wolf Canis Lupus," *https://fieldguide.mt.gov/speciesDetail.aspx?elcode=AMAJA01030#:~:text=Although%20Gray%20Wolves%20dispersing%20from,1967%20(32%20FR%204001,* accessed February 5, 2024; "The Round-Up Meeting," *The Anaconda Standard,* 27 April 1898.

[41] "Losses are Heavy There," *Midland Empire News,* 13 March 1903.

[42] "Cannot Pay the Prices," *The Montana Record-Herald,* 8 March 1903; "Losses are Heavy There," *Midland Empire News,* 13 March 1903.

[43] Whitney Hibbard interview with F.B. McCann, September 17, 1981.

[44] "Cattle and House Account Ledger, 1895–1928," Hibbard family private collection.

[45] Whitney Hibbard interview with Margaret Hibbard, September 20, 1981.

[46] "Plans completed for the Elks Charity Ball," *The Montana-Record Herald,* 19 January 1902; "Leap Year Dance," *The Montana-Record Herald,* 9 April 1904; "A Pretty Party," *The Montana-Record Herald,* 14 May 1904.

[47] Whitney Hibbard interview with Margaret Hibbard, September 20, 1981.

[48] Ibid.

[49] Ibid.

[50] "Helena," *The Butte Miner,* 3 August 1902; "Box Parties at the Tempest," *The Montana-Record Herald,* 21 September 1902. "Reception to Mrs Catt," *The Montana-Record Herald,* 4 May 1902; "Society" *The Montana Record-Herald,* 22 February 1903; "Al Fresco Card Party," *The Montana-Record Herald,* 9 July 1904.

[51] Whitney Hibbard interview with Frank Sterling, August 15, 1981.

[52] "Range Totally Destroyed," *The Billings Gazette,* 3 October 1902.

[53] Whitney Hibbard interview with Ruth Sieben Hagelin, November 28, 1982.

[54] "Another Northern Montana Pioneer Answers Last Roll Call," *The Great Falls Leader,* 8 January 1904.

[55] "Spray of the Falls," *Great Falls Tribune,* 10 December 1902; "Spray of the Falls," *Great Falls Tribune,* 2 July 1903.

[56] Whitney Hibbard interview with Ruth Sieben Hagelin, November 28, 1982; Whitney Hibbard interview with Margaret Hibbard, September 20, 1981.

CHAPTER 7

[1] "Sign of Prosperity," *The Independent Record,* 15 September 1898.

[2] "Malcolm Clarke," *Gold Rush Widows of Little Falls.*

[3] Whitney Hibbard interview with Brian O'Connell, January 2, 1982. Oral Histories about the Life of Henry Sieben, Montana History Portal, Oral Histories about the Life of Henry Sieben, *https://www.mtmemory.org/nodes/view/106564*

[4] Whitney Hibbard interview with Nick Hilger, August 9, 1987. Oral Histories about the Life of Henry Sieben, Montana History Portal, Oral Histories about the Life of Henry Sieben, *https://www.mtmemory.org/nodes/view/106564;* "The Sieben Ranch," *The Great Falls Tribune,* 20 June 2015.

[5] With later additions, the cabin is home of the present ranch owners John F. and Nina Baucus.

[6] Pace, "Henry Sieben," 10-11; Baucus, *Three Gordon Siblings,* 25-26; Baucus, *Henry Sieben,* 22-26.

[7] Bill Lang and Dick Pace in conversation with John "Red" Wolrich, April 4, 1978, Montana Historical Society, SC 1493.

[8] "Heaviest Wool Sales of the Season Conducted this Afternoon", *The Great Falls Leader,* 14 July 1904; "Over One Million Pounds", *The Great Falls Leader,* 5 May 1905.

[9] Whitney Hibbard interview with Margaret Sieben Hibbard, September 20, 1981.

[10] Baucus, *Henry Sieben,* 4; Pace, "Henry Sieben," 12; Margaret Sieben Hibbard in conversation with Red and Viola Wolrich, September 26, 1981; "Society News of the Week," *The Montana Record-Herald,* 15 August 1903.

[11] Whitney Hibbard interview with Margaret Sieben Hibbard, September 20, 1981; "Picnic at the Broadwater," *The Montana-Record Herald,* 11 June 1904.

[12]"Property ledger," Hibbard family private collection; Whitney Hibbard interview with Margaret Sieben Hibbard, September 20, 1981; Pace, *Henry Sieben,* 12; Baucus, *Henry Sieben,* 38.

[13]Kinsey Howard, *Montana,* 108-10; "In Versus Out? Livestock Fence Laws," Jeff Mosley, accessed December 4, 2024, *https://apps.msuextension.org/magazine/articles/5494#:~:text=In%201887%2C%20two%20years%20before,exclude%20all%20free%2Droaming%20livestock.*

[14]"Defending the Fence," *The Montana-Record Herald,* 27 April 1901; "Montana News Brieflets," *The River Press,* 16 August 1905.

[15]"Montana News Brieflets," *The River Press,* 24 May 1911; "Grazing of Sheep Makes War," *The Daily Missoulian,* 20 October 1912; "New Supreme Court Rulings," *The Madison County Forum,* 7 November 1912; Vaughn, *Last Heir,* 74-78.

[16]"To Quiet Title," *The Anaconda Standard,* 6 April 1903; "Phillips et al., vs Coburn," *The River Press,* 29 April 1903; "Damages Sought," *The Montana Daily Record,* 5 April 1906; "People and Events," *The Montana Record-Herald,* 10 July 1906; "Jottings about Town," *The Independent Record,* 6 August 1907; "News of Montana," *The Picket-Journal,* 14 January 1909; "News of Montana," *The Picket-Journal,* 14 January 1909; "Pay Tribute to Mrs. N. Hilger," *The Montana-Record Herald,* 2 June 1910.

[17]"Herders have Fatal Sunday Row," *The Montana Record-Herald,* 2 January 1905; "Sheepherder is Murdered," *Great Falls Tribune,* 2 January 1905. "Lifer Murder Case is Submitted to the Jury," *The Montana Record-Herald,* 14 March 1905; "Helena Interested in Liefer's Trial," *The Anaconda Standard,* 14 March 1905; "Liefer Sentenced to Ten Years in Prison," *The Montana Record-Herald,* 27 March 1905.

[18]"People and Events," *Stevensville Register,* 26 September 1906; "Company Incorporated Now to Attend to Woolgrowing," *Miles City Weekly Star,* 25 October 1906; "To Market Montana Wool," *Dillon Tribune,* 21 November 1906.

[19]"Civic Societies," *The Searchlight,* 28 September 1905; "Local Happenings," *The Searchlight,* 30 August 1906; "Local Happenings," *The Searchlight,* 13 September 1907.

[20]Malone, *Montana,* 232.

[21]Malone, *Montana,* 232-34.

[22]Malone, *Montana,* 236-37; "Frank G. Arnette," *Roosevelt County's Treasured Years,* 264-65; "Frank G. Arnette," *History of Montana,* 921-22.

[23]Whitney Hibbard interview with Jim Spurgeon, September 20, 1981.

[24]"Civic Societies," *The Searchlight,* 28 September 1905; "Local Happenings," *The Searchlight,* 30 August 1906; "Local Happenings," *The Searchlight,* 13 September 1907; Whitney Hibbard interview with Jim Spurgeon, 20 September, 1981.

[25]"Golden Wedding," The Searchlight, 6 December 1907; "George Arnett," *History of Illinois County.*

[26]Malone, *Montana,* 237-41.

[27]Malone, *Montana,* 241.

[28]Malone, *Montana,* 241-42.

[29]"Rich Men of Helena and How They Got It," *The Montana Lookout,* 7 November 1908; "Monied Men of Montana," *Billings Evening Herald,* 12 November 1908.

[30]"Rich Men of Helena and How They Got It," *The Montana Lookout,* 7 November 1908; "Monied Men of Montana," *Billings Evening Herald,* 12 November 1908.

[31]"Local Breezes," *Big Hole Breezes,* 10 May 1907; "Interesting Big Hole Items," *Dillon Tribune,* 31 May 1907; "Local Breezes," *Big Hole Breezes,* 7 June 1907; "Local Breezes," *Big Hole Breezes,* March 20 1908; "Local Breezes," *Big Hole Breezes,* July 1908; "Local Breezes," *Big Hole Breezes,* 12 June 1908; "City and County," *Dillon Tribune,* 28 April 1909; "Butte Current Notes," *The Anaconda Standard,* 1 May 1910; "Many Fat Cattle," *The Madisonian,* 1 December 1910; Henry Sieben pocketbooks 1907-1910, Hibbard family private collection.

[32]Henry's investment in the Big Hole Ranch Company did not end in success. It proved to be impractical with managerial problems and high operating expenses. Henry disposed of his share of the ranch in the 1930s (Baucus, *Henry Sieben,* 30). "800 Feeders," *The Butte Daily Post,* 12 September 1911; "Notes from the Breezes," *Dillon Tribune,* 26 June 1912; Henry Sieben pocketbooks 1911-1916, Hibbard family private collection.

[33]"Cattle account ledger," Hibbard family private collection.

[34]"Henry Sieben Purchases the Cannon Stock Ranch," *The Butte Miner,* 4 July 1907; "Cannon Ranch Sold to Sieben," *Great Falls Tribune,* 4 July 1907; "Rich Men of Helena and How They Got It," *The Montana Lookout,* 7 November 1908; "Monied Men of Montana," *Billings Evening Herald,* 12 November 1908.

[35]Whitney Hibbard interview with Don Brown, May 28, 1981. Oral Histories about the Life of Henry Sieben, Montana History Portal, Oral Histories about the Life of Henry Sieben, *https://www.mtmemory.org/nodes/view/106564*

[36]The Adel post office burned down in the 1920s and no remnants remain today (Whitney Hibbard interview with Peck Warehime, September 11, 1981).

[37]Malone, *Montana,* 242.

[38]Henry Sieben Pocketbooks 1908-1911, Hibbard family private collection; "Adel Expense Ledger 1907-1910," Hibbard family private collection; Whitney Hibbard interview with Brian O'Connell, January 2, 1982.

[39]Whitney Hibbard interview with Frank Sterling, August 15, 1981. Oral Histories about the Life of Henry Sieben, Montana History Portal, Oral Histories about the Life of Henry Sieben, *https://www.mtmemory.org/nodes/view/106564.* "Henry Sieben Pocketbooks 1908-1911, Hibbard family private collection; "Adel Expense Ledger 1907-1910", Hibbard family private collection."

[40]Margaret Hibbard in conversation with Red and Viola Wolrich, September 26, 1981. Oral Histories about the Life of Henry Sieben, Montana History Portal, Oral Histories about the Life of Henry Sieben, *https://www.mtmemory.org/nodes/view/106564*

[41]"Sheepmen in Storage House," *The Montana-Record Herald,* 15 June 1910.

[42]"Capitol Notes," *The Montana-Record Herald,* 5 October 1909; Sieben Live Stock Company headed paper, Hibbard family private collection; "Women Work for

Children," *The Montana-Record Herald,* 8 April 1908; "Plan to Entertain Visitors," *The Butte Daily Post,* 8 January 1908; "Woolgrowers Meeting," *Forsyth Journal,* 15 January 1908; "Explain Cause of Consumption," *The Montana Record Herald,* 22 September 1911; "Forty Thousand for Wesleyan," *The Montana Record Herald,* 30 December 1911; "T.A. Marlow is Honored," *The Montana-Record Herald,* 30 November 1915; Holmes, *Montana,* 297.

[43] Whitney Hibbard interview with Margaret Sieben Hibbard, September 20, 1981.

[44] Ibid.

[45] "Additional Society," *The Great Falls Leader,* 20 August 1910; "Current Notes of Automobile World," *Anaconda Standard,* 5 January 1913; Axline, *Taming Big Sky Country,* 36-37.

[46] "Shean Girls Sue Sieben Estate," *The Montana-Record Herald,* 29 November 1912; "Daughters Enter Suit for $15,000," *The Independent-Record,* 30 November 1912; "Automobilists Sued by Victims Children," *The Butte Miner,* 30 November 30 1912.

[47] Henry Sieben Pocketbooks 1911-12, Hibbard family private collection; Whitney Hibbard interview with Margaret Sieben Hibbard, September 20, 1981.

[48] Mrs Henry Sieben Dies in California," *The Montana-Record Herald,* 31 May 1912; Mrs Henry Sieben Dead," *Great Falls Tribune,* 1 June 1912; "Pay Tribute to Mrs. Sieben," *The Montana-Record Herald,* 5 June 1912.

[49] Henry Sieben Pocketbooks 1911–12, Hibbard family private collection.

[50] "Big Helena Deal," *The Great Falls Leader,* 23 November 1911; "Conrad Bank is Now Open," *The Montana-Record Herald,* 5 October 1910; Henry Sieben Pocketbooks 1911–12, Hibbard family private collection.

CHAPTER 8

[1] "Music is her Dominant Life Theme," *The Independent Record,* February 7 1971; "Society Personals," *The Montana-Record Herald,* July 3 1909; "Green-Sieben," *The Independent Record,* July 18 1915; "Jessie Dean Green Sieben Papers," SC 1875, Montana Historical Society Archives; Broadwater County Historical Society, *Broadwater Bygones;* Whitney Hibbard interview with Margaret Sieben Hibbard, September 20, 1981; "Post-Lenten Ball," *The Independent Record,* April 9 1916; "Dinner," *The Independent Record,* January 16, 1916.

[2] "Funeral Mr Flowerree to be Held Thursday," *The Montana-Record Herald,* November 27 1912; "Jesse D. Phelps Kills Himself," *The Daily Democrat,* May 31 1915; "Jesse I Phelps," *The Independent-Record,* June 4 1915; "Society," *Montana Record Herald,* 28 February 1914.

[3] "Sieben-Sheriff Nuptials," *The Independent Record,* June 15, 1915.

[4] Lewis and Clark County Clerk and Recorder Deeds June 15, 1915; "Thomas A Grimes Buys Old Kessler Residence," *The Montana-Record Herald,* January 16, 1913; Baucus, *Three Gordon Siblings,* 48-53; Burlingame and Toole, *A History of Montana.* Vol. III, 474.

[5] Whitney Hibbard interview with Margaret Sieben Hibbard, September 20, 1981.

[6] "Dinner," *The Independent Record,* August 5, 1917; "Sieben-Hibbard Nuptials," *The Independent-Record,* August 5, 1917; Baucus, *Three Gordon Siblings,* 76-79; Burlingame and Toole, *A History of Montana.* Vol. III, 474.

[7] Malone, *Montana,* 262-66; "Kessler Family papers, 1865-1952," Archives West, accessed December 4, 2024, *https://archiveswest.orbiscascade.org/ark:/80444/xv98170;* "Power Joins the Juveniles," *The Montana Record-Herald,* 24 May 1915; "Julian Anderson," *The Helena Independent Record,* March 25, 2024; Henry Sieben pocketbooks 1919-35, Hibbard family private collection; Whitney Hibbard interview with Margaret Sieben Hibbard, September 20, 1981; Glasrud and Searles, *Black Cowboys in the American West.*

[8] "Hospital Corps Gets Seven in the City: Navy," *The Independent Record,* June 8 1907; Malone, *Montana,* 268-79; Holmes, *Montana,* 314-26.

[9] Kohrs, *An Autobiography,* 1-6; "Conrad Kohrs," accessed December 4, 2024, *https://www.nps.gov/grko/learn/historyculture/conradkohrs.htm.*

[10] "Short Stops," "German School," "German Select School," *The Independent Record,* June 23 1878; "Notes and Personals," *Helena Evening Herald,* May 27 1893; Ellen Baumler, *Helena the Town that Gold Built,* 22; Kohrs, *An Autobiography,* 56-57.

[11] Whitney Hibbard interview with Margaret Sieben Hibbard, September 20, 1981; Holmes, *Montana,* 326-27.

[12] Lewis and Clark County Clerk and Recorder Deeds April 23, 1903; February 27, 1907; August 6, 1907; December 19, 1912; May 2, 1913; October 23, 1915; November 15, 1915; November 2, 1916; Cascade County Clerk and Recorder, April 29, 1910; September 16, 1912; June 28, 1913; July 19, 1920; "Notice for Publication," *The Montana Record-Herald,* January 14, 1913.

[13] Malone, *Montana,* 280-83.

[14] Whitney Hibbard interview with Brian Hilger, August 9, 1987. Oral Histories about the Life of Henry Sieben, Montana History Portal, Oral Histories about the Life of Henry Sieben, *https://www.mtmemory.org/nodes/view/106564;* Baucus, *Three Gordon Siblings,* 76.

[15] "Joe and Carrie Hilger Ranch," National Register of Historic Places, accessed December 4, 2024; *https://npgallery.nps.gov/GetAsset/daf4171a-d73c-4358-a119-fb909b393d07;* Whitney Hibbard interview with Brian Hilger, August 9, 1987.

[16] Whitney Hibbard interview with Brian Hilger, August 9, 1987.

[17] Whitney Hibbard interview with Brian O'Connell, January 2, 1982. Oral Histories about the Life of Henry Sieben, Montana History Portal, Oral Histories about the Life of Henry Sieben, *https://www.mtmemory.org/nodes/view/106564*

[18] Whitney Hibbard interview with Peggy Gordon Lestz, January 15, 1982.

[19] Whitney Hibbard interview with Brian Hilger, August 9, 1987; Whitney interview with Brian O'Connell, January 2, 1982; Whitney Hibbard in conversation with Peggy Gordon Lestz, January 15, 1982; Whitney Hibbard interview with Royal Smith, June 5, 1981; Lewis and Clark County Clerk and Recorder Decree

April 28, 1900; "Funeral of Grimes," *The Independent Record,* November 18 1921; Sieben Ranch Company Minute Book 1915-50, Baucus family private collection.

[20] Whitney Hibbard interview with Brian O'Connell, January 2, 1982.

[21] Whitney Hibbard interview with Don Brown, May 28, 1981.

[22] Whitney Hibbard interview with Royal Smith, June 5, 1981.

[23] Whitney Hibbard interview with Don Brown, May 28, 1981.

[24] Whitney Hibbard interview with Royal Smith, June 5, 1981.

[25] Whitney Hibbard interview with Bill Shanklin, August 1981. Oral Histories about the Life of Henry Sieben, Montana History Portal, Oral Histories about the Life of Henry Sieben, *https://www.mtmemory.org/nodes/view/106564*

[26] Whitney Hibbard interview with Bill Shanklin, August 1981; "6,000-Acre Ranch bought by Sieben," *The Montana Record Herald,* April 17 1920; Whitney Hibbard in conversation with Royal Smith, June 5, 1981.

[27] Whitney Hibbard interview with Brian Hilger, August 9, 1987.

[28] Sieben Ranch Company Minute Book 1915–50," Baucus family private collection.

[29] "Pioneer who Came by Ox," *The Montana-Record Herald,* June 5 1922.

[30] Whitney Hibbard interview with Bill Shanklin, August, 1981; Whitney Hibbard interview with Brian Hilger, August 9, 1987; Whitney Hibbard interview with Nick Hilger, August 9, 1987; Baucus, *Three Gordon Siblings* 53; "Finding of an Ol Ox Shoe," *The Independent Record,* September 10 1922; "New Helena Capital Going into Montana Oil Fields," *The Independent Record,* 14 November 1920; "Helena Stockholders," *The Independent Record,* 10 April 1921; "The City in Brief," *Montana Record-Herald,* August 26 1922; "Sieben Ranch Company Minute Book 1915–50," Baucus family private collection.

[31] "Sieben Ranch Company Minute Book 1915–50," Baucus family private collection.

[32] "Covered Wagon Pioneers Hold Reunion in Geneseo," *Moline Daily Dispatch,* December 4 1926; "Sieben Livestock Company," *National Wool Exchange Reporter,* August 1, 1926.

[33] "Leonard Sieben," Kett & Co., *The History of Henry County, Illinois,* 424.

[34] "Sieben Ranch Company Minute Book 1915–50," Baucus family private collection; Malone, *Montana,* 289-96.

[35] "Sieben Ranch Company Minute Book 1915–50," Baucus family private collection; Malone, *Montana,* 296-303.

[36] Whitney Hibbard interview with Margaret Sieben Hibbard, September 20, 1981.

[37] Whitney Hibbard interview with Bill Shanklin, August 1981.

[38] "Take Plane to Salt Lake City Today," *The Helena Daily Independent,* July 23 1931.

[39] Baucus, *Henry Sieben,* 45.

[40] Whitney Hibbard interview with with Bill Shanklin, August 1981; "Henry Sieben, Oldest of Montana Stockmen," *The Mountaineer,* 17 December 1934; "Henry Sieben, Gold Days Pioneer," *The Montana Record-Herald,* January 24, 1930; Margaret Hibbard interview with Red and Viola Wolrich, September 26, 1981; "Henry Sieben," The Saddle and Sirloin Portrait Foundation, accessed December 4, 2024, *https://www.saddleandsirloinportraitfoundation.org/post/henry-sieben-inducted-between-1920-and-1936.*

[41] Whitney Hibbard interview with Margaret Sieben Hibbard, September 20, 1981; Whitney Hibbard interview with Don Brown, May 28, 1981.

EPILOGUE

[1] "Sieben Ranch Company Minute Book 1915–50," Baucus family private collection.

[2] Minutes of annual stockholder meetings 1938–49, "Sieben Ranch Company Minute Book 1915-50," Baucus family private collection.

[3] Author interview with Chase, Whit and Scott Hibbard. Nina and John F. Baucus, June 2023; Whitney Hibbard interview with Rupert Parsons, October 10, 1987. Oral Histories about the Life of Henry Sieben, Montana History Portal, Oral Histories about the Life of Henry Sieben, *https://www.mtmemory.org/nodes/view/106564;* "Farmers' Memo Book," Hibbard family private collection.

[4] Minutes of annual stockholder meetings 1938–49, "Sieben Ranch Company Minute Book 1915-50," Baucus family private collection.

[5] Baucus, *Three Gordon Siblings,* 64-67.

[6] "Helena Man on Lamb Cooperation Mission, *The Independent Record,* 28 October 1970.

[7] Whitney Hibbard interview with Adolph Johnson, December 22, 1981. Oral Histories about the Life of Henry Sieben, Montana History Portal, Oral Histories about the Life of Henry Sieben, *https://www.mtmemory.org/nodes/view/106564*

[8] "Hibbard and Other U.S. Bond Sale Leaders," *The Independent Record,* 13 January 1952.

[9] "Chase Hibbard: Message to Legislature," *The Independent Record,* 21 February 2023.

[10] "Hibbard, Who I am," *The Independent Record,* 5 June 1972; Baucus, *Three Gordon Siblings,* 88-93; "Ex-Legislator, Henry Hibbard, Ranch Hand Die in Plane Crash," *Great Falls Tribune,* 15 July 1976.

[11] "Mrs. Hibbard: Making the Best of Growing Old," *The Independent Record,* 20 November 1977.

[12] Malone, *Montana,* 314-22.

[13] Malone, *Montana,* 321-22; "Montana Women's History," December 2014, *https://montanawomenshistory.org/things-to-be-done-which-money-and-men-will-never-provide-the-activism-of-montanas-aauw/#more-2746.*

[14] John and Nina Baucus Interview, 2003; OH 2088; Montana Historical Society.

[15] John and Nina Baucus Interview, 2003; OH 2088; Montana Historical Society; Author in conversation with John F. Baucus, April 2024 [e-mail].

[16] John and Nina Baucus Interview, 2003; OH 2088; Montana Historical Society; "Historic Sieben Ranch Thrives in Montana," American Sheep Industry Association, May 2016, *https://www.sheepusa.org/blog/newsmedia-sheepindustrynews-pastissues-2016-may2016-historicsiebenranchthrivesinmontana;* "Baucus' Brother Gets Family Ranch," *The Independent Record,* 1996; Baucus, Three Gordon Siblings, 66-74; Ellis, *Montana Women from the Ground Up.*

[17] "The West will Remain," March 2003, *https://www.angusbeefbulletin.com/ArticlePDF/0303abb_Sieben.pdf.*

[18] "Hunting for Elk Management Solutions," *Montana Free Press,* 13 October, 2022; Author in conversation with Chase, Scott and Whit Hibbard, April 2024 [e-mail].

[19] Author in conversation with John F. Baucus, April 2024.

[20] Bradley, "What is Montana's Top Industry," *https://lmi.mt.gov/_docs/Publications/EAG-Articles/1219-MTsIndustries.pdf* ◈

BIBLIOGRAPHY

ARCHIVES AND MANUSCRIPT MATERIALS

California

- Bob Sieben private collection

Montana

- Cascade County Clerk and Recorder Office, Great Falls, Montana
- The Gallatin History Museum, Bozeman, Montana
- Hibbard Family Private Collection, Helena, Montana
- Baucus Family Private Collection, Helena, Montana
- The History Museum, Great Falls, Montana
- Lewis and Clark County Clerk and Recorder Office, Helena, Montana
- Mansfield Library, University of Montana, Missoula, Montana
    - Collins Land Company Records, 1898–1951, Mss 063
    - Frank Linderman Memorial Collection, 1885–2005, Mss 007
    - Walter H. McLeod Papers, Mss 002
- Meagher County Clerk and Recorder Office, White Sulphur Springs, Montana
- Montana Historical Society, Helena, Montana
    - Jean Baucus Interview, OH 2222
    - John F. Baucus and Nina C. Baucus Interview, 2003, OH 2088
    - Horace Brewster Reminiscences, 1922–1926, SC 468
    - Coburn Family Papers, SC 2064
    - Jessie Dean Green Sieben Family Papers, SC 1875
    - James Fergus papers, 1835–1895, SC 339
    - First National Bank of Kalispell Records, 1891–1903, MC 231
    - Paris Gibson reminiscence, 1914, SC 2172
    - Greenhood, Bohm and Company Records, 1875–1893, MC 130
    - Edith Grimes Waddell Papers, SC 1669
    - Samuel Thomas Hauser papers, 1864–1914, MC 37 (2:4-1)
    - Hershfield Family reminiscences, 1865–1897, SC 2346
    - Chase T. Hibbard interview, 2003, OH 2108
    - E.G. Maclay (Diamond R) Records, SC 415
    - Merchants National Bank records, 1865-1903, MC 115
    - John H. Ming papers 1852-1895 MC 63 (4:4-1)
    - Montana Board of Land Commissioners Records, 1891–1937, RS 29
    - Montana Historical Society Pioneers' Reminiscences, MC 64 (4:4-1)
    - Montana Stockgrowers Association records, 1885-1912, MC 45
    - Eva Nolan James Writings 1950, SC 1719
    - Polk, R.L. Helena City Directories
    - Thomas Charles Power Papers, 1868-1950, MC 55B (2:7-1)

    - Margaret Sieben Hibbard Interview, 1978, OH 989
    - Granville Stuart Papers, 1863-1918, MC 61 (4:3-7)
    - White Sulphur Springs Hotel records, 1893-1900, MC 11
    - John "Red" Wolrich Interview, SC 1493
- Phillips County Clerk and Recorder Office, Malta, Montana
- Roosevelt County Clerk and Recorder Office, Wolf Point, Montana

NEWSPAPERS AND JOURNALS

(Montana unless otherwise noted)

- *The Anaconda Standard*
- *The Benton Record*
- *The Benton Weekly Record*
- *Big Hole Breezes*
- *Billings Evening Herald*
- *The Billings Gazette*
- *The Butte Daily Post*
- *The Butte Miner*
- *The Cheyenne Daily Leader*
- *The Chicago Drovers' Journal*
- *The Chinook Opinion*
- *The Choteau Acantha*
- *The Daily Democrat* (California)
- *The Daily Missoulian*
- *Dillon Tribune*
- *Forsyth Journal*
- *The Great Falls Leader*
- *The Great Falls Tribune*
- *The Harrison Sun* (Nebraska)
- *The Helena Daily Independent*
- *Helena Weekly Herald* (also: *Helena Evening Herald; Helena Semi Weekly Herald, The Daily Helena Herald*)
- *The Independent Record*
- *The Kalispell Bee*
- *The Kalispell Journal*
- *The Livingston Post*
- *The Madison County Forum*
- *The Madisonian*
- *Midland Empire News* (Billings)
- *Miles City Weekly Star*
- *Moline Daily Dispatch* (Indiana)
- *The Montana Citizen* (Glasgow)

- *The Montana Daily Record* (Helena)
- *Montana German Press and Montana Staats Zeitung*
- *The Montana Lookout* (Helena)
- *The Montana Mining Review* (Helena)
- *The Montana Post* (Virginia City)
- *The Montana Record-Herald*
- *The Mountaineer* (Big Sandy)
- *National Wool Exchange Reporter* (National Wool Growers Association)
- *The Old Town Promoter* (Shelby)
- *The Picket-Journal* (Red Lodge)
- *The Rising Sun* (Indiana)
- *The River Press, Daily River Press* (Fort Benton)
- *The Rocky Island Argus* (Illinois)
- *The Searchlight* (Culbertson)
- *The Silver State Post* (Deer Lodge)
- *Stevensville Register*
- *The Stockgrowers Journal* (Miles City)
- *Rocky Mountain Husbandman* (Diamond City, White Sulphur Springs, Great Falls)
- *The Western News* (Libby)

ORAL INTERVIEWS

- Montana History Portal, Oral Histories about the Life of Henry Sieben, *https://www.mtmemory.org/nodes/view/106564*
    - Brown, Don, interviewed by Whitney Hibbard, May 28, 1981.
    - Gordon Lestz, Peggy, interviewed by Whitney Hibbard, January 15, 1982.
    - Hagelin, Ruth Sieben, interviewed by Whitney Hibbard, November 28, 1982.
    - Hibbard, Margaret, interviewed by Whitney Hibbard, September 20, 1981.
    - Hilger, Brian, interviewed by Whitney Hibbard, August 9, 1987.
    - Hilger, Nick, interviewed by Whitney Hibbard, August 9, 1987.
    - Johnson, Adolph, interviewed by Whitney Hibbard, December 22, 1981.
    - Leede Rhein, Pearl, interviewed by Whitney Hibbard, 1980s.
    - McCann, Frank B., interviewed by Whitney Hibbard, September 17, 1981.
    - O'Connell, Brian, interviewed by Whitney Hibbard, January 2, 1982.
    - Parsons, Rupert, interviewed by Whitney Hibbard, October 10, 1987.
    - Shanklin, Bill, interviewed by Whitney Hibbard, August, 1981.
    - Smith, Royal, interviewed by Whitney Hibbard, June 5, 1981.
    - Spurgeon, Jim, interviewed by Whitney Hibbard, September 20, 1981.
    - Sterling, Frank, interviewed by Whitney Hibbard, August 15, 1981.
    - Warehime, Peck, interviewed by Whitney Hibbard, September 11, 1981.
    - Wolrich, John "Red" and Viola, interviewed by Margaret Sieben Hibbard, September 26, 1981.

PUBLISHED WORKS

- Aarstad, Rich et al. *Montana Place Names from Alzada to Zortman.* Helena: Montana Historical Society Press, 2009.
- Axline, Jon. *Taming Big Sky Country: The History of Montana Transportation.* The History Press, 2015.
- Baucus, Jean. *Henry Sieben, 1846–1937: Legacy of Livestock and Land.* Self-Published, 1995.
- Baucus, Nina. *Three Gordon Siblings and Their Montana Family Connections.* Self-Published, 2021.
- Baumler, Ellen. *Girl from the Gulches: The Story of Mary Ronan.* Helena: Montana Historical Society Press, 2003.
- Baumler, Ellen. *Helena, the Town that Gold Built, the First 150 Years.* Helena Area Chamber of Commerce, 2014.
- Broadwater County Historical Society. *Broadwater Bygones: A History of Broadwater County.* Bozeman: Color World of Montana, 1977.
- Burlingame, Merrill A., and Toole, K. Ross. *A History of Montana.* Vols I–III. New York: Lewis Historical Publishing Company, Inc. 1957.
- Clarke, S.J. Publishing Company. *The Biographical Record of Henry County, Illinois.* Chicago: The S.J. Clarke Publishing Company, 1901.
- Coburn, Walt. *Pioneer Cattleman in Montana: The Story of the Circle C Ranch.* Norman: University of Oklahoma Press, 1968.
- Doyle, Susan. *Journeys to the Land of Gold: Emigrant Diaries from the Bozeman Trail, 1863–1866.* Helena: Montana Historical Society Press, 2000.
- Egan Jr., Ken. *Montana 1864: Indians, Emigrants, and Gold in the Territorial Year.* Helena: Riverbend Publishing, 2014.
- Ellis, Kristine E. *Montana Women from the Ground Up: Passionate Voices in Agriculture and Land Conservation.* The History Press, 2018.
- Emmons, David. *The Butte Irish: Class and Ethnicity in an American Mining Town, 1875–1925.* Illinois: University of Illinois Press, 1990.
- Enzler, Jerry. *Jim Bridger: Trailblazer of the American West.* Norman: University of Oklahoma Press, 2021.
- Etulain, Richard W. *The Life and Legends of Calamity Jane.* Norman: University of Oklahoma Press, 2014.
- Glasrud, Bruce A., and Searles, Michael N. *Black Cowboys in the American West on th Range, on the Stage, Behind the Badge.* Norman: University of Oklahoma, 2016.
- Henderson, Roger. "The Pikuni and the U.S. Army's Piegan Expedition: Competing Narratives of the 1870 Massacre on the Marias River." *Montana: The Magazine of Western History* (Spring 2018): 48–70.
- Holmes, Krys. *Montana Stories of the Land.* Helena: Montana Historical Society Press, 2008.
- Hoye, Leota. *Roosevelt County's "Treasured Years."* Great Falls:Blue Print & Letter Company, Printers, 1976.

- Johnson, Dorothy M. "Flour Famine in Alder Gulch." *Montana: The Magazine of Western History* (Winter 1951): 18–27.
- Johnson, Dorothy M. *Some Went West.* New York: The Cornwall Press, 1965.
- Johnson, Dorothy M. *Bloody Bozeman: The Perilous Trail to Montana's Gold.* Missoula: Mountain Press, 1983.
- Johnson, Mark T. *The Middle Kingdom under the Big Sky: A History of the Chinese Experience in Montana.* Lincoln: University of Nebraska Press, 2022.
- Johnson, Mark T. "Great Falls is a White Man's City: Exclusion of Chinese Residents from Great Falls, Montana 1885–1941." *Montana: The Magazine of Western History* (Autumn 2023): 42–59.
- Kett H. F. & Co. *The History of Henry County, Illinois, Its Tax Payers and Voters.* Chicago: Kett H. F. & Co., 1877.
- Kiner, Henry L. *History of Henry County, Illinois.* Vol. 1. Chicago: Pioneer Publishing Company, 1910.
- Kinsey Howard, Joseph. *Montana: High Wide and Handsome.* Lincoln, NE: Bison Books, 2003 (revised edition).
- Kohrs, Conrad. *An Autobiography.* C.K. Warren, 1977.
- Malone, Michael P., Roeder, Richard B., Lang, William L *Montana: A History of Two Centuries.* Seattle and London: University of Washington Press, 1991 (revised edition).
- Martin, Dale. *Ties, Rails, and Telegraph Wires: Railroads and Communities in Montana and the West.* Helena: Montana Historical Society Press, 2018.
- Mueller, Oscar O. "The Central Montana Vigilante Raids of 1884." *Montana: The Magazine of Western History* (Winter 1951): 23–35.
- Pace, Dick. "Henry Sieben: Pioneer Montana Stockman." *Montana: The Magazine of Western History* (Winter 1979): 2–15.
- Paladin, Vivian A., and Baucus, Jean. *Helena: An Illustrated History.* Helena: Montana Historical Society, 1996.
- Petrik, Paula. *No Step Backward: Women and Family on the Rocky Mountain Mining Frontier, Helena, Montana 1865–1900.* Helena: Montana Historical Society, 1987.
- Rowe, Clarence J. et al. *Mountains and Meadows: A Pioneer History of Montana 1805–1925.* Great Falls: Blue Print & Letter Company, Printers, 1970.
- Russell, John C. *Treasure State Tycoon: Nelson Story and the Making of Montana.* Helena: Montana Historical Society Press, 2019.
- Segars, Lorretta. *100 Years in Culbertson 1887–1987.* Culbertson: Culbertson Centennial Steering Committee, 1987.
- Sibell Wolle, Muriel. *Montana Pay Dirt: A Guide to the Mining Camps of the Treasure State.* Denver: Sage Books, 1963.
- Stuart, Granville. *Pioneering in Montana: The Making of a State, 1864–1887.* Lincoln: University of Nebraska Press, 1977.
- Stuart, Granville. *Forty Years on the Frontier.* Lincoln NE: Bison Books, 2004.
- Swibold, Dennis L. *Copper Chorus: Mining, Politics, and the Montana Press, 1889–1959.* Helena: Montana Historical Society Press, 2006.

- Vaughn, Bill. *The Last Heir: The Triumphs and Tragedies of Two Montana Families.* Lincoln, NE: Bison Books, 2022.
- Wilkerson, Miranda E., and Richmond, Heather. *Germans in Illinois.* Carbondale: Southern Illinois University Press, 2019.
- Zion, Candi. *In Between People: The Métis of Central Montana.* Self-Published, 2021.
- Zion, Candi. *Walkin' Down the Middle: The Hi-Line Metis.* Self-Published, 2022.

FILM AND DOCUMENTARIES

- Burns, Ken. *The Civil War.* WETA Washington D.C. Productions for Public Broadcasting Service (PBS), 1990.
- Burns, Ken. *The American Buffalo.* Florentine Films and WETA Washington D.C. Productions for Public Broadcasting Service (PBS), 2023.

ONLINE RESOURCES

- Archives West. "Link and Haire, Architects, records, 1904–1926." *https://archiveswest.orbiscascade.org/ark:/80444/xv73544.*
- Archives West. "Kessler Family papers, 1865–1952." *https://archiveswest.orbiscascade.org/ark:/80444/xv98170.*
- Baumler, Ellen, and Kronholm, Joyce. "A Short Tour of Helena's Historic West Side Neighborhood." *https://mhs.mt.gov/Shpo/docs/WestSide.pdf.*
- Butte-Silver Bow County. "History of Butte." *https://co.silverbow.mt.us/DocumentCenter/View/15538/History-of-Buttedocx.*
- C.M. Russell Museum. "Waiting on a Chinook (Last of 5,000)." https://cmrussell.org/product/waiting-on-a-chinook-last-of-the-5000.
- Davis, John W., "The Johnson County War: 1892 Invasion of Northern Wyoming." 2014, *https://www.wyohistory.org/encyclopedia/johnson-county-war-1892-invasion-northern-wyoming.*
- Legends of America. "Castle Town, Montana." *https://www.legendsofamerica.com/castle-town-montana.*
- Mining History Association, "The Mining History of Butte and Anaconda." *https://www.mininghistoryassociation.org/ButteHistory.htm.*
- Montana Discovery Foundation. "Gates of the Mountains." *https://www.montanadiscoveryfoundation.org/gates-of-the-mountains/.*
- Montana Field Guides. "Gray Wolf—Canis lupus." *https://fieldguide.mt.gov/speciesDetail.aspx?elcode=AMAJA01030#:~:text=Although%20Gray%20Wolves%20dispersing%20from, 1967%20 (32%20FR%204001.*
- The Montana National Register Sign Program, *https://historicmt.org.*
- Mosley, Jeff. "In Versus Out? Livestock Fence Laws." *https://apps.msuextension.org/magazine/articles/5494#:~:text=In%201887%2C%20two%20years%20before,exclude%20all%20 free%2Droaming%20livestock.*
- National Park Service. "Conrad Kohrs." *https://www.nps.gov/grko/learn/historyculture/conradkohrs.htm.*

- National Park Service. "Joe and Carrie Hilger Ranch: National Register of Historic Places Registration Form." *https://npgallery.nps.gov/GetAsset/daf4171a-d73c-4358-a119-fb909b393d07*
- Office of the Illinois Secretary of State, *https://www.ilsos.gov/departments/archives/teaching_packages/early_chicago/doc23.html.*
- Pierce, Morris A. "Documentary History of American Water-Works: Helena, Montana." *http://www.waterworkshistory.us/MT/Helena/.*
- Rea, Tom, "Covering Cattle Kate: Newspapers and the Watson-Averell Lynching." 2014, *https://www.wyohistory.org/encyclopedia/covering-cattle-kate-newspapers-and-watson-averell-lynching.*
- The Saddle and Sirloin Portrait Foundation. "Henry Sieben." *https://www.saddleandsirloinportraitfoundation.org/post/henry-sieben-inducted-between-1920-and-1936.*
- State Historic Preservation Office (Montana). "African American History Timeline." *https://mhs.mt.gov/Shpo/AfricanAmericans/History/Timeline.*
- United States Senate. "Landmark Legislation." *https://www.senate.gov/about/origins-foundations/senate-and-constitution/seventeenth-amendment.htm.*
- U.S. Census. "Population of Montana 1870-1920." *https://www2.census.gov/library/publications/decennial/1920/state-compendium/06229686v20-25ch5.pdf.*
- Walker, Giles E. "Geology and History of the Marysville Mining District." Montana Bureau of Mines and Geology Open-File Report. *https://www.mbmg.mtech.edu/pdf-open-files/mbmg254_text.pdf.* ◈

INDEX

Features on maps or photographs noted in **bold**.

C

D

Originally from Limerick, Ireland, Ciara Ryan fell in love with Montana as a Fulbright Scholar in 2010 and has been researching Montana history and teaching the Irish, Spanish, and French languages here ever since. She earned her PhD from University College Cork and has published numerous articles on the Irish language and history in Montana. Ciara researched and prepared Henry Sieben's biography while in the employ of the Foundation for Montana History. She lives in Helena with her husband, two children, and their goldendoodle. ◈